PARIS UNIVERSAL EXPOSITION, 1867.

REPORTS OF THE UNITED STATES COMMISSIONERS.

EXAMINATION

OF THE

TELEGRAPHIC APPARATUS

AND THE

PROCESSES IN TELEGRAPHY

BY

SAMUEL F. B. MORSE, LL.D.,
UNITED STATES COMMISSIONER.

WASHINGTON:
GOVERNMENT PRINTING OFFICE.
1869.

INTRODUCTION.

An examination of the various objects in this department of the Exposition leads to the conclusion that since the former international exhibitions very little has been presented that is actually new. While displaying a great variety of beautiful modifications of instruments employed in the transmission of messages, showing the utmost mechanical skill and workmanship, deserving of the highest praise, it is found that most of them have already been exhibited in former international exhibitions, and have been noticed and described in the various reports of those exhibitions. Such instruments, for the most part, therefore, will require but a brief mention.

Some of the difficulties that were encountered in the pursuit of inquiries may as well be stated in the outset. The articles to be examined in the Exposition were not collected or arranged in one place as a class, but were widely dispersed under the products of the different countries, and had to be sought for in comparatively obscure parts of the vast area, surrounded by objects of a totally different character. Some of the instruments although named in the catalogue, could not be found; some named were actually not exhibited. Others had their complicated machinery carefully concealed under glass cases, or in their close frames of wood or brass, with the rather repulsive label "*ne touchez pas*, S. V. P.," to be met on the threshold, and which, though more politely expressed than our blunt Anglo-Saxon, "*hands off*," was quite as effective a barrier to free inquiry. To add to this inconvenience, there were, in most instances, no persons at hand, when the instruments were found, to explain the apparatus, and no printed or other description to be obtained. If, therefore, some of the instruments deserving of notice in this report are unnoticed, it will be seen that the neglect is one of necessity, and not of choice.

CONTENTS.

CHAPTER I.

TELEGRAPHS.

CHAPTER II.

SEMAPHORES.

CHAPTER III.

CODES.

CHAPTER IV.

BATTERIES, CONDUCTORS, AND INSULATORS.

TELEGRAPHIC APPARATUS, ETC.

CHAPTER I.

TELEGRAPHS.

DEFINITION OF TELEGRAPH AND SEMAPHORE, DISTINCTION BETWEEN THEM—ETYMOLOGY OF THE TWO WORDS—CHRONOGRAPH AND CHRONOSCOPE—NO EXAMPLE OF A TELEGRAPH UNTIL 1832—EXTENSION OF TELEGRAPHIC AND SEMAPHORIC SYSTEMS THROUGHOUT THE WORLD—RESULTS FLOWING FROM THE INVENTION OF THE GENERIC TELEGRAPH—SCIENCE ADVANCED BY THE TELEGRAPH—PRINCIPAL DISCOVERIES IN ELECTRICITY AND MAGNETISM PRIOR TO THE INVENTION OF THE TELEGRAPH—THE MORSE SYSTEM ADOPTED BY THE INTERNATIONAL CONVENTION AT PARIS—THE MORSE SYSTEM DESCRIBED—THE RELAY OR SECONDARY CIRCUIT—MODIFICATIONS OF THE MORSE APPARATUS—SIEMENS AND HALSKE'S AUSTRIAN MILITARY TELEGRAPH—HUGHES'S PRINTING TELEGRAPH, ITS CONSTRUCTION AND OPERATION—ARLINCOURT'S PRINTING APPARATUS—DUJARDIN'S PRINTING TELEGRAPH—PANTELEGRAPHS—BONELLI'S PANTELEGRAPHIC APPARATUS AS MODIFED BY COOK—ABBÉ CASELLI'S PANTELEGRAPH—LENOIR'S MODIFICATION, THE ELECTROGRAPH.

The telegraph, in the comprehensive sense in which it is usually but erroneously applied to all modes of communicating at a distance, is a very ancient invention, and in this expanded general sense cannot therefore be claimed by any modern inventor. But in the true sense of the word, as signifying imprinting or writing at a distance, the telegraph is a modern invention, and does not date further back than the year 1832. It is, therefore, proposed to use the term telegraph in its strict etymological sense; thus distinguishing it from all other modes of communicating at a distance with which it has hitherto been confounded.

The terms *telegraph* and *semaphore* conveniently comprise, under two generic heads, all the modes of communicating intelligence from a distance not dependent upon actually sending it, either written, printed, or verbal, by some sort of couriers who travel over the interval between two or more points of intercommunication.

If the etymology of the two words telegraph and semaphore be examined, it will be perceived that the term telegraph from τηλε, at a distance, and γραφω, to write or imprint, and the term semaphore, from σημα, a signal, and ερω, to bear or convey, very accurately designate the difference between the two modes of communicating to a distance, to all which modes has hitherto been indiscriminately applied the appellative *telegraph*, but not accurately, for it cannot strictly be applied to the semaphore, since the semaphore neither writes nor prints its signals at a distance. Professor Wheatstone (in a note on page 89, Juror's Report of 1862) makes a very proper discrimination between two instruments which he describes, naming them the chronoscope and the chronograph. A similar discrimination may be very justly made between the telegraph and the semaphore. Professor Wheatstone defines "chronoscope as an instrument by which the interval of time is observed, and chronograph an instrument by which it could be recorded." This is precisely the difference between the semaphore, which shows a signal to be observed, and the telegraph, by which the signal is recorded.

No example of a telegraph, therefore, in the strict sense of the word, appears to have existed previous to the year 1832. All the systems of communication to and from a distance until that date were, without exception, semaphores. True, in most instances, they bear the general name of telegraphs, yet an examination of the end proposed, the modes employed, and the results obtained, will show that none of them had more than a figurative title to the name telegraph. All of them propose but the conveyance of an evanescent signal; none of them propose a written or printed record of their intelligence. None of them, therefore, were strictly telegraphs.

Within a period of about thirty years the telegraphic systems, as well as the semaphoric, by electricity have literally been extended throughout the world, not only covering the vast area of the two hemispheres each with a net-work of these intellectual railways, but the subtle telegraphic thread, through American and British enterprise, has been carried underneath the deep Atlantic, uniting together the two great networks of the two hemispheres.

This vast reticulation of electrical conductors is, for the most part, used for telegraphic purposes; some of the electrical systems for communicating at a distance are, indeed, still semaphoric, but even these are more or less modified by the electrical and mechanical means that have been so efficaciously applied in the modern telegraphs.

The birth and inauguration of the generic telegraph has not only opened a new field for the labors, and given direction to the ingenuity of the mechanician, suggesting numerous varieties of form and distribution of parts, but it has also given a fresh impulse to the researches of the philosopher into the mysteries of its most efficient agent, electricity. It has been the servant of the astronomer; it has assisted in the determination of longitudes;[1] it has promoted the science of meteorology, and been tributary in many ways to the advancement of our knowledge of terrestrial phenomena. It has also directly stimulated and influenced the various systems of electrical semaphores. The application of the

---

[1] "It was suggested by Professor Morse to the distinguished Arago, in 1839, that the electro-magnetic telegraph would be the means of determining the difference of longitude between places with an accuracy hitherto unattainable." The first experiment of the kind resulted in the fulfillment of the prediction. The difference of longitude between Battle Monument Square, Baltimore, and the Capitol at Washington, was accurately determined by Captain Wilkes, by means of the telegraph, June 12, 1844.—See Vail's "American Electro-Magnetic Telegraph," p. 60, 1845.

electro-magnet has produced a great variety of most ingenious semaphoric instruments. It has modified and perfected the needle systems and the dial or cadran systems, as well as the varieties of the letter-printing telegraphs. These all owe to this application their most effective results. These will be noticed in their place. While thus signalizing some of the more important results to science, and to the art of communicating intelligence to a distance, flowing from the invention of the electro-magnetic telegraph, the writer would not assume so much the position of a discoverer in science as the applier of the results of scientific investigators to the practical development of the telegraph. It is, therefore, eminently fitting that the more important and prominent of these discoveries and results should be briefly noticed.

The apparently insignificant and unimportant observation of Galvani rests at the foundation of the brilliant series of discoveries which have made electricity the servant of man in many ways. The first plans of semaphores by electricity were confined, till the year 1800, to machine or static electricity, but from the intractable nature of the agent employed all of them proved unavailable. Semaphores by electricity were at that period, fifty years from the reported first suggestion of the idea by Franklin,[1] abandoned as impracticable. In the year 1800 Volta contrived the pile known by his name. The chemical effects of this pile suggested the idea of electric communication, by the employment of the decomposing effects of Voltaic electricity, and a semaphore based upon this scientific fact received a definite form in the complicated and unavailable plan of Sœmmering in 1811. In the year 1819 Oersted discovered that the magnetic needle could be deflected by the Voltaic current. Schweigger improved upon the primary element of Oersted's discovery just as Volta had done upon his own primary element of a single pair, and demonstrated that the magnetic effect of the current was increased by repeating the primary element, and hence resulted his celebrated multiplier. Arago, and also Davy, in the year 1820, observed the attraction of iron filings by a conducting wire, and Arago subsequently magnetized steel wires by inclosing them in a straight helix of wire, through which the Voltaic current was passed. Ampère discovered that when the Voltaic current is passed in the same direction through two parallel wires they attract each other, and that when passed in opposite directions they repel each other. Upon this observation is founded his theory of magnetism and electro-magnetism, which led to the method of magnetizing adopted by Arago. As early as 1824 investigations had commenced upon the power of wires to conduct Voltaic electricity. Two laws, opposed to each other, bearing upon the conductibility of the current, were announced; the one by Barlow in 1824, the other by Ohm in 1827. Barlow's law was, "that the conductibility was inversely proportionate to the square root of the lengths, and directly as the diameters of the wires, or as the square roots of their sections." The

---

[1] For a note in regard to Franklin's suggestion, see appendix D.

other and the true law is, "the resistance by bodies to the conduction of electricity is directly as their lengths, and inversely as the areas of their cross-sections." This law, says Dr. Page, was proved many years since by Davy, Pouillet, Becquerel, Christie, Ohm, Fechner, and others. It is now known as Ohm's law.

In 1825 Mr. Sturgeon, of England, made the first electro-magnet in the horse-shoe form, by loosely winding a piece of iron wire with a spiral of copper wire. In the United States, as early as 1831, the experimental researches of Professor Joseph Henry were of great importance in advancing the science of electro-magnetism. He may be said to have carried the electro-magnet, in its lifting powers, to its greatest perfection. Reflecting upon the principle of Professor Schweigger's galvanometer, he constructed magnets in which great power could be developed by a very small galvanic element. His published paper in 1831 shows that he experimented with wires of different lengths, and he noted the amount of magnetism which could be induced through them at various lengths by means of batteries composed of a single element and also of many elements. He states that the magnetic action of "a current from a trough composed of many pairs is at least not sensibly diminished by passing through a long wire," and he incidentally noted the bearing of this fact upon the project of an electro-magnetic telegraph, (semaphore?)

In more recent papers, first published in 1857, it appears that Professor Henry demonstrated before his pupils the practicability of ringing a bell by means of electro-magnetism at a distance.

It is claimed for M. Pouillet that in 1830 he constructed very powerful magnets on the same principle of the electro-magnets of the present day; and about the same time Professor Moll, of Utrecht, experimented to produce great magnetic effects with a powerful galvanic battery.

The needle system or electric semaphore owes its origin to a suggestion of the renowned La Place, in 1820, expanded about the same date in more of detail by Ampère; it appears to have been first experimented upon by Schilling, of Cronstadt, but practically realized on a small scale by those distinguished German savans Messrs. Gaus and Weber, of Göttingen, in 1833. It was improved by Messrs. Cooke and Wheatstone in 1837, and extensively introduced into Great Britain, and, so far as European countries are concerned, first transformed by the genius of Steinheil, of Munich, in 1837, from an electric semaphore into an electric telegraph. In the mean time the first electro-magnetic telegraph was devised in the United States in 1832, and shown in practical operation in 1835.

If it be asked what telegraphic system is specifically announced as most developed and extended throughout the world, the answer would seem to be definitely and summarily given in the proceedings of the International Telegraphic Convention held in Paris in March, 1865, composed of the representatives of twenty of the principal nations of Europe, assembled for the special purpose of examining the various projects, in order to adopt a uniform system, and to regulate international telegraphy for their common benefit. They thus decree in their third article: "L'appareil Morse reste provisoirement adopté pour le service des fils internationaux." Concise as is this announcement, as the result of their deliberations, it proclaims that the Morse system—an American system—is preferred for special international service throughout Europe.

Russia, Norway and Sweden, Denmark, Hamburg, Hanover, Prussia, Holland, Belgium, France, Wurtemberg, Bavaria, Saxony, Austria, Spain, Portugal, Baden, Switzerland, Italy, Greece, and the Ottoman Empire, by their respective ambassadors, took part in this convention, and these, it will be seen, comprise all the nations of continental Europe.

Great Britain is the only nation in Europe not represented in this convention; but even in Great Britain the Morse system is the one almost exclusively used in all her colonial possessions, in India, Australia, and Canada, and to an increasing extent also in the United Kingdom, especially in connection with the continental telegraph lines.

In view of these facts, it would seem to be proper, if not indeed necessary, to inquire, as a preliminary step to any examination of the telegraphic and semaphoric instruments in the Exposition, what is this Morse system which has obtained such universal popularity?

THE MORSE SYSTEM.

The Morse system was the introduction and the addition of a new art to the means of communicating at a distance. It is the invention of that art which remained an undeveloped germ until 1832, shut up in the etymology of the word telegraph. It is the art of writing or printing at a distance in one or more places at the same time.

When the first practicable mode for demonstrating such a result was devised in 1832, it was the birth of a new art. It was emphatically the first realization of a telegraph.

An art proposes a result, and includes the means and processes for producing that result.

1. The new art proposes as its result the marking, writing, or printing at a distance.

The means and process consist of—

2. A system of signs, to wit, a conventional code or alphabet adapted to marking, writing, or printing.

3. Of clockwork machinery to regulate the movement of a strip of paper or other material, upon which the signs are to be marked, written, or printed.

4. Of a lever bearing a pencil, fountain pen, printing wheel, stylus, or other marking instrument, for marking, writing, or printing the code of signs upon the paper.

5. Of the application of an electro-magnet, the power of which mediately and mechanically actuates the marking lever, for writing or printing.

6. Of the application of a salt to paper, to prepare it for receiving marks by electro-chemical decomposition.

7. Of a manipulator to close and open an electric circuit at regulated times, to charge and discharge the electro-magnet, or to bring into action the decomposing effects of electricity. Directly connected with the process of writing or printing the signs of the code, the sounds of the lever in writing or printing the letters were found to address the ear, adding a semaphoric result, inherent in the peculiar code of signs devised for writing and printing.

Thus much is new and peculiar to the Morse system. It comprises part of the means for operating the new art, and is precedent to the modes of application of the power, (electricity,) the effective agent for accomplishing the result.

The art thus invented employs as its most effective agent dynamic electricity, generated in some of the well-known methods of generating electricity.

The application of this power is effected by a combination with the preceding means:

1. Of a main line or circuit of electric conductors, connected with the poles of a galvanic battery or other generator of electricity, and having the helices of the electro-magnet as part of the circuit.

2. The armature of this magnet affixed to a lever is operated by the electro-magnet and an adjustable reacting spring, when the magnet is charged and discharged by closing and opening the circuit.

3. The lever bearing a pen, or other marking instrument, is made to mark (as well as to sound) the signs of the code, or by the closing and opening of a second circuit, having within it a battery and electro-magnet, armature, and pen-lever; the pen-lever is made to mark the signs upon the paper, or to sound them at any desired distance, thus producing the final result. This, in brief, is the Morse system.

An instrument embodying these essential portions of the invention was constructed and seen in operation by many witnesses in the autumn of 1835, demonstrating the practicability of the art.

THE RELAY.

The relay or secondary circuit was devised to obviate a foreshadowed difficulty in the possible, not to say probable, weakening of the magnetic power in a long line.

This relay (or, as it was at first named, the receiving magnet, because it received its impulse from the distant station to be transmitted to the register) is simply an electro-magnet, whose only mechanical duty is to close and open another circuit. The accompanying figure explains its office.

M M is the electro-magnet with its coils of wire, the two extremities of which are connected with the main line circuit at L′ L″, thus constituting the coils of the magnet part of the main circuit. When, therefore, the main circuit is charged from the distant station, the electro-magnet M M is charged and becomes a magnet. To utilize the power thus created, a delicate upright lever of metal has at one end a cross-axis *b*, and at the other end it oscillates between the points of two adjusting screws *c* and *d*.

Fig. 1.

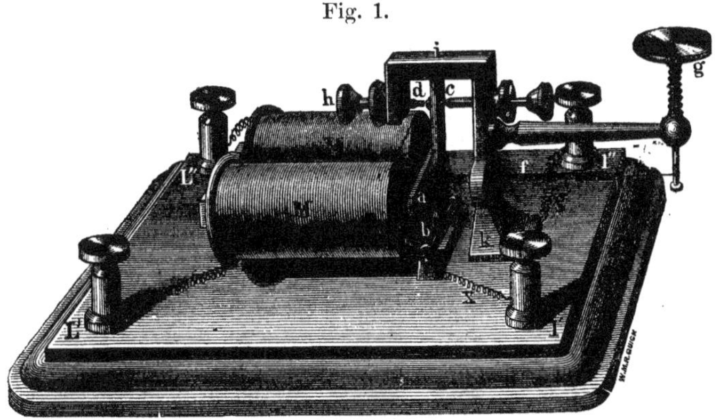

The Relay Magnet.

Erected before the face of the magnet poles, the lever has attached to it a soft iron armature, which is attracted to the point of the adjusting screw *h* at *d*, when the magnet is charged, and brought back to its rest by an adjustable spring *g*, when the magnet is discharged against the insulated point *c* of the other adjustable screw. The circuit called the local circuit, connected by a local battery with the magnet of the register, is connected by its extremities with the relay at the binding screws *l' l''*.

The operation of the relay is as follows: The binding screw *l'*, holding one extremity of the local circuit, is connected with the metal of the lever, which oscillates between the points *d* and *c*, while the other binding screw, holding the other extremity of the local circuit, is connected with the metallic frame *k*. While the lever rests against the insulated point *c*, the local circuit is open, for the insulation prevents metallic contact; but when the relay magnet is charged, it attracts the armature *a*, thus causing the lever to make metallic contact at *d*, and so closing the circuit, as long as the magnet is charged; when it is discharged, the spring *g* brings back the lever against the insulated point *c*, and opens the circuit at *d*.

THE MORSE SYSTEM INTRODUCED IN EUROPE.

In the spring of 1838 this telegraph was introduced to the European world through the French Academy of Sciences, under the auspices of the distinguished Arago, and in the autumn of that year it was breveted in France.

This is the invention which has received the free, unsolicited suffrages of the International Telegraph Convention. It has features of individuality which distinguish it from all other systems of communicating intelligence at a distance, and its universality is undoubtedly mainly due to the result which it proposes and accomplishes, (to wit, a written or printed record,) and also to the simplicity of the mechanism by which that result is obtained.

Adopted in countries renowned for consummate skill in the manufacture of philosophical instruments and delicate instruments of precision, it is natural to expect that the telegraphic instruments constructed by the accomplished mechanicians of these countries, while preserving the essential principles of the original telegraph, would take many forms and display a great variety of mechanical adaptations to produce the result most effectively.

It ought to be here mentioned, however, to the credit of the mechanicians of the United States, to whom was intrusted the manufacture of the first Morse telegraphic instruments in use on the American lines, that most of the instruments, not only in form, but in point of efficiency, compactness, and finish of workmanship, in accuracy of mechanical adaptation and durability, were not inferior to most of those now manufactured and used in Europe. Many of the modifications in form, and the varied distribution of parts of the mechanism in the American instruments, take precedence in time of the European instruments. But the beauty and accuracy of mechanical finish in the great majority of the instruments, it is conceded, are for the most part in favor of the European mechanicians. Especially is this the case in the ingenious instruments used for imprinting the common or Roman letter, first attempted by Vail as early as 1837; afterwards effectively accomplished by House, but subsequently the instruments for which were so admirably perfected by Hughes, and are sent forth from the ateliers of Digney frères, Froment, and others, in France, and Siemens & Halske in Germany.

SIEMENS AND HALSKE'S MODIFICATION OF THE MORSE APPARATUS.

An example is given here of one of the modifications of the Morse apparatus by those distinguished savans and mechanicians, Messrs. Siemens & Halske, of Berlin.

The magnets, two in number, *m m′*, straight, but not united as in the ordinary horseshoe magnet, are placed horizontally instead of vertically, as in the original instruments. The poles *r* of the magnet *m′* have each a facing, outside the coil, of soft iron. The core of the other magnet *m* has a continuation from each pole of soft iron, acting as an armature, to be attracted by the facings of soft iron of the magnet *m′*.

A frame *p p*, from the center of which is the printing lever with its embossing point, is attached to the armature. The ends of the coils of the magnets *a* and *b* are carried to the terminals A and B.

By this arrangement of magnets the attraction of opposite polarities is efficaciously utilized. In all other respects the apparatus is not materially different from the original Morse. Notwithstanding the theoretic advantage of this modification, an experience of some time on the German, Danish, and Russian lines has led to its general abandonment for other modifications, or for the original Morse pattern.

Fig. 2.

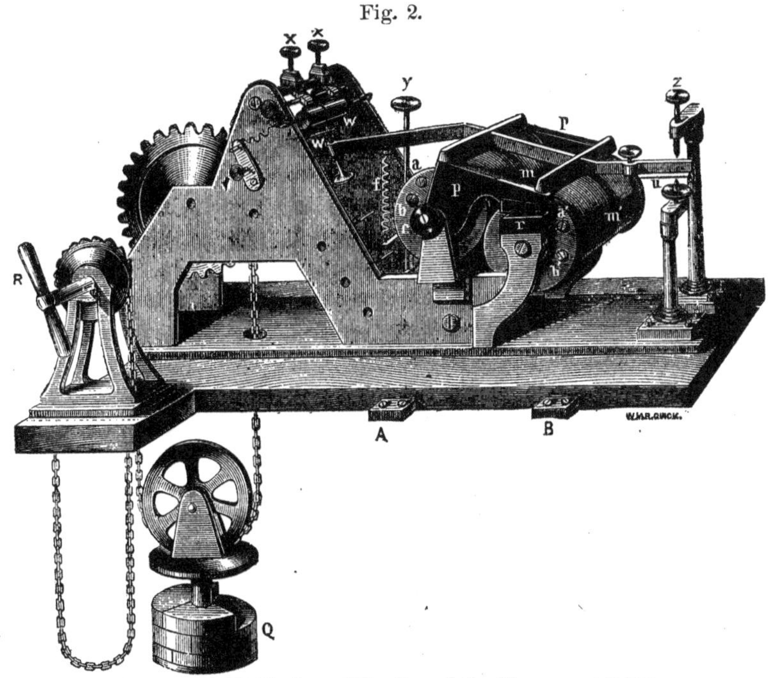

Siemens & Halske's modification of the Morse apparatus.

Another modification of the Morse by Messrs. Siemens & Halske is seen in Fig. 3. It consists in a mode of supplying the ink to the printing wheel.

An inverted bottle B B containing the ink is fixed, with a felt stopper, above and touching the printing wheel *c*. In all other respects it is essentially the original printing-wheel apparatus of one of the first Morse instruments, which was supplied with ink from a sponge. It has, however, in addition, the mode of bringing the paper to the wheel instead of the wheel to the paper, the device of Messrs. Baudouin and Digney frères, which is seen in the next diagram.

Fig. 3.

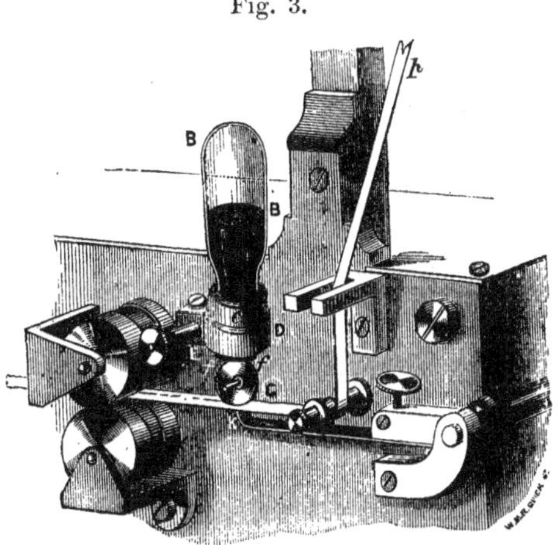

Siemens & Halske's Inking apparatus.

BAUDOUIN AND DIGNEY FRÈRES' MODIFICATION.

This ingenious modification is the invention of Messrs. Baudouin and Digney frères, of Paris, and is a real improvement. It consists in bringing the paper to the inking wheel, instead of the wheel to the paper. The rest of the apparatus is in all essential respects the Morse apparatus.

Fig. 4.

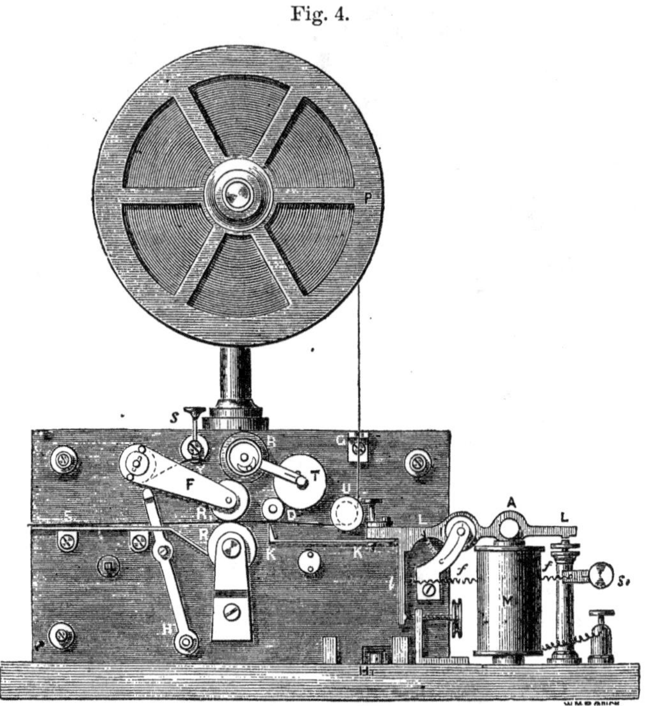

Baudouin and Digney Frères' Inking apparatus.

M is the electro-magnet. A is the armature upon the lever L L, hinged at I. The improvement consists in a prolonging of the lever by attaching to the writing extremity of it a thin metal slip K K, bent slightly upward toward the small printing wheel D. T is a felt ink roller, kept moistened with ink, against which the printing wheel D turns to receive the ink on its edge. The paper from the paper wheel P passes through a guide G down and around a pulley wheel U, and is drawn by the rollers R R′ near but not touching the printing wheel D. So long as the magnet is not charged the paper passes beneath the printing wheel without a mark, but so soon as the magnet is charged the slip, or as it is termed in French, the "couteau," rises, and the edge of the couteau raises the paper against the inking wheel, and a mark longer or shorter, as the magnet continues charged, is made upon the paper. This mode of bringing the paper to the wheel requires so much less power than bringing the wheel to the paper, that for very considerable distances the relay necessary to furnish greater power in order to emboss the paper can be dispensed with. This, we have said, is a real improvement, and its simplicity has given it a wide popularity. It is the simplest of all the modes of recording. It is this instrument that goes by the name of the "ink writer."

Still another modification by Messrs. Siemens & Halske is seen in Fig. 5.

Fig. 5.

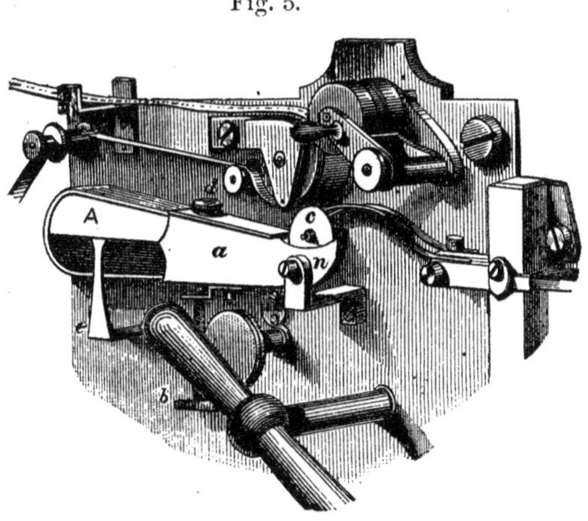

Siemens & Halske's modification of the Ink-writer.

The peculiarity of this modification is in the manner of supplying ink to the printing wheel by a reservoir of ink A *a*, in which the printing wheel *c* revolves, half immersed in the fluid; but in this case the wheel is brought up to the paper.

The reservoir is hinged at *n*, and is raised or depressed by the screw *b* to regulate the flow of ink to the wheel.

Of all these modes of ink-writing that of Messrs. Baudouin and Digney frères is the simplest and best.

Did it not lead too far away from the special duty with which the writer is charged, it would be a most agreeable occupation to notice in detail many of the ingenious, if not always practical, modifications of the telegraph apparatus by the German, French, and English savans and mechanicians, such as the mode of sending dispatches both ways at the same time over the same wire, said to be originally devised by the Austrian savant, Dr. Gintl; and also the modifications of the same, by Herrn Frischen and Siemens & Halske; also the method devised by Stark, of Vienna, of transmitting two messages along a single line in the same direction, together with the modifications of this device by Kramer, Bosseda, Maron, Edlund, and others; also of Wheatstone's automatic printing apparatus, and of Stohrer's double style apparatus.

But inquirers must be referred to the able works of many authors of telegraph treatises, especialy to Sabine's "History of the Telegraph," and to Blavier's "*Nouveau Traité de Télégraphie Électrique.*" To M. Sabine's courtesy the writer is indebted for leave to use many of his engravings of apparatus which are introduced into this report.

AUSTRIAN MILITARY TELEGRAPH.

Among other apparatus is the military telegraph apparatus of Austria, exhibited by the Imperial Royal Direction of Telegraphs in Vienna.

Baron Benedek says, according to the Paris Times of September 1,

1866, that a nation before entering upon a war should provide itself with *three* great elements, and "the Baron classes them in the order of their utiliy. First, *a good commander;* second, *iron roads*, (railroads;) third, *the electric telegraph*."

The whole Austrian group, under the superintendence of the Baron d'Ebner, colonel of engineers, is remarkable for the completeness and beautiful workmanship, as well as scientific skill, of the various apparatus pertaining to electricity and its various uses in modern warfare, These uses, except so far as they include telegraphic service, are irrelevant to the present report, although to the military student in the highest degree instructive and interesting. Through the courtesy of the Baron all were explained, and a pamphlet given entitled "*Notice sur les objets formant l'exposition collective du ministère de la guerre I. R. d'Autriche à l'Exposition Universelle de Paris.*"

The Morse apparatus, compactly and beautifully made by J. Leopolder, of Vienna, is the principal telegraphic instrument used in the military telegraph. The Austrian pamphlet does not, however, give the details of the mode of constructing and regulating the military telegraph. These have been obtained from a very excellent and lucid pamphlet of about one hundred pages by E. Costa de Serda, *capitaine d'état major*, published in Paris.

A short extract from the introduction of this pamphlet supplies some of the desired details. The whole pamphlet is worthy of careful study. Under the head of different species of campaign telegraphs, Capitaine de Serda says:

"Two species of telegraphic apparatus are most usually employed in a campaign:

"I. The Morse apparatus, modified by Digney,[1] comprising—

"*a.* Wagons, with the materiel necessary to the construction of a line of over six miles English.

"*b.* Two wagon stations.

"II. Electro-magnetic dial apparatus, comprising the wagons with the necessary materiel for the construction of a line about six miles English, and the two telegraph apparatus."

Under the head of *Propriétés particulières et emploi de ces deux sortes du télégraphe*, he continues: "The Morse apparatus and its numerous modifications are found in use on the greatest number of permanent lines. This consideration, joined to the facility with which they can be connected with the existing lines, has caused this apparatus to be adopted for the campaign telegraph. The Digney apparatus, in particular, has the advantage of producing the signs printed in ink upon a band of paper, and that which is of greater importance it can be operated without the relay, but it requires experienced operators.

"The magneto-electric apparatus, on the contrary, is much more

[1] The *modification* here spoken of is Digney's mode of using the original *inking wheel*, elsewhere explained in this report.

simple. It is transported upon the wagons at the same time with the materiel, and can be operated by less able telegraphists, but it has the inconvenience of leaving no written record of the dispatch.

"At all times it is essential for military purposes to have both these kinds of apparatus."

NOTE BY MR. DE SERDA.—"These two kinds of telegraph apparatus are not the only ones which can be advantageously used in a campaign. Many models have been proposed or employed, and one is embarrassed to make a choice of them. The essential condition is, that they be strongly made, and easily transportable. Of the number of apparatus fulfilling these conditions, we cite the *Morse apparatus*, which is operated by the Daniel battery, (it is in use in many of the German armies,) and the military telegraph of M. Hipp, described in the Telegraphic Annals, (first year.) As to the two apparatus which we use, in accordance with our instructions, they have already been proved. The telegraph Digney [Morse] was operated in the Italian campaign in 1859. The dial electro-magnetic telegraph [semaphore] of Siemens is used upon the established lines of Bavaria, and has been adopted as the campaign apparatus of the Hanoverian army.

"The more immediate purpose of these telegraphic systems is their employment in the defense of coasts, of rivers, of mountain passes, to put an army in communication with its base of operations."

For more minute details of all that pertains to the construction and organization of the military telegraph, reference must be had to the pamphlet of M. Serda, transmitted with this report, which will amply repay the attention bestowed in its perusal.

From the statement in the pamphlet of the Austrian ministry of war, that "the application of the electric telegraph to military operations dates from the year 1854," it seems not to be known that the proposal for such an application was made to the French minister of war as early as the winter of 1838–'39. The circumstances are these: Morse, in September, 1838, exhibited his telegraphic invention to the French Academy of Sciences. The French minister of war, at that period, was General Bernard, a personal acquaintance and friend of the writer while the general was in the service of the United States, and on my visit to Paris, with my invention, he showed me many attentions. After dinner at the minister's one day, while some of the guests were amusing themselves in the billiard saloon, the writer was engaged in describing the nature of his invention to the general, and incidentally the manner (almost identical with the present plans in use) in which the invention could be used in military operations, stating his belief that the army which first made use of the telegraph in its operations must inevitably be the victor. The general listened with the deepest attention, and requesting reticence on the subject, said, "I will send an officer to you for further explanation." Accordingly, in a day or two afterwards, an officer—a marshal, an aged man—called to see the apparatus, to whom I imparted the plan.

The marshal was skeptical, opposing objections at every step, the principal one, however, being the fact that the telegraph wagon proposed, with the necessary apparatus, would add greatly to the materiel of the army, and so to its incumbrance. No reasoning that any such disadvantage would be more than counterbalanced by the obvious advantages availed to gain his favor to the project. He could not be moved from his position. He left me fully persuaded that it was a chimerical plan, and probably reported against it, for it was not again the subject of conversation with the minister. It should be borne in mind, as an apology for this feeling of the old marshal, that at that time the telegraph had nowhere been practically established, and that serious doubts were entertained, even in high scientific quarters, whether the telegraph could ever be made a practicable, or, at least, a practical enterprise. The skepticism of the marshal, therefore, had a plausible basis. It was not till the telegraphic lines had been extended on the continent, and successfully tested, that the ingenuity of the skillful was turned to the obvious advantage to be derived from a military telegraph. Modern warfare has been materially modified by its means. The Crimean campaign, the campaign in Italy, the civil war in America, and the later campaign in Austria, have all demonstrated that the telegraph is a potent engine, and has become an indispensable agent in military operations.

PRINTING TELEGRAPHS.

HUGHES'S PRINTING TELEGRAPH.

It was the original intention to give full descriptions of the telegraphic apparatus displayed in the Exposition, and in pursuance of this intention much labor and time were expended in examining and describing many of the instruments—labor and time which might have been spared had the fact been earlier recognized that most of the apparatus had been exhibited in previous international exhibitions, and had been fully and much better described in the Juror's Reports of these exhibitions by learned and competent savans. The labors of this report, therefore, are reduced mainly to noticing those which appear to possess some novelty; to giving references to descriptions in former reports and in other published works of the most important apparatus, and to examining and discussing any professed improvements.

A modification of the telegraph, by D. E. Hughes, from the ateliers of E. Hardy, of P. Dumoulin Froment, and Digney frères, Paris, Nos. 4, 10, and 13, of the catalogue, will now be noticed.

Among the many modifications of the telegraph displayed in the Exposition, the adapting of it to the imprinting of the ordinary alphabetic characters is one that early engaged the attention of the ingenious. None, however, have so just a title to pre-eminence as the ingenious printing instrument of Mr. D. E. Hughes. After the operation of the first instrument of Morse, in 1835, demonstrating the practicability of recording intelligence at a distance, the success of the original instrument, in producing this new result, naturally suggested the idea that the ordinary letters of the alphabet might be also recorded or imprinted as successfully as the Morse code of signs, and hence originated the earliest device of Alfred Vail, esq., for printing the Roman letters. Mr. Vail, in 1837, was associated with Morse, and after studying the operation of this first Morse instrument, proposed and draughted his plan of a printing instrument, a description of which he has given in full, with diagrams, in his work entitled the "American Electro-Magnetic Telegraph," published in 1845. The complicated machinery necessary to produce the result, which seemed more curious than useful, and its slowness of operation, compared with the Morse instrument, were obstacles to its practical application. It was never practically tested. The result, however, which was proposed, to wit, the actual printing of the Roman letter, possessed a fascination which took strong possession of the minds of ingenious men, and one of them, R. E. House, esq., devoted his genius and rare mechanical skill to the construction of an instrument of great beauty and effectiveness, which, to a limited extent, is still in operation.

Fig. 6.

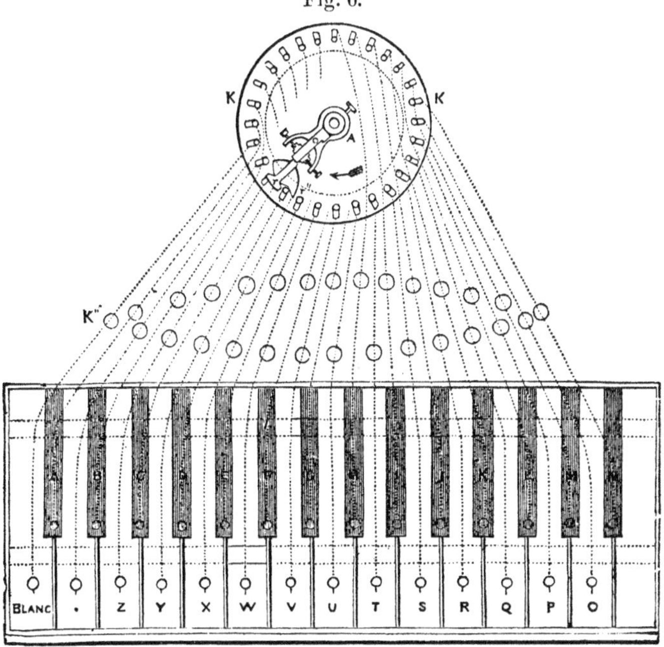

Key-board of the Hughes apparatus.

The Hughes apparatus is of too much importance to pass undescribed, or to be dismissed with merely a reference to a description in books. Not being able to obtain from the accomplished inventor (owing to his absence in the East) a description from his own pen, which would have been preferred, the writer of this report avails himself of the lucid description and illustrations of Robert Sabine, esq., who has courteously permitted duplicate illustrations to be made for this report from his valuable work, "The Electric Telegraph," published in London by Virtue Brothers, in 1867:

"The essential principle of this highly ingenious system is the synchronous movements of the type-wheels at two or more stations, and of the power to press a strip of paper at each of the stations simultaneously against the types on the corresponding parts of the wheels, by the action of a single electric wave or impulse.

"A clockwork at each station turns, with a continuous and uniform motion, an axle, at the extremity of which the type-wheel is supported. The synchronism is attained by the aid of a vibrating spring and anchor escapement. The rotation of the type-wheel is transmitted to a vertical arbor, furnished at its lower extremity with a horizontal arm traveling over a circular disk, in which is arranged a series of contact pins, in number corresponding to the types. Each pin, therefore, represents a letter, and is raised when it is wished to telegraph this letter along the line. The horizontal arm, which travels around the disk with a motion uniform with that of the type-wheel, comes in contact with the pin just at the moment when the corresponding type is at the lowest point and closes an electric circuit, by which the paper is lifted up against the type-wheel and the letter printed.

"The key-board used to elevate the contact pins is shown in Fig. 6. It consists of twenty-eight keys, alternately white and black, marked with the twenty-six letters of the alphabet, a full stop, and a blank, corresponding to an empty space on the type-wheel. Below each of the keys is a movable lever whose fulcrum is at K″, and which terminates at the bottom of one of the contact pins K K, arranged in a circle in the metal box A, in the top and bottom of which are holes for the ends to protrude—the upper holes being long to allow of a radial motion. Each pin is held down by the pressure of a small spring, but may be elevated by pressing down the corresponding key of the piano board.

"Fig. 9 gives a vertical section of the printing instrument and key-board. The section shows a white key hinged at K″, connected to its lever K′, a contact pin k, on the right, and also to a black key, whose lever reaches to a contact pin on the left of the box A. The contact pins are provided with shoulders to limit their movements in each direction.

"The horizontal arm, which travels over the circle of contact points, is attached to the bottom of the vertical arbor Q, to which motion is imparted by the beveled wheel G on the shaft G_2. It is made up of three principal parts: the arm r, jointed at a; the resting piece, or earth contact, r'; and the shovel r''. The vertical shaft of Q is of brass, and is divided electrically into two parts by an insulating ring of ivory q. The lower part is supported by the central pedestal, which is insulated from the box A by a non-conducting ring.

"The continuation of the jointed arm *r*, which is held by the portion of the shaft above the insulating ring *q*, is pressed down by a spring, which keeps a small screw in the middle of the continuation in metallic contact with second piece *r'*, supported by the portion of the shaft below the ring. The shovel *r''* is of steel.

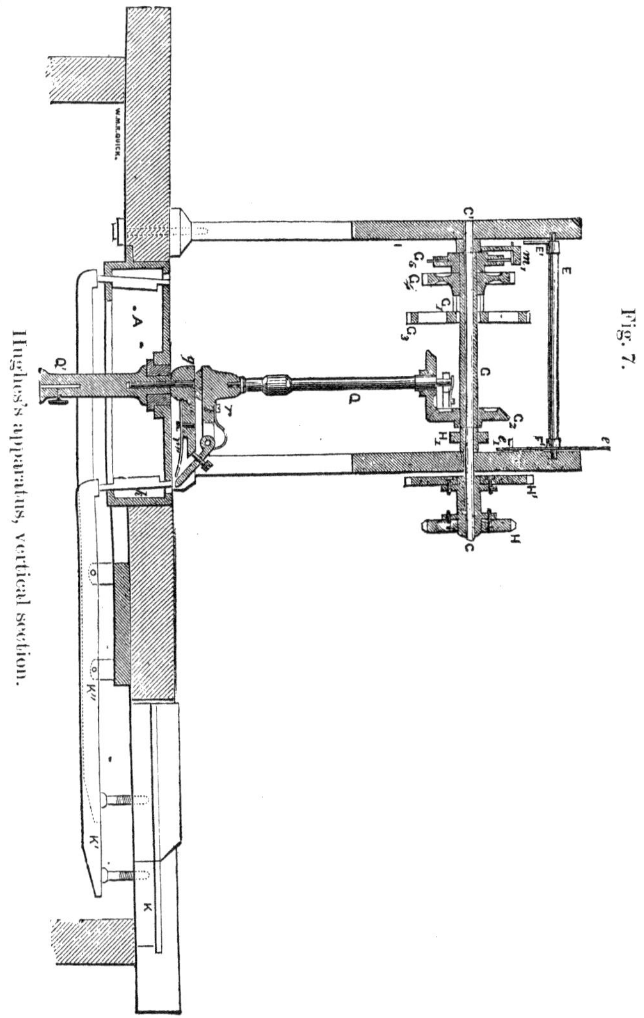

Fig. 7.

Hughes's apparatus, vertical section.

"When a key is depressed the corresponding contact pin is elevated, and if the arbor Q is in motion, the extremity of the arm *r* mounts upon the elevated pin, by which contact between *r* and *r'* is interrupted and that of *r* with *k* established. The arm *r* having made contact with the shovel *r''*, which immediately follows it, pushes the pin *k* in its slot outside the circumference swept over by *r*; so that if the latter made another revolution while the finger is kept down on the key, no second contact is made, and the same letter is not repeated. The operator feels a vibration of the key as the shovel passes by the pin, and is thus made aware that the letter has been printed.

"The type-wheel H contains on its circumference, in twenty-eight equal spaces, twenty-six letters of the alphabet, a dot, and a blank space; it is fixed to the extremity of the axis C C′, which is put in motion by means of the hollow axis G enveloping it in the greater part of its length. The connection between C C′ and G is made by the mediation of a fine ratchet-wheel G_5 attached to the axis G, the click m_1 being on the axis C C′. On the latter are supported, besides the type-wheel and the click, a corrector H′, or wheel with long narrow teeth, equal in number to the types, serving to establish precision between the movements of the horizontal arm r and the type-wheel. On the same axis is a wheel H_1, having a notch at one part of its circumference for stopping the type-wheel when the blank space is opposite the printing press, in case it should spring forward.

"The hollow axis G is turned by clock-work moved by a weight, a wheel of which engages with the pinion G_1, and supports besides the ratchet G_5 and beveled wheel G_2, already mentioned, the escape wheel G_4, and a tooth wheel G_3, which locks into the pinion I′, Fig. 8, of the printing shaft I.

"The printing-shaft turns seven times as fast as the type-wheel, and carries a fly-wheel I″ at one extremity, in order to overcome the inertia of a small shaft, whose duty is to lift the paper up to the type-wheel at the other extremity. This is shown partly in section in Fig. 8. The printing-shaft I, and its continuation i, are locked together by means of a ratchet-wheel I_1 and click i'.

Fig. 8.

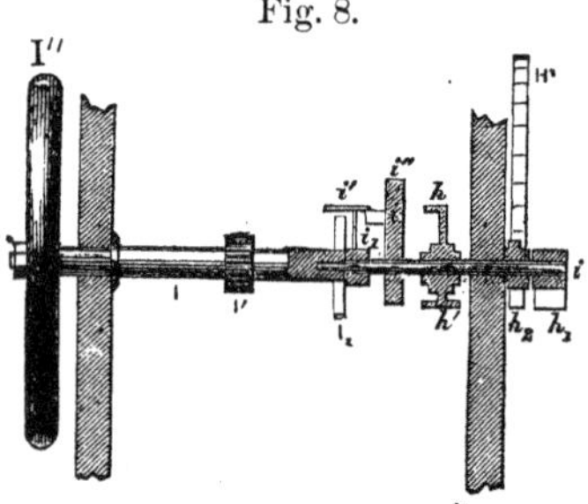

"At the end of the continuation shaft i is a cam h_1, for lifting the press and the paper against the type-wheel.

Fig. 9.

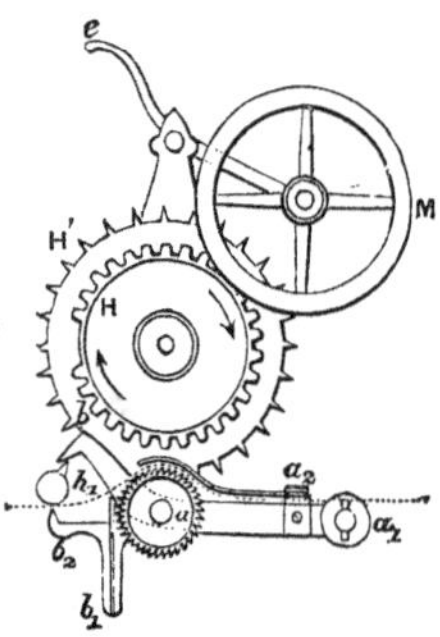

"The printing press is shown in Fig. 9. Underneath the type-wheel is a small cylinder a, over which the paper is led, its axis being in the middle of a bent lever b, turning at a_1; attached to it is a ratchet-wheel in the teeth of which catches a click affixed to a movable piece b_1, terminating in the rectangular arm b_2, which is forced upward by a spring, attached to the frame of the apparatus, but is stopped against the axis i. When i makes one revolution, the cam lifts the arm b of the lever, together with the cylinder a and paper strip up to the lowest tooth of the type-wheel, by which the paper strip is impressed with the print of the type, kept inked by an inking-roller M. The cam being very sharp, the movements of ascent and descent are proportionally rapid, and the paper touches the type during only an infinitely short space of time. The axis continuing to turn, the cam meets the arm b, and depresses it, causing the click to draw round the cylinder and advance the paper a certain distance.

"By the side of the ratchet-wheel I′, the printing-shaft carries an escapement h h', arrested by a continuation of the lever L L′, moving with the armature of the electro-magnet. The armature is of soft iron, supported at the extremity of a lever D, over the poles of the electro-magnet, Fig. 10. The lever turns between supports on the axis, and

Fig. 10.

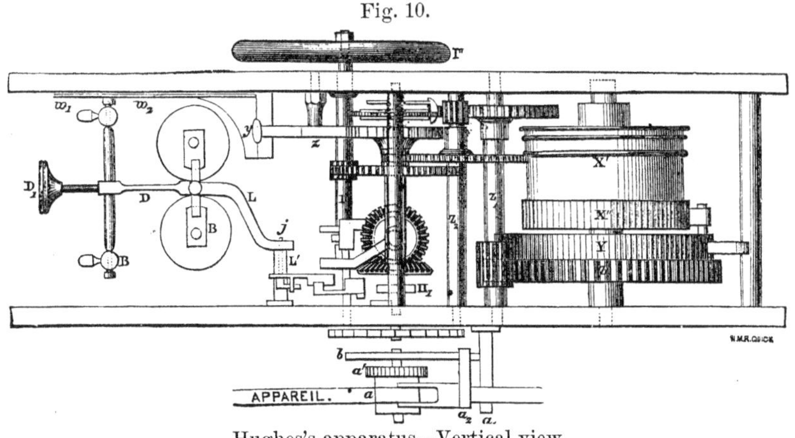

Hughes's apparatus—Vertical view.

tends to rise by the force of a spring regulated by the adjusting-screw D′.

"The screw d', Fig. 11, on the end of the lever L L′, turning on the axis j, sits over the armature; the other end of the lever engages with one of the pallets of the escapement h h', and governs the motion of the axis i. When a current traverses the coils of the electro-magnet, the armature and lever are depressed, the click is put in gear, and the pallet h of the escapement, released, turns with the axis i. At the moment when the pallet h' passes under the lever, it relifts it, and depresses the screw d', returning thereby the armature to the poles of the electro-magnet, and at the same time throwing the click out of gear.

Fig. 11.

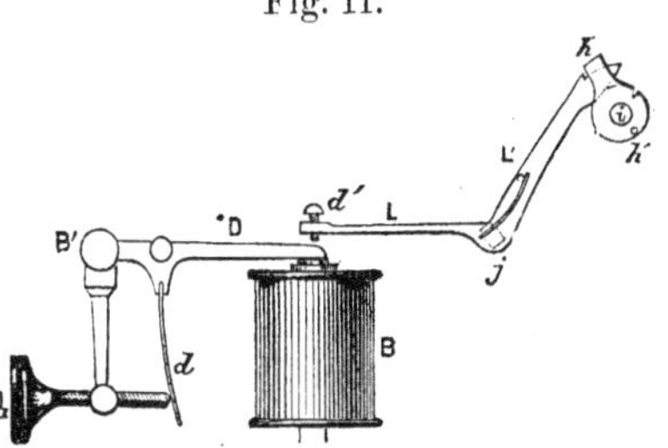

"The magnet B is of novel construction. It consists of a permanent horseshoe magnet, with soft iron cylindrical continuations on the poles. These continuations are each encircled by a coil of wire. When no current passes through the coils, the armature is attracted to the poles by the magnetism distributed in the iron. This force is opposed by the adjusting spring, which is so regulated that, the armature being in contact, a very weak current is able to neutralize the attraction.

"The printing-shaft has also the duty of correcting the movement of the type-wheel, and of insuring always that, at the moment of printing a letter, the type is in its proper position. This is effected by means of a curved cam h_2 on the axis *i*. The instant the cam *h′* lifts the arm *b* of the frame carrying the printing roller, the projection h_2 locks into the teeth of the wheel H′, and adjusts, if it be necessary, its position. If, on entering the teeth of H′, the cam has to push the wheel forward, or to accelerate the motion of the axis C C′, the click *m* is pushed onward, passing over one or more of the teeth of the ratchet-wheel G_5. If, on the contrary, the cam has to retard the motion, the click pulls the ratchet-wheel backward, for which purpose the latter is not made rigid on the axis, but is formed of a disk held between leather washers, supported by two plates of metal fixed on the hollow shaft G.

"The electric circuits of the apparatus are very simple. The bottom of the vertical shaft Q is connected to earth, and the upper part to one end of the coils of the electro-magnet, the other end being to line. One pole of a battery is connected to the levers *k* of the contact pins; the other pole to earth. At two corresponding stations the plates of the batteries must always be looking the same way, because the home apparatus is intended always to work as well as that of the distant stations, and the armature of its magnet is only liberated by currents in one direction.

"When a current arrives, therefore, from the line, it passes first through the coil B of the magnet, then through the vertical shaft Q, which it descends and goes over from the screw in the jointed arm *v* to the resting-piece *r′*, and from this to earth. When a current is to be transmitted, the operation consists principally in interrupting the earth circuit, and inserting the battery into the break. This is done by the contact-pins and jointed arm of *r*. A key being depressed, the arm *r*, in its journey, rides over the pin, and its screw is lifted up from contact with *r′*, which breaks the direct earth circuit; at the same time the contact of *r′* with the pin *k*, which is in communication with a pole of the battery through the lever K, sends a current from the battery (K *k* *r* Q) through the coils of the magnet into the line, &c.

"Suppose two such apparatus, properly adjusted, at the extremities of a line of telegraph, the clock-work wound up, the electrical connections properly established, and the type-wheels locked; the employé who desires to transmit presses down the key of his instrument; this pushes up the corresponding contact peg in the circle K, and when the chariot arrives over the pin, the extremity of the piece *r* rides over it, separating the earth contact and introducing the battery into the line circuit. The current passes through the vertical shaft, the coils of the magnet, and line wire to the other station, where it circulates in the coils of the magnet, the vertical shaft, &c., and goes to earth.

"In traversing the coils of the magnets of both instruments, the current weakens the attractions of the armatures to the poles of the electro-magnets; the former are forced off by the spring, the screws *d′* are raised and the levers L at the same time depressed. The pallets *h* of the escapements *h h'* are thereupon released, the axis *i* put into gear with I, and the type-wheels released. During the revolution made by the axis *i*, the cylinders *a* are raised by the cams, and lift the paper up to the printing-wheels at the moment when the latter are unlocked. No letter is printed, because the blank space in the type-wheel occurs just there. The paper strips and cylinders descend again, the former advancing a step. The clicks are then disengaged from the ratchets, and the pallets *h* recaught by the levers L', which were lifted up, causing the armatures to be pushed down again to the poles of the magnets.

"If a key answering to any letter be now pressed down, the current is repeated the moment the chariot passes over the raised contact pin; the printing axis is put in motion, the letter printed, and the paper pushed on as before, and so on, until the message is completed.

"It sometimes happens that the apparatus do not agree when one of the stations sends its message. In this case the employé at the receiving station advises his correspondent of it by giving him a signal; both then arrest their type-wheels, and the transmission is recommenced, beginning always with the blank.

"To avoid the inconvenience of irregular working, which might arise from changes in the battery power, Professor Hughes has adopted a method of short circuiting the coils of the electro-magnet the instant after the armature is released, that the current, whatever may be its intensity, comes into play only long enough to effect the required weakening of the magnetic attraction. This is done by connecting one end of the electro-magnet coils with D, and the other end with L, in addition to the other connections, and by adjusting the screw *d'*, so that, when at rest, the armature reposing on the poles does not touch it; but as soon as the neutralization occurs it is lifted up by the force of the spring, and the coils short circuited by contact of D with *d'*.

"The speed of transmission attained by this apparatus is very great. The chariot and type-wheel revolve about one hundred and twenty times in a minute, and an expert manipulator can transmit on the average two letters during a single revolution of the shaft.

"The word '*telegraph*,' for example, is completed in six turns, as follows:

First turn	*blank* and *t*.
Second turn	*e l*.
Third turn	*e*.
Fourth turn	*g r*.
Fifth turn	*a p*.
Sixth turn	*h*.

"The French word '*bonté*' is done in four turns—

First turn	Blank.
Second turn	*b o*.
Third turn	*n t*.
Fourth turn	*é*.

"Another example is the word '*dintz*,' more fortunate than either, being transmitted during a single revolution."

In summing up the advantages and disadvantages of the Hughes apparatus, Mr. E. E. Blavier, vol. II, pp. 268, 269, says:

"The dispatches by the Hughes apparatus received upon the strip of paper are directly transmitted to those for whom they are destined without any transcribing. The strip of paper is cut off and pasted in lines upon a leaf of ordinary paper. * * *

"The strip upon which is the impression at the place of departure is preserved for the control. The errors and the delays which attend the copying of the dispatches, and the expense of clerk-hire, are thus diminished.

"Errors can also be *revised* during the transmission made by incorrect manipulation, or erroneous reading of the text to be transmitted. But there occurs no confusion in the signs received, as may happen in the Morse system when certain letters resemble each other, or in the apparatus for fugitive signals where all depends upon the attention of the operator.

"These advantages are common to all the printing apparatus, but that which distinguishes the apparatus of M. Hughes is the great speed of transmission that he gives, which is due to this, that each letter requires but a single passage of the current, and to this that there is no stopping of the apparatus during the transmission.

"This speed surpasses greatly that attained by all the other systems.

"Upon the lines of four hundred or five hundred kilometers, (thirty-one miles English,) for example, fifty-five to sixty dispatches of twenty words in an hour can be easily transmitted with the Hughes apparatus on condition that the labor is continuous and the order of transmission is not often changed. Under the same conditions from thirty-five to forty dispatches can with difficulty be obtained by the Morse apparatus,[1] and from twenty to twenty-five with the dial apparatus or escapement printing instruments.

"On the other hand, the manipulation of the Hughes instrument requires expert and intelligent operators; for the want of skill cannot be remedied by a slower transmission, as with the dial or Morse instruments. It is very complicated, and in consequence is liable to frequent derangement. It cannot, therefore, be used for ordinary stations, *(postes secondaires,)* where the Morse instruments will always be preferred because of their great simplicity. For the important offices connected directly by the wires, it is eminently practical, and it has already rendered great services; its use is daily extending."

It is to be remarked, in regard to this extremely ingenious instrument, that it is not the special result, to wit, the printing of the ordinary letter of the alphabet, that gives to it its prominence and its great excellence; these are due rather to the greater quantity of intelligence it pro-

[1] For correction of these erroneous figures, see *Statement of comparative speed*, &c., Chap. v.

fesses to transmit in a given time. It must be admitted that aside from the simplicity of the apparatus by which the Morse characters are transmitted, one of the chief merits of the Morse apparatus has hitherto been that a greater amount of intelligence in a given time, and by simpler means, can be transmitted and recorded by it than by any other system. It is now asserted that the Hughes apparatus transmits more than the Morse, as the latter is now usually operated. If, however, it shall be ascertained that the Morse has been underestimated in its speed of transmission, or if, by some modification or improvement in manipulation, or skill in the operator, it should be demonstrated that the Morse transmits as rapidly as the Hughes, or even if it should be with somewhat less rapidity, the improvement of whatever nature would in all probability cause the Hughes apparatus to give place to the improvement, provided it was not encumbered with great complication. For, be it remarked, the public as well as the telegraph administrations are most interested in having the greatest quantity in the shortest time, and will care very little whether the telegraph clerk who receives a dispatch has come to the knowledge, for example, of the letter E by the simple dot [.] of the Morse code, or by the usual E of the Roman alphabet. It is the same letter in either case, and that process which can with due economy and least complication send the greatest number of them in a given time will be preferred to all others[1].

ARLINCOURT'S PRINTING APPARATUS.

For a clear description of this very ingenious Roman-letter printing apparatus, (which was also exhibited at the great exhibition of 1862, and is briefly noticed in the record in the Practical Mechanics' Journal,) the inquirer is referred to the excellent work of Blavier, vol. II, pp. 226 to 233. Mr. Blavier, however, after describing it, says: "This apparatus, notwithstanding its apparent complication, gives good results, and has been employed with success upon some lines. It, nevertheless, has the inconvenience common to the dial apparatus of requiring a great number of emissions of the current for each letter, and cannot be used but upon short lines."

Many of the instruments in the Exposition bear only the name of the mechanician in whose ateliers they have been constructed, but in the apparatus mentioned in the catalogue under the following numbers, as well as in some of the apparatus of Messrs. Digney frères, there is a distinct recognition of the original inventor. These instruments differ very little from each other, and not at all in the essential features of the original Morse apparatus. They are, without exception, well made and practically effective.

[1] The above remarks were made in the autumn of 1867, just after the close of the Exposition. Since that time, as will be seen by reference to experiments on rapidity of transmission with the Morse apparatus in the United States, the rapidity of the manual operation of the Morse apparatus is shown to far exceed the rapidity of Mr. Hughes's apparatus.

"No. 64. Longoni & Dell Acqua, of Milan—The Morse Telegraph, modified by Moroni.

"No. 61. Joseph Pik, Warsaw—Telegraph, Morse system.

"No. 66. Joseph Poggioli, Florence—The Morse apparatus complete.

"No. 7. T. A. M. Sortirs—The Morse apparatus.

"No. 49. Leon de Hamar, Pesth, Hungary—Telegraph apparatus of Morse.

"No. 50. Jean Leopolder, Vienna—Typographic telegraph, with the Morse characters."

DUJARDIN'S PRINTING TELEGRAPH.

This apparatus is composed of a manipulator (Fig. 12.) and a register (Fig. 13.)

Fig 12.

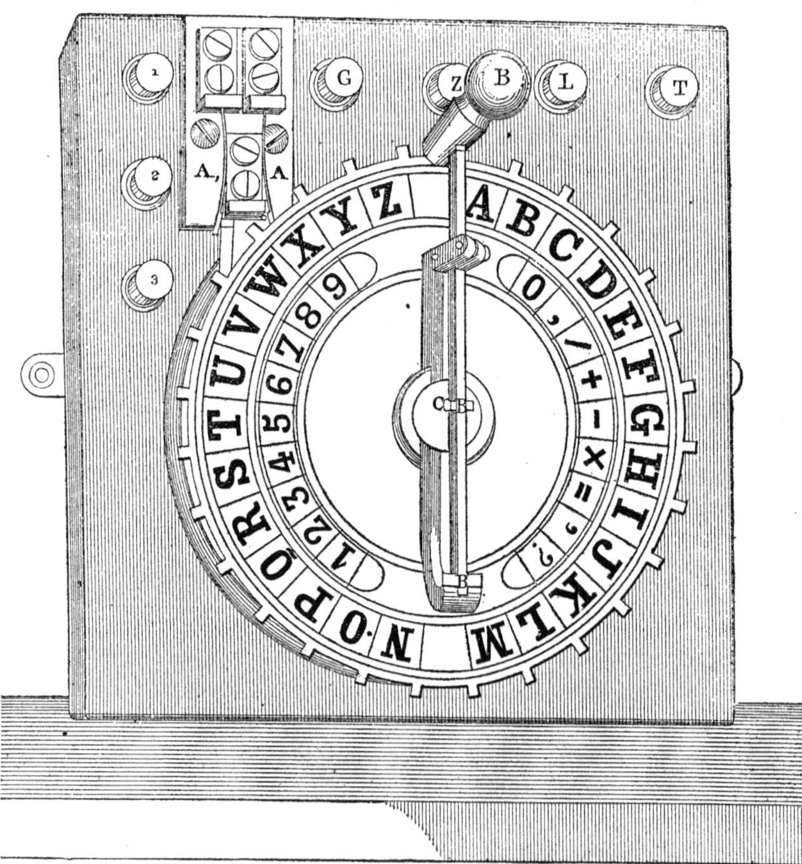

Printing Telegraph of Dr. Dujardin, of Lille—Manipulator.

The manipulator consists of a wheel (*à gorge sinueuse*) of fourteen undulations, making the commutator A oscillate, which sends over the line at each turn of the wheel twenty-eight currents, alternately positive and negative, succeeding each other without any appreciable interval.

The axis of this wheel bears a crank B, which moves above a divided dial, upon which are engraved, upon two concentric circles, the let-

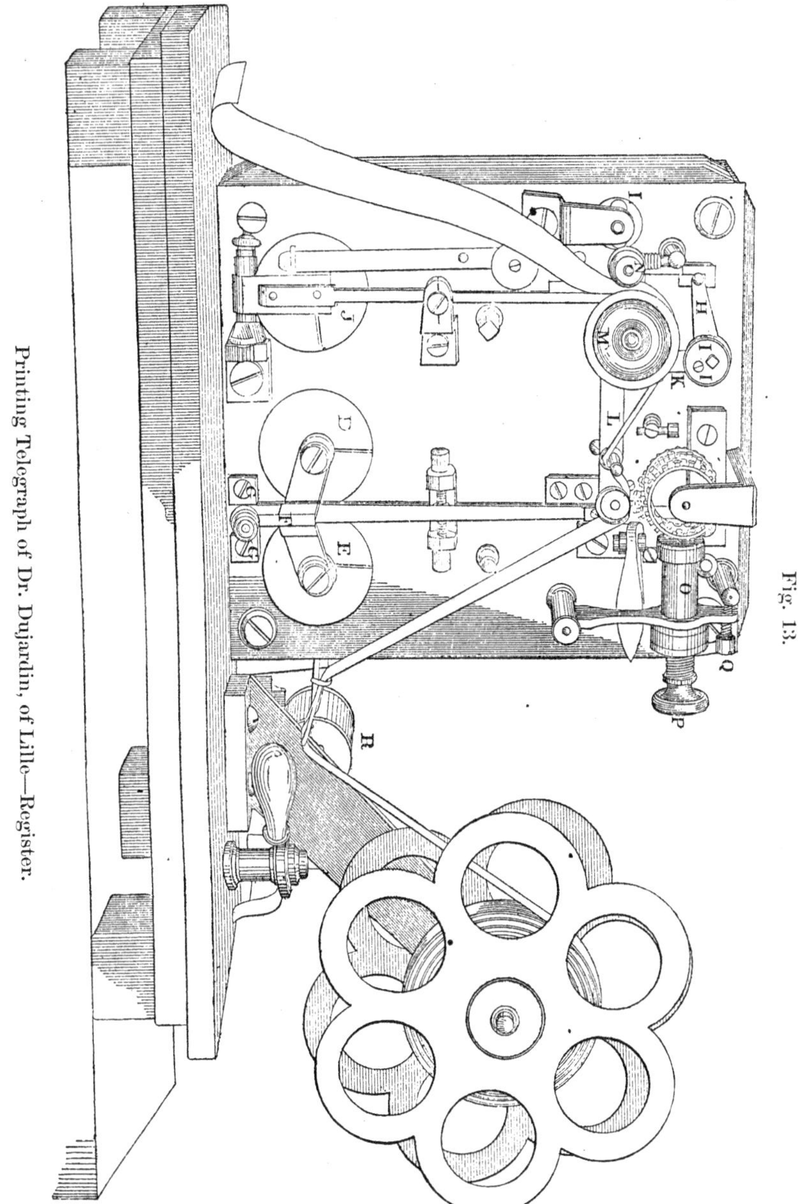

Fig. 13.

Printing Telegraph of Dr. Dujardin, of Lille—Register.

ters, the numerals, and other conventional signs. When the crank is stopped before any letter, and is sunk in the corresponding notch, the shaft C, which is articulated with this crank and traverses the axis of the dial, is pressed down, and causes to move under the manipulator a double commutator, which produces an impression of the letter by means indicated presently. During the reception, the crank of the manipulator ought to be constantly kept down.

The receptor or register is composed of two trains of wheels serving the one to turn the type-wheels, the other to produce the impression, and (*déclanchés*) each by a special electro-magnet. The last movable wheel of the first train of wheels carries an escapement wheel of fourteen teeth, and two type-wheels—the one for letters, the other for numerals—acting alternately. These wheels are cut out in the form of rings and fitted into one another, so that they resemble an ×, whence their name of cross-wheels. The electro-magnet D E oscillates the pallet F, polarized by the piece of iron G, which is itself polarized by the magnets placed under the register. The last movable wheel of the second train of wheels carries the stop H and the eccentric I. The halting magnet (*aimant boiteux*) J, by the intervention of a fork with two prongs, serves to release the stop H, and allows it to make a complete revolution. During this revolution the eccentric I, by means of a crank K, raised above the lever L, is made to strike the paper against the types. The axis of the second movable wheel of the impression wheel carries the cylinder (*entraineur*) M and the roller N, which moves forward the paper during the revolution of the stop. The plug or ink-stopper O presents a particular arrangement; it is a brass tube, in which is moved a piston by a screw P, and which contains an oleaginous ink. A disk of velvet, which gives passage to the ink, shuts the tube, and is found constantly in contact with the types of the wheel which does the work. The screw of the regulator Q allows to the velvet to press more or less upon the types. The electro-magnet shut up in the box R serves to cause the local current in the printing electro-magnet to pass at the proper time.

When it is desired to transmit, the crank of the dial is turned, and, from this movement of rotation, a series of currents, alternately positive and negative, result, which, in a biforked manner in the electro-magnets D, E, and R, produce on the one part the rotation of the type-wheels, and on the other the permanent attraction of the pallet of the electro-magnet R, which carries the current by which the printing is done. When the crank is pressed into the notch corresponding to the letter which it is desired to print, the double commutator under the manipulator is brought into action. This double commutator serves on the one part to break the current of the line and to put into a position of reception the apparatus of the operator who transmits, and on the other part to transfer the battery current of the line to the local circuit which is employed, it may be altogether or only in part. Upon the divided dial and at the extremities of the same diameter are found two empty divisions, which serve to make the spaces between the words, and work the change of the type-wheels. When the crank is pressed into the division between Z and A the wheel for the letters is brought into action, and when the crank is pressed into the division between M and N it is the other wheel which is brought into action.

The apparatus which is here described permits the transmission of twenty-three words per minute, and has operated actually between Paris and Lille in a very satisfactory manner. The speed of transmission amounts to from thirty to thirty-five words, by substituting for the dial manipulator a key manipulator, and employing a little different register from that described. The apparatus thus modified can operate at very great distances. It has operated thus very regularly during six months between London and Edinburgh, and if it has not been definitely adopted in England by the Electric Telegraph Company, it is that at the present time it does not print the numerals.

PANTELEGRAPHS.

One of the two modes by which writing or printing was to be effected at a distance was the mode of recording by the chemical decomposition of a metallic salt by means of the electric or galvanic current. Although the earliest experiments successfully proved the practicability of this mode of recording, yet the simplicity aimed at by the writer of this report in devising his process, turned his attention more engrossingly to the second or mechanical mode of recording by means of the electro-magnet. Subsequent to these results, obtained as early as 1835, Davy, in England, devised and patented, in 1839, a plan of marking by chemical decomposition which, however, has never been in practical use. Bain, still later, in 1846, proposed his method of marking the Morse alphabet by the successful application of a more sensitive salt than had been employed. Bakewell, in England, in 1851, further developed the electro-chemical mode of marking, by devising and accomplishing an interesting result, which has since been expanded and improved by Bonelli,[1] of Florence, and more recently by Caselli and Lenoir. By the genius and skill of these distinguished men, the electro-chemical process has been successfully applied to the production at a distance of perfect fac similes of writing and drawing.

BONELLI'S APPARATUS MODIFIED BY COOK.

Just at the moment of transmitting this report to Washington, an interesting article from the Anglo-American Times, London, February 27, gives the latest information respecting this ingenious modification by

[1] The lamented death of the gifted Italian, Bonelli, has retarded the perfecting of his autographic system. It is, nevertheless, advancing to perfection through the genius, perseverance, and energy of his friend, Henry Cook, esq., who showed in Paris the instrument in a progressive state. It gave great promise of taking a high position among the telegraphic instrumentalities of the day.

Henry Cook, esq., of Bonelli's automatic instrument. The article is given entire:

"We translate the following from a French paper:

"'NEW SYSTEM OF TELEGRAPHY.

"'This morning the Emperor Napoleon III condescended to examine at the Tuileries the new telegraphic system invented by the late Mr. Bonelli and Mr. Cook, partner of the American banking house of Messrs. Norton & Co. After a practical and complete examination of the new apparatus, his Majesty expressed his satisfaction on all points, and invited the inventor to come the following day at noon to show the Empress the rapidity and accuracy of the instruments, which far surpass all yet seen in telegraphy. The advantage of Mr. Cook's system consists in the absolute exactness of the messages transmitted, and we need not point out this value to men of business who are aware what errors are committed with the instruments in use, occasioning inconvenience and pecuniary loss. Mr. Cook's system also enables three messages to be transmitted in the time now taken for one. In short, his Majesty considered the benefits of the new system so important that he has authorized M. the Count de Vougy, director general of telegraphs, to give the inventor every facility necessary to bring his telegraphic apparatus into general use.

"'Mr. Cook, in connection with the celebrated Italian telegrapher, M. Bonelli, has devoted many years and very large sums of money to the perfection of Bonelli's system. Since the decease of the latter, the improvements made by Mr. Cook have been so satisfactory as to attract much attention to the system, not only in Europe, but in the United States, where plans are being arranged for its general introduction. For Great Britain it has been most favorably considered by Lord Clarendon, who has had an opportunity for a careful examination of its merits. At the second interview, both the Empress and Prince Imperial were present. The printing and autographic instruments were tested with great success. The special objects of the improvements of Mr. Cook are perfect accuracy and great rapidity in all seasons. No action of temperature or climate have any detrimental effect on these instruments, which so far have worked better in bad weather than in fair. The special importance of positive accuracy cannot be denied, and with these instruments it is insured. Mr. Cook's system is grounded on Chevalier Gaetano Bonelli's patent, which he purchased in 1860, and by years of labor and outlay improved into the instrument just submitted to the Emperor. The original instrument constructed from this patent was automatic, and required fifty wires, working simultaneously yet independently, while the present needs but one. The first improvement was the production of a telegraphic machine reducing the number to eleven wires, then to five, though even this number barred its general adoption, notwithstanding its power to print forty messages per hour, insuring accuracy, and being independent of synchronism. The present instruments were further modified by Messrs. Bonelli and Hipp, but to Mr. Cook is due the final improvements which now make them so nearly perfect. The machinery is simple and strong, the parts delicate in substance, are of steel, and there is nothing which with ordinary wear should get out of order. The instruments are said to be capable of transmitting one hundred and sixty messages per hour, but in reality they can accomplish from eighty to one hundred, the maximum of other instruments being forty. The system also permits greater speed in delivery. The address is first printed, and the envelope can be addressed while the rest of the dispatch is printing off. When finished, the paper is passed between rollers of blotting paper, and dispatched—no need to read it, its accuracy is sure. The simplicity of the plan enables the authors of the system to engage to send messages cheaply—children, boys, or girls being soon able to set up the type. Experiments prove that fourteen and a half words per person per minute ean easily be attained; thus machines, at the rate of eighty messages per hour, would transmit one thousand six hundred words per hour; two type-setters would compose one thousand seven hundred and forty; one machine clerk and two type-setters can, therefore, keep the instrument at the maximum pace of work. During the interruption of a line, the time by existing systems is now lost; by Mr. Cook's apparatus the messages are set up as they arrive. The moment a line is reported good the messages are sent through at the utmost speed, and lost time may thus to a great extent be retrieved.'"

It may be remarked that, properly to estimate the value of this modification, the actual result must be considered, assuming that, other things being equal, that system which can transmit the greatest quantity of dispatches in a given time is the best.

In this, as in the other automatic devices, the time required to prepare the dispatches for transmission is an essential element in the calculation. Whether this time of preparation can be economically lessened by dividing the labor of preparation among several persons is a matter mainly of finance. Whether it is economy to employ one person for a particular work, or whether several persons can accomplish it sooner, is outside the merits of the transmitting machine. The preparation is a work to be accomplished precedent to the duties of the machine. The ability of the instrument to transmit that which has been prepared is the main point to which attention will be directed.

The instruments are said to be "capable of transmitting one hundred and sixty messages per hour," but this, we presume, is the maximum under the most favorable circumstances, for it is immediately added, "that in reality they can accomplish from eighty to one hundred."

In the preparation for transmission it is stated that "experiments prove that fourteen and a half words can be set up by one person in a minute;" that is to say, if one person is employed to prepare a dispatch for transmission of sixteen hundred words, then twenty words (or one dispatch) would require five and a half words more than could be prepared in one minute. But allowing that even eighty dispatches, equaling sixteen hundred words, could thus be prepared in one hour, it will be perceived by reference to the speed tests of the Morse, given in the table, Chapter V, that Morse operators have far exceeded that rate, having in fact transmitted the entire eighty in the time that the Bonelli instrument was ready to commence transmission.

Nevertheless, the beauty and (compared with the automatic methods of other modifiers of the system) the simplicity of Mr. Cook's modification and improvement of Bonelli's method were greatly admired. Experience alone will determine whether it can be economically and advantageously used.

It is to be heartily and sincerely hoped that its ingenious improver may realize his most sanguine expectations, and the objections we have hinted at find a successful solution.

From the well-known liberality of the French administration, under the able guidance of its distinguished chief director, it is sure to have a fair trial.

APPARATUS OF THE ABBÉ CASELLI.

The apparatus of the Abbé Caselli is somewhat complicated, and is very expensive, but it is a beautiful and efficient apparatus, producing its results with perfect success.

It is easy to imagine many cases in the affairs of a government, as well as in common life, where the result accomplished by such an apparatus would be of immense advantage, and, although too expensive for general or ordinary use, it is destined to become a necessity to governments as an adjunct to other systems, furnishing, in many exigencies, a verification of official orders and other acts, demanding a more immediate conveyance than by the mail.

For a complete description of this exceedingly beautiful apparatus, the inquirer is referred to the lucid and accurate description of it in Blavier, vol. ii, from page 274 to 301.

LENOIR'S MODIFICATION—THE ELECTROGRAPH.

No. 13 of the catalogue is an apparatus for producing a similar result, by M. E. Lenoir, which he calls an "electrographe." It is much less complicated in appearance than the Abbé Caselli's, occupying scarcely more space than an ordinary Morse apparatus. A specimen of its results in fac-simile drawing is transmitted to the department.[1] The specimen was produced in the Exposition on a short circuit, and no opportunity was afforded of proving its efficacy at a distance, or to ascertain at what distance it was capable of operating. It is regretted that a description promised has not been received, as the apparatus, from its simplicity, prepossessed one strongly in its favor. Specimens by Lenoir's process are also transmitted.[1]

[1] Deposited in the library of the Department of State.

CHAPTER II.

SEMAPHORES.

THE DIAL OR CADRAN SYSTEMS—THEIR ADAPTATION TO SPECIAL SERVICE—PERFECTION OF WORKMANSHIP IN THE INSTRUMENTS EXHIBITED—SOUNDERS OR ACOUSTIC SEMAPHORES—CATON'S SOUNDER FOR USE IN THE FIELD—ORIGIN AND NATURE OF THE ACOUSTIC SEMAPHORE—THE MORSE CODE ADAPTED TO RECOGNITION BY EACH OF THE FOUR SENSES—PROFESSOR STEINHEIL'S BELL SOUNDER—BRIGHT'S BELL SOUNDER—MORSE'S ORGAN-PIPE SOUNDER—SIGNAL SEMAPHORES—NIGHT SIGNALS BY MADAME COSTON—COSTON FIRE SIGNALS—AUSTRIAN FIELD SIGNAL APPARATUS.

DIAL OR CADRAN SYSTEMS.

In the semaphoric class of instruments, for communicating at a distance, a great variety of forms adapted to various service were displayed in the Exposition. The most common form was that of the dial or cadran, containing around the circumference of a disk the letters of the ordinary alphabet and the numerals. This kind of instrument is operated by a handle, which moves an indicator to the desired letter upon the disk. This movement causes, by a "step by step" action, an index upon a dial at a distance to move and stop at the same letter. The interior machinery of these various instruments is as various as in ordinary clock movements for the indication of time. All of this class of semaphores have long been invented and in use in the United States, and are well adapted to special service, usually on more limited circuits, and for private use, between places of business in or near cities, between private residences, and between railway stations. The indication of the common letter on the dial dispenses with the necessity, in the ordinary operator, of becoming familiar with a conventional code; but the operation is necessarily slow, and, therefore, not so well adapted to administrative or commercial purposes as the telegraphic apparatus, which has the paramount advantage of leaving its record, a convenience which the simple dial or cadran apparatus does not possess. Many of these dial semaphores in use in Europe are admirably constructed in the ateliers of those accomplished mechanicians Digney frères, Bréguet and Froment, in Paris, Siemens & Halske, in Berlin, Hipp, in Neufchatel, and many in England and in other countries, displaying the greatest beauty and perfection of workmanship.

SOUNDERS, OR ACOUSTIC SEMAPHORES.

CATON'S FIELD SOUNDER.

No. 75 is designated in the catalogue as "Pocket field telegraph apparatus," and is exhibited by J. D. Caton, esq., of Ottawa, Illinois. It is what is called a sounder in some of the treatises on the telegraph. It is a direct offspring of the semaphoric quality of the Morse recording in-instrument. The sound of the pen lever in recording with the Morse apparatus indicates also to the *ear* the signs of the Morse code that are at the same time being indicated to the *eye* upon the moving strip of paper. The sounds of these letters hold the same relation to the written telegraphic letters that speech does to written or printed language.

As some misapprehension exists as to the origin and nature of the acoustic semaphore, a few words of explanation and correction will not be considered out of place.

There is a peculiarity inherent in the nature of the original Morse code, which adapts it for recognition by each of four at least of the senses. It addresses not merely the sight by its written character, but the hearing, the taste, and the touch. It allows therefore, of course, recognition by sound. This quality of the Morse code, of being recognized by more than one of the senses, does not belong to ordinary alphabetic characters, and arises from its novel construction. The principle of the Morse code is this: it is formed from broken or unequal parts of a continuous line. It is composed of shorter and longer lines, or, as they are usually styled, dots and dashes, the shorter line being a dot, and the longer a dash. Each letter therefore is a line, or group of lines of different lengths, each group being a combination of these elementary parts, differing from all the other groups. For example, A is represented by a short and a long line, thus, - —; B, by a long line and three short ones, thus, — - - -; N, by a long line and a short one, thus, — -, and so on. These differences are at once recognized by the eye when written, but in the process of writing them by the Morse apparatus each group or letter is also indicated to the ear by its sound. The rationale of this peculiarity is this: in writing or printing either the dot or the dash in these groups the pen-lever produces two sounds, as well in making a dot as in making a dash. One of the two sounds is caused by the stroke of the pen-lever against the stop, which limits its motion in one direction, and the other of the two sounds is caused by the stroke against the stop, which limits its motion in the other direction. These sounds are the natural and ordinary accompaniment of the process of writing or printing the letters.

It might seem, at first blush, that, as each dot and each dash has equally two sounds, the one would be confounded with the other; but the difference by which a dot and a dash is distinguished the one from the other is, not by the number of the sounds, but by the difference of the interval, in the respective cases, between the first and second sound. In the one case, that of the dot, the two sounds which indicate it are separated by a short interval of time; in the other case, that of a dash, the two sounds have a *longer* interval between them. This difference of interval very soon becomes familiar to the ear, and enables the operator to hear as well as to see the transmitted dispatch. This acoustic effect is, in fact, the half-way result of a process arrested before its entire completion; completed, indeed, to the ear, but not, as yet, to the eye. Or the whole process may perhaps be better described as producing two results, either of which suffices, and therefore either may be dispensed with at pleasure, or both used together. This choice of results is exemplified in the various instruments using the Morse code. This sounder, for example, dispenses with the writing apparatus, and thus becomes a semaphore; on the other hand, the various inking instruments dispense with the sound, and are wholly dependent upon the written record, while the embossing instruments using the dry point have the double advantage of both results: they have the aid of the ear as well as of the eye. The inking process, therefore, it will be perceived, while gaining an advantage in one direction, loses an advantage in another. It is noiseless, and in consequence has the disadvantage of the electro-chemical process. On this point Mr. Sabine hints at this disadvantage of noiselessness as a probable cause that the electro-chemical process has not been popular. He says (p. 180) "the noiseless operation of the electro-chemical telegraphs may have assisted in keeping this method of recording out of more general use. It is always indispensably necessary to combine an alarm with the system, to call the attention of the manipulator—not so necessary with the Morse, which is, in working, always accompanied by the rattle of the beam and armature." Another disadvantage of the electro-chemical process is hinted at—that it lacks an economic arrangement for translation; that is, as a relay or means of repetition, which is an inherent, natural advantage in the Morse embossing system.

The first acoustic semaphore using the Morse code was the original recording instrument shown by the writer in 1835, at which time this acoustic peculiarity was not only noticed, but was then made known to others, and was considered of sufficient importance to be secured by letters patent drawn up in 1837. The claim therein is for a mode of communicating intelligence "by signs and sounds, or either."

The pen-lever in all the earlier instruments, as at this day, had this acoustic character, and whether recording or not upon the moving strip of paper, distinctly indicated the letter by its sound. It should be remarked that this acoustic quality rendered any other alarm unnecessary.

The sounder exhibited in the American section is the Morse pen lever, without the pen, thus separating from the register the acoustic portion, which is neatly compacted in a box no larger than a snuff-box. The following description of the instrument is taken from the report upon the United States section: "This instrument consists of a pair of helices, each two inches long and three-fourths inch in diameter, encased in a thin cylinder of hard rubber. They are wound with No. 36 insulated copper wire. The armature is one and five-eighths inch long, one-twentieth of an inch thick, and one-quarter of an inch wide. The sounding lever, of brass, is one and a half inch long, is placed horizontally, from the center of which drops a perpendicular arm, to which the armature is attached. The free end of the sounding lever plays between the milled heads of two set screws, the upper of which is inserted in the lower. This connects with a branched anvil, the two legs of which rest upon a brass sounding board, one and three-eighths inch in diameter, which is concave beneath, and is attached with three screws to the bottom of the case, a diminutive adjusting spring, actuated by a milled head, adjusting post with milled headed connecting screws. At the opposite end of the magnet is a key of very thin tempered brass, one-quarter of an inch wide and one and three-quarters inch long, with ivory finger-piece, connecting points of platinum, and a current breaker with ivory handle. This completes the mechanical contrivances, and the whole is inclosed in a hard rubber case, with a cover like a snuff-box.

"The external dimensions, when shut, are, length, five inches; breadth, two and a quarter inches; height, one and a quarter inch. The ends of the box are semi-circular. The case stands upon four brass legs, three-eighths of an inch diameter and three-eighths of an inch long. Entire weight, ten and a quarter ounces.

"Here are all the instruments necessary for a complete telegraph office, where the operator receives by sound. No local circuit is required, but it is operated on the main circuit. The report is as clear, distinct, and audible as that of an ordinary sounder actuated by a local circuit. It is designed for use in the field or out of doors. A telegrapher will attach it to the main line anywhere in the country in five minutes, when he can send and receive messages with the same facility and accuracy that he can in a regular telegraph office. Mr. Caton states that during the war he supplied the government with a large number of these instruments, but was unable to fill all of the orders of General Stager, who had charge of the government telegraph department. Nearly all telegraph superintendents are supplied with them, as well as very many operators, who never travel without them. Their invaluable services in case of railroad accidents may be readily appreciated, and at the west they are in constant use. An account of their services thus rendered each year would fill a volume, and, really, no train should ever move without one, in the hands of a competent operator."

It was beautifully finished, and was sent to the Exposition by Judge J. D. Caton, of Ottawa, Illinois, and manufactured in Ottawa by Mr. Robert Heming, whose telegraphic instruments are among the best in the country.

Various modifications of the acoustic apparatus have subsequently been made in Europe.

PROFESSOR STEINHEIL'S SOUNDER.

Professor Steinheil was the first in Europe, who attempted an acoustic method by causing the magnetic needle, by which he also recorded signs, to strike upon two bells of different tone, according as positive or negative currents were made to pass through the conductor.

SIR CHARLES BRIGHT'S SOUNDER.

Sir Charles Bright, in England, introduced, at a still more recent date, an efficient modification of the acoustic apparatus upon the lines of the

British and Irish Magnetic Telegraph Company. The modification consisted in substituting two bells of different tones to indicate the Morse code in place of the stops used in the original Morse instrument, by which a louder as well as a varied sound was given, and utilizing the negative and positive currents to operate the bells. Experience would seem to have proved that of the two modes originally indicating the Morse code, to wit: by writing and by sound, the acoustic mode is becoming more extended and is even preferred in large districts for ordinary communication. The reports from various parts of the United States, from Great Britain, and from the East Indies show that it has some advantages over the writing mode; but when used as an instrument separated from the writing apparatus, it has the disadvantage common to all semaphores of having no record for justification or control. The bell apparatus is also said to be complained of in the larger offices, on account of the greater noise they produce creating confusion, but this defect is easily obviated by deadening the sound to any desired degree of loudness.

The substantial improvement, however, in Sir Charles Bright's modification of the sounder consists in applying the Morse adaptation of the electro-magnet to Steinheil's plan of using two bells of different tones, and operating them by the alternations of the positive and negative currents of electricity. In a recent letter of Sir Charles Bright to Professor Morse he says: "The sound instrument which I adopted for the magnetic company consists of two bells, dull in sound and differing in note, placed on each side of the operator about on a level with his ear. These are worked by a relay sending currents through one or the other, according to the signals required. Two keys are used for sending, one for the right hand, or positive current, the other for the left, or negative current. One wire is, of course, used. There is no difference in the duration of either signal, and in this is the saving of time, compared with the sounders (the Morse) used here, (in the United States,) where, in employing dots and dashes, the latter (I take it) require three times the duration of a dot. In the other the signals are all dots, but a Morse operator can use it by considering one key as a dot, the other as a dash, but sending dots on both. It is the quickest instrument of a non-mechanical kind."

On this it may be remarked that, theoretically at least, this modification of Sir Charles Bright's is the perfection of the sounder. In view, however, of the skill and ability displayed by the American operators in their results in speedy transmission with the Morse sounder, it is difficult to conceive that, practically, any improvement of it could be made. Yet, as there is theoretically an economy of time in Sir Charles Bright's modification, it may prove to be practically as well as theoretically better.

MORSE'S ORGAN-PIPE SOUNDER.

One of the modifications by Morse himself, experimented upon by him as early as 1845, gives the sound of each letter of the Morse code more accurately than any yet devised; and although not practically adopted, because of the greater advantages of the written mode in simplicity of apparatus, is yet, perhaps, worthy (at a time when the acoustic method is received with favor) to be revised and made practical, at least so far as to satisfy curiosity. The method devised by him was by an organ pipe so connected with a small bellows as to be opened and closed by the pen-lever, in the act of writing a dot or a dash. It is at once obvious that in indicating a dot, the pipe would give a short, sharp sound, but in indicating a dash the sound would be correspondingly prolonged. The short and long intervals, therefore, by which the dot and the dash are now distinguished, in the ordinary acoustic instruments, are, by this method, more completely expressed, reducing the code to *musical expression*, to crotchets, and semibreves. The disadvantage which suggets itself is the necessity of a bellows apparatus for a constant supply of air to the pipe, adding materially to the complication of the machinery; and it has also the inconvenience just alluded to, by its loudness, (which indeed might easily be moderated,) of confusing the ear where many instruments are within hearing of each other.

SIGNAL SEMAPHORES.

NIGHT SIGNALS, BY MADAME MARTHA J. COSTON.

This is a very ingenious and effective semaphore, which commends itself from its simplicity. Three lights of different colors, white, red, and green, are so flashed or burned in combinations representing the numerals 1, 2, 3, 4, 5, 6, 7, 8, 9, 0, and also two letters A and P—in all twelve combinations. The light is produced by the combustion of a peculiar pyrotechnic composition for each of the desired colors.

A handle or holder is all that is necessary, ordinarily, to hold the selected color:

A flash of white indicates the numeral........................... 1
A flash of white followed by red.................................. 2
A flash of white followed by green................................ 3
A flash of red.. 4
A flash of red followed by white.................................. 5
A flash of red followed by green.................................. 6
A flash of green.. 7
A flash of green followed by white................................ 8
A flash of green followed by red.................................. 9
A flash of white, red, and green.................................. 0
A flash of white, red, and white.................................. P
A flash of red, white, and red.................................... A

When a communication is to be made, the white, red, and white are quickly and successively flashed, indicating the letter P, (prepare,) and when answered by red, white, and red, indicating the letter A; the correspondence commences by flashing the respective colors of the numbers desired to be sent.

Experience has demonstrated the usefulness of the "Coston fire signals," and they have passed the practical test with success. They have been approved and recommended, not only by our own accomplished naval officers, and our marine department, but also by the French ministry of the marine, and distinguished French officers. They have been definitively introduced into our own service, and also into that of France.

The accomplished inventor has more recently improved her system, by the use of what she calls parachute rockets discharged from a pistol or gun; but on the same principle of colored lights.

AUSTRIAN FIELD SIGNAL APPARATUS.

The semaphoric apparatus No. 52, "Austrian field apparatus," is an example of the adaptability of the Morse code not merely to the telegraph, but to almost every kind of semaphore, whether they be signals on land, or through the Atlantic cable, or by flags in the marine. Various semaphores have adopted this convenient code, by some modification of it on the same principles.

This field apparatus consists of a pole some fifteen feet in height, having at its top three disks of thin metal, each turning upon a horizontal axis within a circular frame, so as to present, at will, its full orb, or the thin diameter. These three disks are thus arranged ○ ○○. The upper disk represents, when shown singly, the dot of the Morse code; the two lower disks, shown together, represent the dash or line of the Morse code. The mode of its action may be illustrated by describing the process in conveying to a different station the word *fire.* This word in the Morse code would be thus written, [– – —– – – – – —– – –.] The disks in their normal state are supposed to present to the spectator their thin edge, and so are invisible at a distance. The first movement, therefore, in conveying to a distance the word fire, is to darken the upper disk, by turning it so as to show its full orb thus, ◉ ○○; when this is recognized at the distant station, by a similar movement there, the disk resumes its normal condition, having indicated a dot. This movement is repeated, conveying a second dot, and then the two lower disks are darkened ○ ◉◉, indicating a line, after which the upper disk is once more darkened, adding another dot to complete the letter F, its completion being indicated to the distant station by the darkening of all the disks at once. In this manner all the letters, numerals or signs of the Morse code can be indicated, and correspondence to any extent may be carried on semaphorically by this simple arrangement. This mode is slow, but other circumstances being favorable, it is efficient.

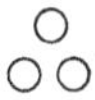

CHAPTER III.

CODES.

ETYMOLOGY OF THE WORD CODE—THE ORIGINAL MORSE CODE AND THE MODERN MODIFICATIONS—ITS UNIVERSAL ADOPTION—THE ALPHABET, CYPHERS, PUNCTUATION MARKS, AND OFFICIAL SIGNS—SPACE-LETTERS—INVESTIGATION OF THE FREQUENCY OF OCCURRENCE OF THE VARIOUS LETTERS IN THE LANGUAGE—INCONVENIENCE OF CONFOUNDING THE SPACE-LETTERS WITH OTHERS—THE EUROPEAN MORSE CODE CONTAINS FIVE ADDITIONAL SIGNS—DIFFICULTIES ATTENDING A CHANGE IN THE ESTABLISHED CODE—PROPOSED IMPROVEMENT OF PUNCTUATION AND OFFICIAL SIGNS—THE MORSE CODE AS MODIFIED AND ADOPTED IN EUROPE SHOULD BE ADOPTED IN THE WESTERN CONTINENT.

THE MORSE CODE.

Without occupying time in discussing the etymology of the word *code*, (which strictly means a digest or collection of laws reduced to order,) or the propriety of its use in the present connection, it is found to be applied in the various reports on telegraphy, and it is therefore adopted as a concise term to designate the system of signs, or signals, employed in the telegraphic and semaphoric instrumentalities of the present day.

As pertinent directly to these instrumentalities the codes adopted and proposed come to be treated of.

Given the first idea of a telegraph in its strict etymological sense, or the possibility of writing or printing at a distance, the most natural first thought would be to devise some mode of expressing, by writing or printing, at a distance, the letters or numerals of the inventor's native language.

The complication of machinery required for this purpose was then the first serious difficulty to be overcome. To express numerals by dots seemed to be the simplest mode of obviating this difficulty, for when this simplicity was left out of view, the complication of machinery to produce the ordinary letters or numerals seemed an insurmountable obstacle.

Therefore, in considering the mechanical means at command for producing at a distance any permanent mark, it was perceived that by means of the electro-magnet the motion of a lever, up and down, could be easily and surely commanded; and if a pencil at one extremity of it were made to strike upon a piece of paper a dot would be made whenever the magnet was charged and quickly discharged. This action, however, without a further device, would be unavailing to produce variety, since the lever motion is limited to the simple movement of up and down. Hence the idea of moving the paper at a regular rate beneath the pencil. Thus a dot could be made on the moving ribbon of paper, which, passing onward, the paper was ready to receive (after an interval more or less extended) another dot or series of dots. Thus the ability

The original Morse code and its modern modifications.

ORIGINAL MORSE CODE.		MODERN MODIFICATIONS.		
	Units. 1 2 3 4 5 6 7 8 9 10 11 12		Units. 1 2 3 4 5 6 7 8 9 10 11 12	
Letters—				
A	· —			
B	— · · ·			
C	· · ·	C	— · — ·	
D	— · ·			
E	·			
F	· — ·	F	· · — ·	the original Q.
G	— — ·			
H	· · · ·			
I	· ·			
J	— · — ·	J	· — — —	
K	— · —			
L	———	L	· — · ·	the original X.
M	— —			
N	— ·			
O	· ·	O	— — —	
P	· · · · ·	P	· — — ·	the original 1, numeral.
Q	· · — ·	Q	— — · —	
R	· · ·	R	· — ·	the original F.
S	· · ·			
T	—			
U	· · —			
V	· · · —			
W	· — —			
X	· — · ·	X	— · · —	the original 9, numeral.
Y	· · · ·	Y	— · — —	
Z	· · · ·	Z	— — · ·	
&	· · · ·			
Numerals—				
1	· — — ·	1	· — — — —	
2	· · — · ·	2	· · — — —	
3	· · · — ·	3	· · · — —	
4	· · · · —	4	· · · · —	
5	— — —	5	· · · · ·	
6	· · · · · ·	6	— · · · ·	
7	— — · ·	7	— — · · ·	
8	— · · · ·	8	— — — · ·	
9	— · · —	9	— — — — ·	
0	————	0	— — — — —	
Punctuation signs—				
Period .	· · — — · ·	.	· · · · · ·	Period.
Comma ,	· — · —	;	— · — · — ·	Semicolon.
Interrog. ?	— · · — ·	,	· — · — · —	Comma.
Exclam. !	— — —	:	— — — · · ·	Colon.
Quota. " "	· — · — · — · —	?	· · — — · ·	Interrogation.
Parenth. ( )	· — · · —	" "	· — · · — ·	Quotation.
		!	— — · · — —	Exclamation.
		-	— · · · · —	Hyphen.
		'	· — — — — ·	Apostrophe.
		/	— — — — — —	Sign of fraction.
		( )	— · — — · —	Parenthesis.
			· · — — · —	Underscore.

to produce dots in groups at pleasure was demonstrated, and, consequently, groups of dots expressive of the various numerals were devised. In pursuing the experiments with the numerals whose elements were a simple dot and space, it was perceived that, by means of the moving paper, not merely a dot could be produced at pleasure, but if the magnet was kept charged while the paper was in movement, the pencil produced a line long in proportion to the time in which the magnet was charged. This fact introduced a third element for combination, to produce variety in the groups, indicating letters as well as numerals, to wit: the line or dash, so that dots, spaces, and lines, in any variety of combination, were at command for forming a code of signs. Hence originated what is now universally recognized as the Morse code.

ORIGINAL MORSE CODE.

To enable the inquirer to understand the modifications of that code which has become the universal telegraphic means of correspondence, the original code is given, (see diagram) together with the slight modern changes which experience has suggested as improvements.

THE MODIFIED MORSE CODE.

The following is the modified Morse code, adopted throughout the world, as used in France, Belgium, Holland, Prussia, Austria, Italy, Spain, Portugal, Switzerland, Russia, Sweden, Denmark, Norway, Turkey, Greece, Syria, Persia, Egypt, India, Africa, Great Britain, and also in Australia, and in other countries:

1. *Alphabet.*

Letter.	Sign.	Letter.	Sign.	Letter.	Sign.
A	· —	J	· — — —	T	—
Ä	· — · —	K	— · —	U	· · —
B	— · · ·	L	· — · ·	Ü	· · — —
C	— · — ·	M	— —	V	· · · —
D	— · ·	N	— ·	W	· — —
E	·	O	— — —	X	— · · —
É	· · — · ·	Ö	— — — ·	Y	— · — —
F	· · — ·	P	· — — ·	Z	— — · ·
G	— — ·	Q	— — · —	Ch	— — — —
H	· · · ·	R	· — ·		
I	· ·	S	· · ·		

2. *Ciphers.*

Cipher.	Sign.	Cipher.	Sign.
1	· — — — —	6	— · · · ·
2	· · — — —	7	— — · · ·
3	· · · — —	8	— — — · ·
4	· · · · —	9	— — — — ·
5	· · · · ·	0	— — — — —

3. *Punctuation, &c.*

	Sign.		Sign.
Full stop .	· · · · · ·	Sign of exclamation !	— — · · — —
Semicolon ;	— · — · — ·	Hyphen -	— · · · · —
Comma ,	· — · — · —	Apostrophe '	· — — — — ·
Colon :	— — — · · ·	Line of fraction $\frac{x}{x}$	— — — — — —
Sign of interrogation ?	· · — — · ·	Parenthesis ( )	— · — — · —
*Inverted commas " "	· — · · — ·	*Sign for underscoring, <u>John</u>	· · — — · —

* To be placed before and after the respective signs.

4. *Official signs.*

	Sign.		Sign.
Public message	· · ·	Interruption	· · · · · · · · · ·
Official telegraph message	· —	Conclusion	· — · — · — ·
Private message	· — — ·	Wait	· — · · ·
Call signal	— · — · — · —	Receipt	· — · · — · · — ·
Understood	· · · — ·		

The length of a dot being taken as a unit, the lengths of the different signs will be as follows:

A dash =3 dots.
The space between the signs of a letter=1 dot.
The space between the signs of 2 letters=3 dots.
The space between the signs of 2 words=6 dots.

On examining these codes with their modifications it will be seen that there are six letters or signs in the original Morse code, to wit, *C, O, R, Y, Z, &*, called *space letters*, because they are distinguished by spaces in the body of the letter. These letters were devised on the basis of simplicity, or economy of space, the inventor being anxious that no letter should exceed the extent of five units or dots in length, and it will be perceived that, with the single exception of the letter J, none of them exceed that number.

Another principle in constructing the code was also specially observed, the frequency of occurrence of the various letters in the language was studied, and for this purpose the arrangement of the type boxes in the cases of a printing office was examined in order to ascertain the relative frequency of the letters by the size of the type boxes. Those found to be most used were E, I, T, A, N, O, S, the letter E being the most copious of all; then followed the letters C, D, F, H, L, M, R, U. These letters occurring most frequently in the language were, therefore, constructed of the fewest and shortest elements. The letter E is represented by a single dot [-]; the I and T within the space of two dots or units; and so on, none of the rest (with the single exception mentioned above of the letter J) exceeding five dots or units.

All the numerals, the more readily to distinguish them from the letters, were each comprised within the value of six dots or units.

The space letters were very early found in practice to have the inconvenience of being confounded with other letters. For example, the C, [- - -] was apt to be mistaken for I, [- -], E, [-], or, if not well rendered, for S, [- - -], &c. But after the introduction of the alphabet into practical use, it became next to impossible to make the desired change, which was attempted by the inventor, even on the first public line; so it was reluctantly suffered to exist. Notwithstanding the defect has always been acknowledged by the inventor, and the substitution of other combinations for the space letters often proposed, yet so soon as the first operators had acquired the practical use of the original code, the change seemed hopeless.

The construction of this code originally on the basis of simplicity and economy of space, resulting in economy of time, furnishes an example of a good general principle, the principle of simplicity, carried to excess.

This defect in the code through the ingenuity of European savans, who have given it their attention, has been remedied in conformity with the general principles of the original code, but it still required more than ingenuity to accomplish the remedy. Governmental power was necessary to command the change, and thus to overcome the difficulty of change so early encountered in the United States in attempts to improve the original code.

The remedy consists in the substitution of other combinations of the short and long lines, in place of the space letters. This has been done, indeed, by some sacrifice of simplicity, and an increase of the aggregate amount of units in the entire code, but the inconvenience of the space letters has thus been remedied, and the modification is a substantial improvement.

The substituted groups for the space letters, however, were but five in number. In five other instances, indeed, the combination of dots and dashes in the original code representing a particular letter is changed to represent another. The original Q [. . — .] now represents F; the original X [. — . .] represents L; the original numeral 1 [. — — .] represents P; the original F [. — .] represents R; and the original numeral 9 [— . . —] represents X. These latter changes appear to be arbitrary, and no improvement. On the contrary the change adds a unit in extent to each of four of the letters, while the fifth alone (the R) remains the same in length as before.

The original F is.........	4 units.	The new F is...........:	5 units.
The original L is.........	4 units.	The new L is............	5 units.
The original P is.........	5 units.	The new P is............	6 units.
The original R is.........	4 units.	Tne new R is............	4 units.
The original X is.........	5 units.	The new X is............	6 units.
	22 units.		26 units.

It will be noticed that the established European Morse code contains five additional signs constructed on the same general principles, to represent peculiar accented letters not in the English alphabet, but necessary in the alphabets of the continent; these are:

A [· — · —] = 6 units.
É [· · — · ·] = 6 units.
Ö [— — — ·] = 7 units.
Ü [· · — —] = 6 units.
CH [— — — —] = 8 units.

Each of the numerals in the original Morse code is of the value of six units. The ten characters, therefore, for numerals amount, in aggregate value, to sixty units, while the aggregate value of the new signs for numerals is seventy-five units. Notwithstanding this addition, there is a substantial improvement in the construction of the new signs for numerals. Although the first four numerals, 1, 2, 3, 4, of the original code were as readily recognized as in the new arrangement by the number of dots commencing the sign, yet the last six numerals were not so ingeniously arranged for recognition as in the new arrangement, which is perfect. The first five numerals are readily recognized by the number of dots, while the last five, by counting each line of the sign as two, and adding the number of dots which end the sign, the cypher intended is unerringly given.

As a rule, it is not well hastily to insist on changes in the established code, to the disturbance and discomfort of so large and skillful a body as are the telegraph operators, for by every change they are compelled not merely to learn a new sign, but to *forget* an old one; and it is a question for international settlement whether it is not better to suffer a little inconvenience from an acknowleded imperfection than to attempt a remedy which must necessarily give annoyance to thousands.

IMPROVEMENT OF PUNCTUATION AND OFFICIAL SIGNS.

This remark is not intended to deter from the attempt to improve the defective punctuation signs and official signs which appear cumbersome and wasteful of space, and therefore of time. The inventor suggests the following substitute for these signs:

Proposed punctuation signs.

		Letters.	No. of units.	No. of units in adopted code.
Period	.	E ·	1	6
Semicolon	;	S · · ·	3	9
Colon	:	SS · · · · · ·	7	9
Comma	,	M — — (with dot above)	4	9
Interrogation	?	T —	2	8
Quotation	" "	U · · —	4	8
Exclamation	!	X — · · —	6	10
Hyphen	-	N — ·	3	8
Apostrophe	'	A · —	3	10
Sign of fraction	\	R · — ·	4	12
Parenthesis	( )	I.I. · · · ·	5	10
Underscore, or italics	——	I · ·	2	9
			44	108

This proposed improvement condenses this part of the code by reducing the aggregate value of the eleven punctuation signs to forty-four units of space; the original punctuation signs, only six in number, being of the aggregate value of forty-seven units of space, and the punctuation signs of the present adopted code being of the aggregate value of one hundred and eight units of space.

In this proposed change in the punctuation signs, two of the official signs are appropriated which can be transferred to the punctuation signs, and their places supplied in the official signs by other letters, to wit: The S [. . .] now used to signify "Public message," and proposed by the inventor to be transferred to signify "semicolon," may be supplied by I [. .], K [— . —]; and the A [. —] now used to signify "Official telegraph message," and proposed by the inventor to be transferred to signify "apostrophe," may be supplied by F [. . — ·]. This adds, indeed, seven units of space to the aggregate length of the sum of official signs, but the "call signal" might easily be reduced to C [— . — .], which at once subtracts five units from the seven, and "conclusion" might be represented by D [— . .], which subtracts six units more; and "receipt" would bear reduction to R T [. — . —], which subtracts five units more from the aggregate, resulting in an aggregate gain of nine units.

The comparison between the present and the proposed "official signs" gives the following result.

The present official signs contain in the aggregate sixty-six units of space.

The proposed official signs contain in the aggregate fifty-seven units of space, thus:

Official signs.

		Units of Space.
Public message	· · — · —	8
Official message	· · — ·	5
Private report	· — — ·	6
Call signal	— · — ·	6
Understood	· · · — ·	6
Interruption	· · · · · · · · ·	9
Conclusion	— · ·	4
Wait	· — · · ·	6
Receipt	· — · —	7

Since the Morse code as modified prevails throughout the eastern continent, it is very desirable that in the United States—and, indeed, throughout the whole western continent—also, the slight changes adopted and proposed should be practically carried out by the telegraph companies, thus producing a *uniformity* in one great element of international intercourse, the *telegraphic alphabet of language*, and furnishing one realized example of that uniformity which so many of the master minds of the world at this day aspire to create in other world-wide interests.

For some further remarks on the principles of the code, see the article in this report on the *acoustic* character of the code, in treating of *semaphores* and the *sounder*.

CHAPTER IV.

BATTERIES, CONDUCTORS, AND INSULATORS.

FAILURE OF ALL ATTEMPTS TO EMPLOY FRICTIONAL ELECTRICITY FOR COMMUNICATING AT A DISTANCE—USE OF VARIOUS FORMS OF BATTERIES FOR GENERATING DYNAMIC ELECTRICITY—USE OF MAGNETO ELECTRICITY—FARMER'S THERMO-ELECTRIC BATTERY—LECLANCHÉ'S BATTERY—THE MAGNETÓ-ELECTRIC BATTERY OF S. HJORTH, OF COPENHAGEN—LADD'S DYNAMO-ELECTRIC APPARATUS—LETTER FROM DR. WERNER SIEMENS—OBSERVATIONS UPON THE CONVERSION OF MECHANICAL EFFECT INTO ELECTRIC CURRENTS WITHOUT THE EMPLOYMENT OF PERMANENT MAGNETS, BY DR. WERNER SIEMENS—SULPHATE OF MAGNESIA BATTERY—SUBMARINE TELEGRAPH CABLES—FARMER'S COMPOUND TELEGRAPH WIRE—THE MORSE BATHOMÈTER—PROPOSED NEW MODE OF LAYING AND RAISING SUBMARINE TELEGRAPH CABLES—INSULATORS AND INSULATION—BROOKS'S PARAFFINE INSULATOR—INSULATION TEST OF THE BROOKS AND OTHER INSULATORS—DAY'S KERITE INSULATOR—MEMOIR BY PROFESSOR SILLIMAN UPON INSULATION AND PROTECTION OF ELECTRICAL CONDUCTORS—ACTION OF OZONE UPON TELEGRAPHIC INSULATION—LETTERS UPON THE VALUE OF KERITE AS AN INSULATOR.

BATTERIES OR GENERATORS OF ELECTRICITY.

Static or frictional electricity has long since been discarded as an agent in the electrical instrumentalities for communicating at a distance. All attempts hitherto to make it practicable have failed, and all the devices for that purpose, however ingenious, as most of them were, must be consigned to the category of failures. The principal form of electricity, which has been effective, either in the semaphore or in the telegraph, is dynamic electricity, usually generated by the chemical action of acids upon metals, or the decomposition of metallic salts. The earliest form of Voltaic battery, even the first column of Volta, is available to produce the actual result required either of showing a signal, as in the semaphore, or making a record, as in the telegraph. The earliest form employed by Morse in 1835, and with success so far as to show the practicability of recording, was the well-known Cruikshanks battery. Since this early period many modifications and substantial improvements in the battery have been made, and the constant batteries of Daniel, of Grove, and of Smee, in England, and others on the European continent, have given greater facility in operating the instruments both of the telegraph and semaphore. But the introduction of magneto-electricity, one of the grand results of the generic discovery of Oersted, and of the more recent discoveries of Faraday, have furnished the means of constructing a new generator of electricity, which takes its place intermediately between the frictional and the Voltaic, having less quantity than the Voltaic and less uncontrolable intensity than the frictional instruments. The Voltaic, however, has the quality of giving more readily a continuous current, and is therefore better adapted to recording in all the instruments using the Morse code.

FARMER'S THERMO-ELECTRIC BATTERY.

The batteries exhibited have little of originality. With one or two exceptions, they generally show unimportant modifications of those long known.

The thermo-electric battery of Farmer, of Boston, (No. 74,) is one of novel construction, and deserving of special notice.

Fig. 15.

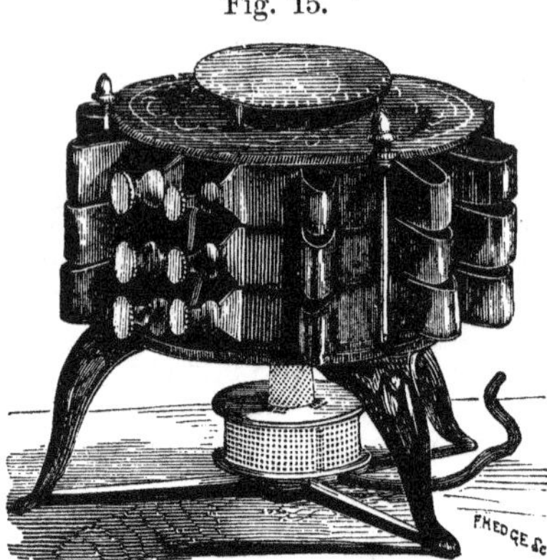

Farmer's Thermo-electric Battery.

The engraving (Fig. 15) represents this battery. It consists of three rings of nine pairs each. A common rubber tube conveys ordinary street gas to a gas burner or gas stove under the center of the battery. A deflector is placed at the top to keep the heat down in the center. All that is required to put the battery in operation is to turn on the gas and light at the burner. The battery acquires its maximum activity in a few moments, when it works continuously and constantly as long as it receives heat.

These batteries are made of various sizes, weighing from a few pounds to half a ton. One of this larger class is now in operation, and is capable of depositing about one pound of copper per hour, at an expense of five or six pounds of coal in the same time.

The smaller batteries are more conveniently operated by gas or lamp. These latter are very convenient for medical use or for telegraph local batteries. The somewhat larger battery gives all the effects of a series of cells, (of the acid batteries in common use.)

These batteries are admirably suited to the wants of the exact experimenter, and render the most useful assistance in their investigations where an absolutely constant current is required, being capable of working for an indefinite period without a perceptible variation in the strength of current which they deliver. Their utility is very apparent to the electrotyper who desires a uniform current, and to the electro-gilder and silver-plater they are especially commended, because they require no acids, mercury, or liquids of any kind in their operation.

The saving which they effect in time, attention, waste, their cleanliness, the readiness with which they can be put into operation, the small expense of working them, and their durability, commend them to all.

Where an establishment is doing sufficient work to require the use of one of such size as can be operated by coal as a fuel, the economical production of electricity by their use is very obvious, five or six pounds of coal being capable of evolving as much electricity as one and a half pound of zinc, five or six pounds of sulphuric acid, and one ounce of mercury.

These batteries, like any series of cells, can be coupled to suit the work they have to perform. As compared with the acid batteries, these batteries have been worked with Boston gas as follows: ten pairs equal to one Smee cell in power; twenty-four pairs equal to one Daniels cell in power; forty-four pairs equal to one Grove cell in power. But in calculating for a battery to perform work for an indefinite period, an addition of 50 per cent. upon the above list is recommended, as the heating power of gas differs very materially in different places. Naphtha has been used with perfect success, and found very economical.

The principal objects kept in view in this invention are, first, to make a battery of sufficient power to be available for industrial uses; second, that it should be reasonably durable; third, that it should be convenient to use; fourth, that it should not be too costly.

With regard to the first object, one has been constructed and used which has deposited 12 pounds of copper, from a sulphate of copper solution, in twenty-four hours, by the consumption of less than 110 pounds of anthracite coal. Smaller ones have been constructed that are most conveniently operated by a gas flame, and which will evolve 50,000 feet-pounds of electricity by the consumption of one pound of common coal gas.

These latter are made of various sizes, and capable of evolving from 20 to 300 feet-pounds of electricity per minute. A common pint-cup Grove cell will evolve 80 feet-pounds of electricity per minute. The current from this (gas-consuming) thermo battery is the most constant and uniform of any that I have ever used, and is admirably adapted to the requirements of exact research.

With regard to the second head, the durability of the thermo battery depends much on the temperature at which it is worked. At all temperatures there appears to be a gradual increase in the specific resistance of the alloys which enter into its composition, but the more slowly the lower the temperature of the heated junction. One of about 150 feet pounds per minute power has been in nightly use for nearly a year. Its power has not been recently measured, but it is still in working order. Some have been in almost daily use by physicians for nearly two years.

Third. The gas-consuming batteries are as convenient as need be, requiring only to be attached by a flexible or other pipe to a gas-burner. The large battery fired with coal needed attention every three or four hours.

Fourth. The thermo battery is much more costly than an acid battery of equivalent power, in the first instance; but the cost of daily maintenance is less. A thermo battery, equivalent in power to four or five Grove cells, costs about ninety dollars.

A thermo battery, to be heated by waste steam, could be operated at trifling cost, and would be very durable, but the amount required to do a given amount of work with only 120 degrees difference of temperature between the junctions, might be of inconvenient size and first cost.

In this battery the two elements used are, German silver for the negative pole, and an alloy of zinc and antimony for the positive pole. The proportions of the zinc and antimony used are, about ninety-six parts antimony and fifty-three parts zinc, as mixed in the melting pot. The pairs are arranged around a central source of heat; and the outer junctions are cooled by radiation and connection.

LECLANCHÉ'S BATTERY.

This battery is much in use in the French telegraph administration. It consists of a prism of carbon for its positive pole, which is surrounded by a mixture of peroxide of manganese and carbon pulverized, filling the porous jar. This jar is put into the glass jar containing a solution of sal ammoniac; within the same glass jar and solution is a prism of amalgamated zinc, forming the negative pole. Its action is thus: On closing the circuit, the sal ammoniac is decomposed, the chlorine of the solution is absorbed by the zinc, the negative pole; while the hydrogen and the ammoniac pass to the positive pole, reducing the peroxide of manganese. According to the inventor's explanation, "the peroxide of manganese mixed with carbon being a good conductor of electricity, the system may be considered as a single fluid element, in which the positive pole is formed of an artificial metal having a great affinity for hydrogen."

MAGNETO-ELECTRIC BATTERY OF S. HJORTH.

This invention by S. Hjorth, of Copenhagen, relates to improvements introduced into the construction of magneto-electric batteries, with a view to obtaining by a slow motion of the armatures any required quantity or intensity of electric fluid.

The improved battery may be constructed of different circles of bar magnets, set partly around and partly above each other, with corresponding intermediate armatures mounted on wooden or other suitable disks on a central shaft, made to rotate by suitable mechanism.[1]

When quantity of the electric fluid is required, the currents are collected by rings, and from thence pass by conductors to a commutator mounted at the upper end of the central shaft. When intensity is desired, the conductors may be connected in one length according to circumstances.

The armatures are provided with false poles, the dimensions of which correspond with those of a certain number of magnets of similar polarity; say for instance eight or nine bars. The changes of polarity in the armatures at each revolution will consequently be equal to the number of these armatures multiplied by the respective series of magnets of similar polarity.

The power developed being in ratio with the number of changes of

[1] Drawings of this apparatus, submitted with the report, are deposited in the library of the Department of State.—EDITOR.

polarity produced at each revolution, an advantage may be obtained by the application of equal numbers of armatures and magnets. This arrangement is composed of three disks, each provided with ninety-six armatures, corresponding with the same number of magnetic bars, so that each revolution gives rise to changes of polarity equal to

$$96 \times 96 = 9{,}216 \times 3 = 27{,}648.$$

The armatures are coiled with wire internally and externally. The two intermediate circles of permanent magnets are fixed to brass rings.

The armature wheel or disk is formed of hard wood or other suitable material, and is provided with two rings, composed of vertical bars overlapping each other, in which the armatures are geared.

It is evident that the concentric series of magnets and armatures, as also the number of these elements, may be increased or decreased according to the effect to be produced. In all cases, the armature disks should be arranged "step-ways," so that when the armatures of the first series have completely passed between the magnets, those of the following series reach but half way, and those of the third series only commence to be drawn in between the magnets. The force of attraction being thus added to the power applied to the central shaft, the motion of the latter is necessarily facilitated by increase in the power of the magnets.

The form, dimensions, and general details of construction of the apparatus above described may be varied according to its intended application.

LADD'S DYNAMO-ELECTRIC APPARATUS.

This apparatus is not in the catalogue, but was exhibited in the English department.

A French journalist thus enthusiastically speaks of it:

"In the judgment of all competent persons, the most astonishing object in the galleries of the Champ de Mars is the machine of Mr. Ladd, constructor of physical instruments, of London, exhibited under the name of Dynamo-Electric Apparatus. Very extraordinary in its principle, in its construction, and in its action, it is composed essentially of two plates of soft iron about two feet long, one foot wide, and four inches thick, kept at a distance of a few inches from each other. They are both of them attached by their ends to two kinds of cylindrical surfaces, also of soft iron, in the bosom or hollow of which turn two armatures of Siemen's cylinders, of soft iron, grooved upon their two faces and covered according to their length by insulated copper wire. An insulated copper wire sufficiently large surrounds also the two plates in compacted spirals perpendicular to their length, and going from one plate to the other, so as to form a closed circuit. The current pervades it through a commutator designed to maintain it always in the same direction. The second armature, on the contrary, is entirely out of the circuit of the first armature and of the plates of soft iron. It turns simply opposite the second poles of the plates, and becomes the seat of an induction current always in the same direction, which, conducted by the wires soldered to the two poles, goes to produce outside the effects of light, of heat, of motion, of affinity, or of chemical decomposition, as may be desired.

"It is perceived that in itself this whole mass of soft iron, of copper wires, without steel, without magnets, is absolutely inert. How can life and activity be given to it? By providing it with a small quantity of magnetism, by priming it magnetically. It is sufficient for this strictly to place properly the plates by putting them in the magnetic meridian, so that the terrestrial magnetism may communicate to it a slight magnetism. But it is better to make to pass once, and once for all, through the wire which surrounds the plates, the current from a Daniels's, Smee's, or Bunsen's battery, which, after having made them temporarily electro-magnets, leaves them, the circuit being broken, with a little of residual magnetism, which magnetism for the future (and if they are not left too long to themselves) renders them always ready for action, or to create torrents of electricity of which they become the source. We have thus passed from absolute inertia to static or powerful activity. Motion completes all the rest. It is sufficient, in fact, to turn at the same time the two armatures, so that in returning constantly upon itself, the inductive current engendered at first by the residual magnetism incessantly increases the polarity or the activity of the plates, which have become powerful electro-magnets, and so that the second armature becomes the point of departure of an electric current of quantity and intensity proportional to the rapidity of rotation of the armatures, or to the force expended by the operator. With the machine exhibited, of which we have given the dimension so small, the exterior current is equivalent to that of twenty-five or thirty Bunsen elements.

"It supplies a Foucault regulator of medium size, and maintains at a white heat a platinum wire of more than a yard in length and half a millimeter in diameter. Here then is the immediate transformation, from the only condition, a small quantity of residual magnetism, by means of mechanical motion, first of power, next of electrical effects, then luminous, calorific, and chemical, &c. Nothing in fact is more simple, more effective. Nothing also is more grand, more unexpected, more mysterious. Mr. Ladd has borrowed from Mr. Wyld his plates, leaving out the magneto-electrical apparatus, substituting for it simply the residual magnetism and adding a second armature, which is the new element of his invention. He has taken from Messrs. Wheatstone and Siemens their return of the current upon itself, forcing it thus to increase itself, constantly multiplying itself, and like them rejecting the battery, for which there is no necessity."

If others do not go quite so far as this earnest French writer in designating the apparatus of Mr. Ladd as the "most astonishing object" in the whole Exposition, they will certainly agree with him in his admiration of the *effects* of this beautiful instrument, and in his designation of them as "grand, unexpected, and mysterious." Mr. Ladd is stated to have borrowed from Messrs. Wheatstone and Siemens their method of causing the current to return upon itself.

An account is given of this discovery from the pen of the discoverer, the eminent Dr. Werner Siemens, of Berlin, who seems to have observed this effect and utilized it, apparently concurrently with Professor Wheatstone, but in reality a little before him, as will be seen by the following letter addressed to Professor Morse:

"BERLIN, *December* 30, 1867.

"Herewith I send you the translation of my communication to the Academy of Sciences in Berlin. I have had it done in London, for we are very weak in English here. As you see by the date of the communication, the publication took place about one and a half month sooner than my brother's and Mr. Wheatstone's speech in London. Already, in November of last year, my first machine was in working and made known to the scientific men here. Wheatstone added something new to it. Ladd has the merit of having shown a larger machine than that in operation in Paris. I had not enough machine power in the Prussian department, and on that account did not take a very large machine with two cylinders, like Ladd's. If you should visit Berlin on your return journey, (which I hope,) I can show you this machine, which gives a brilliant electric light and produces ten cubic centimeters of oxygen and hydrogen gas per second. I could also show you other interesting apparatus. A new mechanical tachygrapher for Morse writing, and an electric distance measurer. This would be especially useful to steamships, as with them we can measure the exact distance of steamers, light-houses, coasts, &c., while in motion."

"ON THE CONVERSION OF MECHANICAL EFFECT INTO ELECTRIC CURRENT WITHOUT THE EMPLOYMENT OF PERMANENT MAGNETS.—When two parallel wires forming part of the circuit of a galvanic battery are approached to or separated from each other, a diminution or augmentation of the strength of current in the whole circuit is observed, according as the movement is in the direct or the inverse direction of the forces which the currents in two wires exercise reciprocally upon each other.

"The same phenomenon is observable still more remarkably when the poles of two electro-magnets, whose wires form parts of the same galvanic circuit, are made to approach or recede from each other. If the direction of the current in one of the wires is changed at the moment of their greatest or least distance, as is the case in all electro-dynamic rotating apparatus, a lasting diminution of the current occurs as soon as the apparatus is put into motion. This diminution of the current of the battery by opposite induction current it is which renders it impossible to employ galvanic electricity successfully as a motive for the production of mechanical effects. Suppose such a machine to be turned backward by some foreign force, it is evident that these induction currents must add themselves to that of the battery, which they proportionally strengthen; and since an increase of this circuit current is necessarily followed by an increase of magnetism in the soft-iron cores, and then again by a further corresponding increase of currents, and so on, the accumulation very soon reaches a point at which the galvanic battery may be removed from the circuit without occasioning any perceptible diminution in the resulting current. The moment the rotation is interrupted, however, the current ceases and the magnetism vanishes. Sufficient magnetism remains, nevertheless, in the iron to cause the process of accumulation to recommence from the moment that the rotation is renewed. It is only necessary, therefore, to magnetize the iron once by a galvanic current of short duration in order to render it forever afterwards capable of being recalled into action by simple rotation.

"The direction of the current depends upon the polarization of the residuary magnetism; and it can only be changed when, by means of a galvanic current, the residuary magnetism of the iron is changed.

"The effects here described take place also with every electro-magnetic machine whose movements depend upon the attraction and repulsion of electro-magnets whose wires form a single circuit. Nevertheless, in order to provide apparatus especially for showing powerfully the phenomena of the dynamo element, a particular construction is found to give the best results. The wire of the stationary electro magnet must have a sufficient magnetic inertia, so that the strength of the attained magnetism does not diminish during the reversing of the current in the wire of the rotating armature. It is also essential that the armature should be so constructed that during its rotation the opposite polar faces of the electro-magnet should be always magnetically closed. These conditions are best fulfilled by the employment of the band form of armature proposed by me some years ago, and which has since then come very generally into use. The armature in question consists of a cylinder of soft iron rotating upon its axis. It carries an insulated wire wound in two deep longitudinal grooves, one in each side. The poles of a battery of permanent magnets, or, in this case, those of the stationary electro-magnet, are cut out so as to let the armature rotate with the least possible space between them.

"By means of a machine constructed upon this principle, if the proportions of the various component parts are justly determined and the commutator properly placed, and a sufficient velocity of rotation given to the barrel armature, a current may be produced in the wire which is so intense that it develops heat enough to burn the covering with which the wire is insulated. This accident, however, can be avoided, when the machine is required to be kept in constant action, by the introduction of resistances or by moderating the velocity of rotation.

"Magneto-electro inductors do not increase in power proportionally with an increase of dimension, whereas with the machine in question the reverse is the case. The reason of this is that in permanent magnets the magnetism increases in a very small ratio to the weight of metal of which they are made, and that with a battery of permanent magnets it is impossible to concentrate their action upon a limited surface without their mutually diminishing their strength to a very material extent. On this account steel magnets are not well adapted for employment in magnet inductors which are required to produce very strong currents. It is true that such machines have been made with permanent magnets, which have given an intense electric light, but, in order to attain this, they were required to be of colossal dimensions, and were correspondingly expensive. In addition to this, the magnets lost very soon the major part of their magnetism, and the machine therefore its force.

"Mr. Wyld, of Birmingham, has lately constructed a machine for the production of powerful magneto-electric currents, whose capability he has increased by the employment of two barrel inductors of my construction, as described above. In the larger of the two he has substituted an electro-magnet for the battery of permanent magnets, setting it in action by the current of the smaller one, and as the electro-magnet becomes more strongly magnetic than permanent magnets could, the resulting current is correspondingly stronger.

"It is easily seen that Wyld has, by this construction, considerably obviated the difficulties found in employing steel magnets. But independently of the inconvenience attending the use of two inductors, his apparatus has still the disadvantage that it is directly dependent upon the steel magnets of the first inductor for the efficiency of its operations."

SULPHATE OF MAGNESIA BATTERY.

A new battery is described by Mr. McGowan, general superintendent of telegraphs in Victoria, Australia, as producing an economy over the sulphate of copper battery, used for the local battery to work the register.

This form is known as the sulphate of magnesia battery, and has been patented. "The containing cell is of more than ordinary large dimensions; the negative and positive elements are copper and zinc, cylindrical in form, and the exciting fluids are, 1, sulphate of magnesia, in the form of a nearly saturated solution; 2, sulphate of copper in broken crystals. The former surrounding the metals in the containing vessel; the latter, in partial solution, admitted through a perforation at the extremity of a conical glass receiver placed within the interior cylinder."

CONDUCTORS, CABLES, ETC.

SUBMARINE TELEGRAPH CABLES.

In consequence of the success which has attended the use of submarine telegraph cables, and especially the great success of the Atlantic cable enterprise, the attention of the skillful has of late been turned to the importance of improving and perfecting them.

There were many electrical experiments made with submarine conductors for various scientific purposes previous to their application to telegraphy.

It is believed that the first submarine telegraph line was laid and operated in New York harbor by Morse, in October, 1842. Although destroyed early after its submersion, by the anchor of a vessel getting under way, it was not destroyed until the fact of its ability to transmit dispatches was fully demonstrated. The gold medal of the American Institute was bestowed for this success.

Since that date the skill of European, especially of English, French, and Prussian savans, has succeeded not only in improving the construction of submarine cables, but in extending them in various directions from the United Kingdom across rivers, straits, and channels, and through seas, until the islands and continents of the eastern hemisphere are to a great extent telegraphically united, and the great enterprise of the day, the Atlantic telegraph, through the skill and perseverance and capital of English and Americans, has been the overcoming of the apparently insurmountable obstacle of an ocean deemed until recently unfathomable. It is unnecessary here more than to allude to this well-known enterprise, since the exhaustive history of it is familiar to all who have read the history of the Atlantic telegraph in the graphic pages of Doctor Russell and the Reverend Henry Field.

COMPOUND TELEGRAPH WIRE.

As directly connected with the improvement of submarine cables, attention is drawn to the "compound telegraph wire," the invention of Moses G. Farmer, esq., of Boston, who exhibited the thermo-electric battery, already described, page 52.

Mr. Farmer, in a letter to Professor Morse, dated Boston, July 29, 1868, thus describes this valuable improvement, and the tests to which it has been subjected:

"I sent to you, a little time since, a pamphlet relating to our new compound telegraph wire, composed of a steel core and a copper covering, the whole coated with an alloy, principally tin, for preservative purposes. You will take in at a glance the numerous advantages of this wire.

"As has been most fully shown by Thomson's researches, and amply demonstrated by the working of the Atlantic cable, the speed at which a line can be worked is directly as its conductivity, and inversely as its electro-static capacity. The distance, also, which can be reached is directly as the conductivity, and as the degree of insulation. Anything, therefore, which improves the conductivity, or diminishes the static capacity, or increases the insulation, is a benefit.

"Let us look for a moment at the comparative conductivity, strength, and specific weight of iron, steel, and copper. I have carefully measured and recorded one or all of these elements for more than fifty samples in common use. I find upon an average that from two and three-quarters to three miles of common telegraph iron wire would break of its own weight if suspended vertically; about one mile and three-quarters of copper, and about seven and a half miles of the steel which we use. I copy my coefficients:

Steel, 7.47
Galvanized iron, 2.91 } $\left(\frac{Tl}{w}\right)$
Copper, 1.72

"Now, for weight per mile, take the diameter of the wire in inches, and multiply its square by—

For steel, 13373.
For iron, 13800. } $\left(\frac{w}{ld^2}\right)$
For copper, 15400.

"The result will be the weight per mile, 5280 feet.

"Now, for conductivity, assume as unity a round wire of chemically pure copper, one-twentieth of an inch in diameter; it would weigh thirty-nine and one-ninth pounds per mile. I will copy my latest coefficients, which, if multiplied by the weight per mile, will give the actual conductivity in terms of the unit above assumed, viz:

$$\left(\frac{cl}{w}\right)$$

For steel, .00262.
For copper, .02045.
For galvanized iron, .00355.

"The coefficient for copper, .02045, is one for commercial copper, which I used in making up the tables in the pamphlet referred to. We now use a copper, for which the proper coefficient is .02301, or ninety per cént. of pure copper, (which would be .02556.)

"The resistance of 5280 feet of pure copper wire, weighing 39.11 pounds, would be about 21.3 B. A. units.

"Now, with the help of these coefficients, let us examine two or three wires. No. 8 iron wire weighs three hundred and seventy-five pounds per mile. (*Vide* Shaffner, L. Clark, M. G. Farmer.) Hence its tensile strength, or the weight which would break a short length of it, would be $T=2.9\times375=1087$ pounds, and its conductivity would be $C=.00355\times375=1.331$—Farmer's latest; ($C=1.298$, L. Clark.) This refers to ordinary galvanized iron wire, at about ten or ten and a half cents per pound, and not Washburn's best at fourteen cents.

"Now, take fifty-six pounds per mile of steel:

Its $T=7.47\times56=418$.
Its $C=.00262\times56=.1467$.

"Take, now, fifty-six pounds of copper per mile, and we have:

Its $T=1.72 \quad \times56= \quad 96$.
Its $C= .02045\times56=1.145$.
Or its $C= .02301\times56=1.288$.

"Now the combined strength of the two would be—

T steel + T copper = T compound.
$418+96=514$ pounds.

"And the combined conductivity would be—

C. steel + C. copper = C. compound.

.146+1.145=1.291.

"Or, as we now make it—

.146+1.288=1.434.

"Thus we have a compound wire weighing one hundred and twelve pounds per mile, having a conductivity of from 1.291 to 1.434, according to the copper used, fully equal, if not superior, to that of average No. 8 galvanized iron wire, (1.298 to 1.331,) which compound wire will require $\frac{514}{112}$=4.58, or four and a half miles, to be suspended vertically to break of its own weight, being more than fifty per cent. stronger than iron wire in proportion to the weight which it has to sustain. Hence it can probably be put up with fewer poles per mile, thus increasing the degree of insulation.

"I will here insert two tables:

Galvanized iron wire.

Posts.	Sag.	Ti	C	T	$\frac{w}{l}$	$\frac{Ti}{T}$
38	1	144.3	1.136	928	320	.155
38	2	72.2	1.136	928	320	.077
38	3	48.1	1.136	928	320	.052

Compound wire.

Posts.	Sag.	Ti	C	T	$\frac{w}{l}$	$\frac{Ti}{T}$
23	1	140	1.331	.514	112	.272
23	2	70	1.331	514	112	.136
22	3	47	1.331	514	112	.091

"So that with twenty-three posts per mile, instead of thirty-eight, the insulation would be 33—23÷23=$\frac{65}{100}$= sixty-five per cent. better, and with a sag of two feet, the strain on the wire at the insulator would be only about one-seventh of that required to break a short length of the wire; and with a sag of only one foot, the strain would be less than one-third of its ultimate strength. The uniformity and homogeneity of the steel render it less likely to break from flaws, (and the short experience which we have had with it shows this.) The saving of cost per transportation is evident at a glance.

"Now let us look at a larger wire. Suppose 187 pounds per mile of steel and 188 pounds per mile of copper equal 375 pounds per mile, (same weight as a No. 8 galvanized iron, which has a tensile strength of 1087,) and a conductivity of 1.331 (at best average:)

	$\frac{w}{l}$	T	C	$\frac{Tl}{w}$
Steel	187	1397	.490	7.47
Copper	188	329	4.324	1.72
Summary	375	1720	4.814	4.59

"Here we have an increase over No. 8 of 1720−1087÷1087=$\frac{58}{100}$, or fifty-eight per cent. in tensile strength, an increase of 4.814−1.331÷1.331 =261 per cent.; or, in other words, we could reach three and a half times as far with the compound wire as with the iron of equal weight per mile, while the insulation could be improved by the use of fewer poles per mile, this wire being nearly sixty per cent. the stronger."

Table showing the relative weight, strength, and conductivity of the compound and other wires.

	$\frac{w}{l}$	T	C	$\frac{C}{C\,fe.}$
Table No. 1	375	1091	1.331	1
Table No. 2:				
Steel	187	1397	.490	......
Copper	188	325	4.324	......
Compound	375	1722	4.814	3.61
Table No. 3:				
Steel	119	889	.311	......
Copper	119	205	2.737	......
Compound	238	1094	3.048	2.29
Table No. 4:				
Steel	52	388	.136	......
Copper	52	89	1.196	......
Compound	104	477	1.332	1
Table No. 5:				
Steel	78	583	.204	......
Copper	297	511	6.831	......
Compound	375	1094	7.035	5.28
Table No. 6:				
Steel	357	2768	.935	......
Copper	18	31	.414	......
Compound	375	2799	1.349	1
Table No. 7:				
Steel	136	1016	.356	......
Copper	43	74	.989	......
Compound	179	1090	1.345	1
Table No. 8:				
Steel	56	418	.147	......
Copper	56	96	1.288	......
Compound	112	514	1.435	1.07

Explanation of Columns.—1st, $\left(\frac{w}{l}\right)$ weight per mile; 2d, (T) tensile strength; 3d, (C) conductivity; 4th, $\left(\frac{C}{C\,fe.}\right)$ conductivity compared with common No. 8 galvanized wire.

Table No. 1 contains the elements for the average of No. 8 galvanized iron telegraph wire; table No. 2, compound wire of equal weight; table No. 3, compound wire of equal tensile strength; table No. 4, compound wire of equal conductivity; table No. 5, compound wire of equal weight and tensile strength; table No. 6, compound wire of equal weight and conductivity; table No. 7, compound wire of equal tensile strength and conductivity; table No. 8, compound wire, our ordinary equivalent of No. 8 galvanized iron wire, such as costs ten to eleven cents per mile at present.

The improvement of Mr. Farmer in the construction of telegraph wire is considered of so much importance as to warrant the insertion here of a more detailed specification of its advantages; and in view of the obstacles encountered in the construction of lines in the Ottoman Empire, to which the energetic director of Turkish telegraphs alludes in his letter to the United States minister resident in Constantinople, inserted in Chapter VI, (obstacles occasioned by the accumulation of ice upon the wires in certain localities,) we specially commend the fact that the compound wire seems specially adapted to obviate these difficulties:

"There is a growing tendency in this and other countries to employ larger wire for telegraph purposes, in order to obtain a greater conducting capacity.

"Notwithstanding the many disadvantages attending the use of large telegraph wire, No. 4 has been adopted on important lines and for long circuits, in England, Russia, and other countries, solely for its superior conductivity; and it is well understood by telegraphers in general, that for the rapid and successful operations of the circuits, much depends upon this element. Especially is this the case in wet weather and upon long lines.

"Under certain conditions of the lines, consequent upon wet weather, *superior conductivity* will accomplish that which increased battery power utterly fails to do; and repeaters at intermediate offices, with their necessary main batteries, accomplish but imperfectly and unsatisfactorily, as a general rule, and in many cases fail to do altogether.

"Pure copper wire, having a conducting capacity of nearly seven times that of galvanized iron wire, has, of course, a great advantage in this respect for telegraph purposes. Its use, however, has been prevented in consequence of lack of sufficient strength to sustain itself.

"In the American compound telegraph wire this vital objection to the employment of copper alone for this purpose is obviated, and a conductivity and relative strength, superior to that of galvanized iron, are combined in a lighter wire.

"The composite parts of this wire are steel and copper, the steel forming the core, and serving mainly for strength, while the copper serves more especially as a superior conductor.

"In regard to relative strength it is well known that the breaks in ordinary galvanized telegraph wire, occasioned by accumulations of ice and snow, and from other causes, occur at weak points, or at imperfections which are caused by flaws existing in the iron before galvanizing, as well as from the effects of that process.

"We therefore claim that our compound wire, even with a relative strength no greater, theoretically, than that of a galvanized iron wire, will be much less liable to breakage from these causes, in consequence of the uniformity of strength in the steel core, while, in fact, the relative strength itself, of the compound wire, is very much the better of the two. (See table beyond.)

"Steel wires, of sizes varying from No. 12 to No. 16, stretched from pole to pole, across streams from one-quarter to three-quarters of a mile in width, in the United States, which have withstood the accumulations of ice and sleet for years, are good illustrations in this connection. One special instance may be cited of a No. 16 steel wire, between fourteen hundred and fifteen hundred feet in length, which has been in operation across the Kennebec River, in Maine, for the past eight years; and which, we are informed by the superintendent of the line, has parted twice only during that period—in each case having been untwisted at a joint by the great strain upon it caused by an immense accumulation of ice, the wire itself remaining intact.

"The advantages of increased conductivity and strength having been briefly set forth, there are other practical advantages to be gained in the use of the American compound telegraph wire, to which we would respectfully call the attention of contractors and telegraph companies.

"Large wire is used only because of its superior conductivity; and it is obvious that a light wire is preferable in handling and stringing, which can be done with less labor.

"Also, maintaining a superior conductivity and relative strength, the lightness of this wire will admit of an average of at least ten poles to the mile less than would be otherwise necessary.

"This reduction in the number of poles per mile will not only conduce to economy in construction, but it will effect a decrease of twenty-five per cent. or more in escape of the electric current.

"In stringing over the tops of buildings, stretches may be safely made double the length of those taken with the ordinary telegraph wire, and yet with less strain upon the insulators.

"Another point in its favor is the imperishable nature of copper, which, in this wire, is the exposed metal; the zinc coating of the galvanized iron being deteriorated near the sea, and from the effect of gases, &c., from chimneys, while copper will remain, under such conditions, unimpaired. In fact, under all circumstances, the durability of the com pound wire is greatly superior to that of the galvanized wire in general use.

"In the construction of lines there are many cases in which the expense of transportation of telegraph wire from the manufactory to its destination is an item of considerable magnitude. By reference to the accompanying table it will be readily seen that with the same or a much greater conductivity, as compared with galvanized iron, the compound wire weighs very materially less, with no disadvantage whatever arising from its lightness.

"Referring again to 'conductivity,' which has been the chief objective point in the production of this wire, it will be observed that this element may be largely increased without sacrificing strength, and without recourse to an unwieldy and cumbersome medium for conduction.

"Increased conductivity admits of a reduction in battery power, with a consequent decrease in the escape of electricity. Long circuits are worked with greater facility, and the rains and the fogs lose their time-honored power to prevent the passage of the electric current where it should properly flow.

No. I.—Commercial table showing the absolute and relative strength and conductivity of the compound wires.

GALVANIZED IRON WIRE.				COMPOUND STEEL AND COPPER WIRE.				
Size.	Weight per mile.	Relative strength.	Conductivity.	Conductivity.	Relative strength.	Weight per mile.	Sizes of steel.	Size of compound.
12	161	2.9	.53	.53	5.5	62	17	16+
11	208	2.9	.69	.69	5.1	70	17	15—
10	263	2.9	.87	.87	4.7	79	17	15+
9	313	2.9	1.03	1.03	4.9	99	16	14
8	375	2.9	1.29	1.29	4.6	112	16	14+
7	449	2.9	1.48	1.48	4.4	121	16	13—
6	525	2.9	1.73	1.73	4.5	147	15	12—
5	610	2.9	2.02	2.02	4.3	161	15	12
4	720	2.9	2.38	2.38	4.0	179	15	12+
3	835	2.9	2.76	2.76	4.2	216	14	11—
2	969	2.9	3.20	3.20	3.9	238	14	11+
1	1121	2.9	3.71	3.71	3.8	263	14	10—

Special table No. II.

GALVANIZED IRON WIRE.				COMPOUND WIRE.			
Size.	Relative strength.	Weight per mi .	Conductivity.	Conductivity.	Weight per mile.	Relative strength.	Size.
4	2.9	720	2.38	2.65	198	4	11—
6	2.9	525	1.73	1.86	139	4	13+
8	2.9	375	1.29	1.35	101	4	14
9	2.9	313	1.03	1.12	83	4	15
10	2.9	262	.87	.95	71	4	15—

Special table No. III.

GALVANIZED IRON WIRE.				COMPOUND WIRE.			
Size.	Relative strength.	Weight per mile.	Conductivity.	Conductivity.	Weight per mile.	Relative strength.	Size.
4	2.9	720	2.38	2.65	257	5	10—
6	2.9	525	1.73	1.86	181	5	12+
8	2.9	375	1.29	1.35	131	5	13+
9	2.9	313	1.03	1.12	108	5	14+
10	2.9	262	.87	.95	95	5	14—
12	2.9	161	.53	.60	58	5	16

Special table No. IV.

GALVANIZED IRON WIRE.				COMPOUND WIRE.			
Size.	Relative strength.	Weight per mile.	Conductivity.	Conductivity.	Weight per mile.	Relative strength.	Size.
4	2.9	720	2.38	2.65	160	3	12
6	2.9	525	1.73	1.86	112	3	14+
8	2.9	375	1.29	1.35	81	3	15
9	2.9	313	1.03	1.12	67	3	16+

"The term relative strength, used in the preceding tables, denotes the quotient obtained by dividing the strain which would break the wire by its weight per mile.

"The gauge here used is that employed by Washburn and other telegraph-wire makers.

"Table I compares several sizes of galvanized iron wire with the American compound telegraph wire of equal conductivity and a relative strength from thirty to ninety per cent. greater, showing that the compound wire need have only about one-third the weight of galvanized iron wire to be relatively stronger, and at the same time to possess equal or greater conductivity.

"It is evident why this should be so, since the best commercial copper possesses more than six times the average conducting capacity of galvanized iron wire; and the steel which enters into the compound wire has nearly three times the tensile strength of galvanized iron wire of equal size.

"The relative strength of the steel which is used in the American compound telegraph wire averages 7.47; that of the copper, 1.72; while the average relative strength of galvanized iron wire, as found by testing various samples of the best in the market, is only 2.9.

"Hence it is clearly evident that, by varying the proportions of steel and copper in the compound wire, any desired relative strength can be given between the limits of 1.72 and 7.47; and, at the same time, any desired conductivity can be had along with it.

"It will be seen, however, that a high relative strength is more costly than a low one, for the reason that steel possesses a less specific conductivity than copper, and this difference of conductivity is greater than the difference of cost.

"But, in the construction of lines of telegraph, while an increased relative strength adds to the cost of the wire used, it, on the other hand, effects a saving in the number of poles and insulators required, thus reducing the total cost of material and its transportation, which is often of great importance; therefore increased relative strength is, on the whole, more economical.

"Table II shows wires of different conductivities, all possessing a relative strength of four.

"In table III the wires all show a relative strength of five, while

"Table IV shows wires with a relative strength of only three, which is at least three per cent. better than the average of telegraph wire, and the strength of the larger sizes is certainly ample. From this table it appears that we can get the conductivity of a No. 8 galvanized iron wire by using a compound wire weighing only eighty pounds per mile. Such a wire would be handled with the greatest ease, as a man could readily carry a mile or more upon his back.

"By using either of the two larger sizes shown in this table, all the advantages of a heavy iron wire, which would weigh from five hundred to seven hundred pounds per mile, can be secured by a compound wire weighing less than one hundred and seventy-five pounds per mile.

"Other sizes than these in the above tables can be made possessing intermediate or greater relative strength and of any desirable conductivity.

"The foregoing tables are based on the employment of a copper which shall possess seventy-eight one-hundredths of the conductivity of a chemically pure copper wire.

"The standard unit of conductivity here employed is that of a round copper wire one-twentieth of an inch in diameter, chemically pure, and one foot in length.

"In making up the coefficients of tensile strength, conductivity, and weight per mile of galvanized iron wire, for comparison with the compound, as per tables, careful tests were made and an average taken from several samples, including some of the best qualities found in the market."

At the risk of some repetition the following observations upon conductors and insulation are extracted from a more recent publication by the American Compound Telegraph Wire Company, of which Mr. Moses G. Farmer is the consulting electrician:

"The method most commonly in use now, and always likely to be, for the construction of lines of telegraph, is to stretch a line of wire in the air from one pole to another, attaching it to the pole by the intervention of an insulator, connecting each end of the circuit with the ground. The reason we use an insulator is that we wish to transmit as much as possible of the current to the far end of the line before it enters the ground.

"Now, as a current of electricity divides itself into as many branches as there are paths open for it to travel in, and since the proportion of the whole current flowing in any particular path depends on the conductivity of that particular path, in comparison with the sum of the conductivities of all the paths, we wish to diminish the number and value of the paths of escape down the several posts which support the line.

"To maintain a current of electricity in a line of telegraph we employ some form of galvanic battery. Those most generally used are the Grove nitric acid and the Daniel's sulphate of copper battery. About five of the latter are equivalent to three of the former in ability to work a long line.

"Since, however good the insulator may be, some small portion of the current escapes from the line, over it, down the post to the ground, it is manifest that if the line be long, the posts many, and the insulators very poor, a small portion only of the entering current may reach the far end of the line.

"The law which governs this may be thus enunciated. If the current upon the line near the battery be called the entering current, and that upon the distant end near where it enters the ground be called the arriving current, then the distance to which any stated fraction of the entering current will reach is proportioned directly to the square root of the conductivity of the wires, to the square root of the insulating power of the insulator, and inversely to the square root of the number of poles per mile used. It is customary, of late, to compare the resistance of different wires with one another, by referring them to the standard adopted by the British Association for the Advancement of Science.

"This unit is sometimes called an ohm, or an ohmad, a name given in honor of Dr. G. S. Ohm, who so fully developed the laws which govern the distribution and action of a galvanic current; an unit a million times larger than this, and called a megohm, is used to compare the resistance of insulators.

"A round wire of pure copper, one-twentieth of an inch in diameter and about two hundred and fifty feet in length, nearly represents this unit of resistance; a nearer representation of it is a round wire one foot in length, and one hundred and forty-eight one-thousandths of an inch in diameter, made from an alloy composed of two parts of silver and one part of platinum.

Since a pure copper wire is from six to eight times as good a conductor as an average iron wire of the same size, and since the distance to which we can work a line of telegraph depends, among other things, upon the conductivity of the line, it is plain that it would be desirable to use copper if it answered as well in other respects as it does for conductivity; and the first lines in this country were actually constructed of copper, but it was soon found that its ductility and inferior tenacity rendered it inapplicable to the purpose. So iron wires soon came to be substituted for copper, and size No. 9, weighing about three hundred and twenty pounds per mile, was selected, as it seemed to generally possess about the same conductivity as did the No. 16 copper wire, which had been hitherto used.

"Since 1847 iron wire has been almost wholly used in this country, until within the past year, when the American compound telegraph wire made its appearance. This wire is the result of almost numberless attempts which have been made to utilize the well-known conducting power of copper; and it is at last accomplished by uniting copper, the best conductor, with steel, the strongest known material; thus at once securing lightness and strength with great conductivity in the same wire, copper being six or eight times as good a conductor as iron, and steel being twice or thrice as strong.

"The American compound telegraph wire has a core of carefully-selected and well-manipulated steel, which core is first tinned, and then has drawn upon it a strip or ribbon of the very best Lake Superior copper, which is selected with the greatest care.

"In the course of its manufacture it goes through a great number and variety of processes, such as annealing, tempering, drawing, &c., and the completed wire is finished by passing it through a bath of melted tin, by which the copper and steel are welded into and made one complete whole.

"The smaller sizes are generally drawn into lengths of one thousand to fifteen hundred feet, and are put up in mile bundles, three or more pieces being carefully joined together at the factory.

"A wire of ordinary iron, weighing about three hundred and twenty pounds per mile, and known to the trade as No. 9, will offer from seventeen to twenty-two units of resistance or ohms to the mile. A compound wire composed half of steel and half of copper, offering the same mileage resistance, will weigh only about one hundred pounds per mile; an iron wire of average quality, weighing three hundred and seventy-five pounds per mile, and known as No. 8, will offer the same mileage resistance as a compound wire of less than one-third that weight.

"None is suffered to go out from the factory as first-class wire, in which the conductivity of the copper is less than ninety per cent. that of chemically pure copper.

"It is manifestly a great advantage to use a light wire, if it presents the required ability to sustain itself, since it produces less strain upon the insulators, which are always brittle, and requires posts of less strength to sustain it. The cost of transportation is also less, as also is the cost of handling in stringing, &c.

"The compound wire possesses another advantage, based on the fact that steel, even at a low temper, possesses a great degree of elasticity, so much so that it can be stretched or elongated one two hundred and fiftieth part of its length without taking a permanent set; but will, upon removal of the strain, return to its original length; and it is a fact that when a tree falls upon a line of the compound wire and does not break it, when the tree is removed the wire returns nearly or quite to its original position, instead of remaining stretched as does an iron wire.

"From this cause a line of compound wire keeps up to its original height, and does not sag more and more year after year, as an iron wire does.

"In order to show clearly the advantages which the compound wire offers in the construction of lines of telegraph, it may be well to compare the relative conditions as to strength and ability to work lines built of iron wire, with equally efficient lines constructed with compound wire.

"A very common mode of construction has been to use No. 9 iron wire, weighing three hundred and twenty pounds, and putting it up on thirty-five poles per mile, with glass insulators on wooden pins, which insulators, in a long-continued rain-storm, would not offer more than two or three megohms of resistance. We will suppose one wire used, the posts to be twenty-five feet above ground. If the wire be of very good quality it will offer eighteen ohms per mile of resistance, and if it be soft it will generally break at a strain of about one thousand pounds; but there being always more or less of flaws in a mile of the wire, if it be put up very taut it will break a few times the first year. We will suppose the posts one hundred and fifty feet apart, and the sag of the wire midway between the posts to be nine inches; this would be called pulled up pretty straight. The strain on the wire near the insulator would be two hundred and fifty pounds, or twenty-five per cent. of the ultimate strength of the iron; and it would be more than that, as the strength of a wire is that of its weakest cross-section, and there being occasional flaws, two hundred and fifty pounds would sometimes be as much as one-third of the real strength of the wire.

"With a mileage resistance of eighteen ohms, and with thirty-five insulators per mile, which offer three megohms resistance each in a very rainy day, the fraction of the entering current which would reach the end of the line, two hundred and fifty miles distant, would be about five and one-third per cent. The apparent resistance of the line, measured from one end, would be only about two hundred and thirty-eight ohms, instead of four thousand five hundred, which it would be if the line were insulated to absolute perfection. Suppose now that ordinarily thirty Grove cups are used at one end only, the total electro-motive force of the thirty cups will be about forty-eight volts, and the internal resistance of the thirty cups should not exceed twelve ohms; then the total resistance of the circuit, with all the relays cut out, would be $238 + 12 = 250$ ohms, and the strength of the entering current would be one hundred and ninety-two thousandths of a megafarad, or one hundred and ninety-two thousand farads.

"This is from ten to fifteen times as much strength of current as is ordinarily required to work a relay; and, indeed, the five and one-third per cent. of it, or ten thousand one hundred and seventy-six farads is amply sufficient to work the relay at the distant end of the line.

"We will now suppose that we employ a compound wire weighing two hundred pounds per mile, ninety pounds of this wire being steel and one hundred and ten pounds of it being copper—its breaking strain will be about one thousand and forty pounds; one-fourth of this will be two hundred and sixty pounds, and if it be put up on nineteen posts per mile, with a sag of sixteen inches midway between the poles, the ratio of the span to the sag will be the same as in the former case. The tension on the wire will be the same fraction of its ultimate strength, as in the case of the iron wire on thirty-five poles per mile; and from its superior homogeneity it will be less likely to break.

"Now, on a line thus constructed, the conducting resistance being 7.72 ohms per mile, and there being only nineteen insulators of three megohms each per mile, we shall find that *thirty-four per cent.* of the entering current arrives at the terminal station, two hundred and fifty miles distant, instead of five and one-third, as with the No. 9 iron wire; and we shall find that twelve cups of Grove's battery will cause as strong a current to arrive at the distant end as did the thirty cups on the previous iron wire.

"Some of the best constructed lines in the United States use a wire of extra quality, weighing three hundred and eighty pounds per mile, with as low a mileage resistance as thirteen ohms.

"These lines are built on thirty-eight to forty posts per mile, with glass insulators that in a hard rain do not show more than nine megohms resistance each.

"A line so constructed would be capable of transmitting ninety per cent. of the entering current to a terminal station seventy miles distant, and ten per cent. of the current to a terminal station four hundred and eighty-four miles distant.

"But if a compound wire, half of steel and half of copper, weighing one hundred and forty pounds per mile, and having a mileage resistance of twelve ohms, be put on twelve posts instead of thirty-eight, with the same kind of insulators, we should find that ninety per cent. of the entering current could be transmitted over a line one hundred and thirty-one miles long, and ten per cent. over a line seven hundred and fifty miles in length.

"If, instead of the compound wire, weighing one hundred and forty pounds—only about three-eighths the weight per mile of the iron—we make it weigh the same, namely, three hundred and eight pounds per mile, its mileage resistance would be only four and five-tenths ohms; and if it be put up, as in the last example, we should find that ninety per cent. of the current would be received at a terminal station two hundred and thirteen miles distant, and similarly ten per cent. at a station twelve hundred and twenty-five miles away.

"It is clear that the principle involved in the foregoing examples, namely, transmitting an increased percentage of the current by means of superior conductivity, or insulation, or both, is applicable to the double transmission and other intricate systems, as well as to the working of long circuits, and general operations in humid weather.

"*Increased conductivity* becomes of special importance to those systems which strive for greatly increased rapidity of transmission, particularly on long lines, as *this feature alone* aids us to overcome the retardation due to lateral induction.

"Its special advantages are also manifest on lines which may be liable to contact with trees, as the percentage of a current which will pass beyond a given local fault will be greater as the conductivity of the wire is increased. In other words, the greater the conductivity of the wire the less the escape from it.

"We have thus endeavored briefly to set forth a few of the advantages which this wire offers to enterprising contractors and companies which desire to remove the odium that has hitherto been the standing reproach of American lines."

THE MORSE BATHOMETER.

This is an instrument designed to aid submarine telegraphy exhibited by Sidney E. Morse and G. Livingston Morse, of New York. In regard to this bathometer the pertinent remarks of C. W. Siemens upon the apparatus in the Exhibition, in England, of 1862, may be quoted. He says: "New discoveries and inventions, represented most likely by some ill-executed model, will naturally occupy only a modest position among the great crowd of brilliant objects surrounding us at a great exhibition, and are overlooked, or only half appreciated, until their real worth becomes gradually apparent, in the course of years, through the results they are destined to produce." This it is believed very aptly applies in the present case. The instrument referred to attracted little attention, from its unpretending size and appearance, and the jurors who examined it evidently misapprehended or overlooked its peculiarities. Its main principle was supposed to be the compression of air, which experience has long since proved cannot be successfully used as a means of ascertaining the depth of very deep water, and this erroneous impression probably turned away the attention of the jurors from the novel contrivances in this curious instrument.

The Morse bathometer is a double bathometer, by which the depth of the water in the deepest parts of the ocean may be ascertained, at one sounding, by two entirely distinct and independent methods. Messrs. Morse, in the course of their experiments, made the remarkable and, in its applications to investigations of the bottom of the sea, inestimably important discovery that small hollow glass spheres can be constructed which will retain their buoyancy in the deepest parts of the ocean, being neither crushed nor permeated by water under the enormous pressure at those great depths. They have made hollow glass spheres so light that they would float in water with more than half of their bulk above the surface, the spheres being between three and four inches in diameter, and the glass less than a tenth of an inch thick, and they subjected these light and fragile bodies, in the cistern of an hydraulic press, to a pressure of seven tons on the square inch, which is the pressure at the depth of about thirty thousand feet, or nearly six miles in the ocean. The spheres came out from this severe trial of their strength and impermeability whole, and empty of everything but air. In the construction of their bathometer Messrs. Morse deposit these spheres, in any required number, in a tube of tin, wood, or other suitable material, the tube being commonly of four inches interior diameter, several feet long, ballasted at its lower end so that it will stand and float upright in the water, and surmounted at the upper end by a conical or parabaloidal cap, having a socket on the top, in which a very light straight rod of any desired length may be securely fastened. When a sounding is to be made an elongated weight, sufficiently heavy to carry the whole instrument rapidly down, is attached to the lower end of this upright, ballasted tube, and so attached that the moment a small weight, which moves in advance, strikes the bottom of the sea, the large weight will be infallibly detached and allow the tube, by its own buoyancy, to ascend with the rest of the apparatus to the surface. As this instrument is not encumbered with a line, or with anything causing irregularity of motion, it moves through the water with uniform velocity, both in its descent and ascent, and the time of its disappearance below the surface may, therefore, be taken as a correct measure of the depth of the water. If, for example, it should be found to occupy just ten minutes in descending to and ascending from a depth of one thousand fathoms, its disappearance for just twenty minutes would indicate that the depth was two thousand fathoms. The rapidity of the descent and of the ascent of each instrument will be regulated, of course, by the amount of weight suspended from, and of buoyancy inclosed in, the tube. It can easily be made to go down and return in very deep water in less than a tenth part of the time required when a line is used.

But this bathometer, as has already been remarked, is double. In determining the depth of the water at any point, Messrs. Morse do not confine themselves to calculations based on the interval of time elapsing between the disappearance and reappearance of their instrument at the surface. They inclose in any convenient part of their tube, to be carried down and brought back with it, another instrument, which enables them, on its return to the surface, to mark, with the greatest precision, the true depth of the sea at the place of the sounding. This instrument, which is based on the principle of the compression of water, and is the proper Morse bathometer, is thus constructed. A glass bottle (it may be of the capacity of a pint, more or less) is completely filled with freshly distilled water, and closed at its neck with an India-rubber stopper. Through the center of this stopper passes, longitudinally, a short glass tube of very small bore, open at both ends, and extending beyond the stopper in both directions, namely, an inch or more within the bottle and two or three inches on the outside. One end of an India-rubber tube three or four inches long, open at both ends, and, when open, of about an inch in diameter, is then passed over the neck of the bottle and made tight there by winding around it fine wire or cord, which presses it close to the glass. The bottle is then sunk in a vessel of distilled water till the water rises above the mouth of the India-rubber tube, which is held up and open to receive it. Mercury, sufficient to fill the tube to the extent of one-half or more of its capacity, is then poured in, the mouth of the tube closed, and a cord or wire wound tightly around at the end, under water, thus converting the India-rubber tube into a bag filled in nearly equal portions with mercury and distilled water. On inverting the bottle, the mercury, from its specific gravity, occupies the lower half of the India-rubber bag, and keeps the water from access to the lower orifice of the glass tube, which passes now from the bottom of the bag through the stopper into the bottle. When this bottle of water, thus prepared, is placed at the bottom of the sea, the pressure of the external sea water, acting through the India-rubber bag, and through the mercury in the bag and in the glass tube, compresses the fresh water in the bottle, and the mercury is forced from the bag into the bottle to fill the void caused by the compression. The quantity of the mercury forced into the bottle is a perfect measure of the extent of the compression of the water, and this compression is always exactly proportioned to the height of the compressing column—that is, of the depth of the sea. It is only necessary, therefore, to measure the mercury forced from the bag into the bottle to know with the greatest precision the depth of the sea at the lowest point of descent of the bottle. To facilitate the measuring of the mercury, Messrs. Morse, in constructing their bottle, cause a glass tube several inches long, of even bore and closed at the outer end, to be inserted in the end of the bottle opposite to the neck, so that on inverting the bottle the mercury, which at first rests in the neck on the stopper, falls into this meter tube, which is graduated, and thus shows the depth of the sea by the height of the mercury, as in the barometer and thermometer the height of the mercury indicates the weight and heat of the air.

As the bulk of all liquids is greatly affected by temperature, as well as by pressure, the indications of any bathometer based on the principle of the compression of water, in the construction of which this consideration has been overlooked, will be wholly unreliable. Messrs. Morse have guarded effectually against all error from this source, as the bottle containing the water which they compress is kept during the whole period of every sounding in a small wooden case surrounded by ice, and the temperature of its contents, therefore, is always precisely thirty-two degrees of Fahrenheit. It is, of course, not necessary to send down a deep-sea thermometer with their instrument.

The following are among the advantages of the Morse bathometer:

1. *The rapidity with which it does its work.*—Six hours and more, it is said, are commonly consumed in paying out and hauling in a line with a sinker attached to it in water two thousand fathoms deep. The Morse bathometer, it is estimated, can be made to go down to this depth and return in less than thirty minutes.

2. *The certainty of its operation.*—When properly constructed, it it can never fail. The various contrivances for sounding the sea by sinking weights or instruments, which are raised again with a line from the bottom, fail so frequently in very deep water that explorers have now abandoned the tral of them there, and it seems to be generally admitted by scientific men that in the greatest depths of the ocean no reliable sounding has ever yet been made. In the Morse bathometer the weight always carries the instrument to the bottom; the detachment

of the weight at the bottom is made by their device perfectly certain, and when the weight is detached the rest of the apparatus can never fail to rise to the surface.

3. *The Morse bathometer is automatic.*—The momentary attention of a single operator is all that is necessary to effect a sounding in the greatest depths of the ocean. He puts ice into the case with the bottle, marks the latitude and longitude on the tube, screws the long, straight rod into the socket at the upper end of the tube, hangs the weight on the hook at the lower end, and drops the instrument into the sea. It then takes care of itself. By its own power it moves, rapidly and uniformly, from the surface to the bottom, deposits its load there, and returning as rapidly, or (if desired) more rapidly, to the surface. The operator need not even wait to pick it up. The tube, with the bottle which it incloses and the rod which rises from it into the air, will live and ride triumphantly above the surface, amid the lashings of the waves and winds of all the storms it may encounter, and whoever picks it up, at any time or at any place, however distant, may know, merely by examining the bottle, the true depth of the sea at the point marked on the tube, and may publish the information to the world. If he chooses he may then mark on the tube the time when, and the latitude and longitude of the place where, the instrument was picked up, adjust the bathometer by dropping the mercury into the bag, and re-inserting the stopper in the neck of the bottle, put ice in the case, hang a new weight on the hook of the detaching apparatus, and cast the whole instrument again into the sea, to be again picked up by another person at another place; and thus one instrument, in process of time, may be used to make scores or hundreds of soundings, at the cost for each sounding of only the bag of sand required to sink the instrument, the few ounces of ice that surround the bottle, and the few minutes of time occupied in readjusting.

4. *The mathematical accuracy of its marks of depths.*—The Morse bathometer in its indications of depth is not affected by currents. A line, during the long time consumed in its descent, may be so swayed by currents and counter-currents that a length of twice, and more than twice, the perpendicular depth of the water may be required to reach the bottom. The measure of the depth of the sea by a line is therefore eminently unreliable; but this instrument, constructed on the principle of the compression of water, which is always precisely as the perpendicular height of the compressing column—that is, as the depth of the sea, without regard to currents—must mark this depth with scientific precision.

5. *The cheapness of the instrument.*—A tin tube a few feet long and three or four inches in diameter; four or five hollow glass spheres of a size adapted to the tube; a small glass bottle in a wooden case; three or four ounces of mercury; a light fishing rod, ten or twelve feet long, with any glittering substance at the end that will attract attention

at a distance; and a twenty-pound weight, which can be made for a dime by casting plaster of Paris into the form of a long narrow bucket, and filling the bucket with sand or stones—these are the items in the cost of an instrument with which the greatest depths of the ocean can be sounded, quickly, certainly, automatically, and with perfect scientific exactness.

Is it too much to expect that, with the facilities afforded by this instrument, we shall soon have at least one sounding on every square mile accessible by ships of the three-fourths of the surface of the earth covered by water, and that with these soundings artists will construct a perfect model of the bottom of the sea, in which all its depressions below the level of the surface will be minutely and accurately represented? How long will it be before we can have an equally accurate map-in-relief of the one-fourth of the earth's surface that rises above the water? Not until man has visited every square mile of Central Africa, of Central Australia, and of every empire, and every island from which he is now excluded by inhospitable climates and inhospitable men.

Strange! that the bottom of the sea—the widest field of the geographer, three-fourths of his entire field, hitherto covered with a thick veil, defying all attempts to penetrate it—should at last, by such simple means, be opened everywhere for the investigation of everybody, so that the true shape of its whole vast expanse can now be more readily, accurately, and minutely dotted down on paper, and represented in sculpture, than the true shape of any large district of the dry land inhabited by man and revealed daily in the light of the sun!

PROPOSED NEW MODE OF LAYING AND RAISING SUBMARINE TELEGRAPH CABLES.

Messrs. Sidney E. Morse and G. Livingston Morse, of New York, propose a new method of laying submarine telegraph cables. Submarine telegraph cables have hitherto been laid, as nearly as possible, in one continuous straight line on the bottom of the sea. It is obvious that when a cable has been thus laid, it cannot be raised from the bottom to the surface in the deep sea without breaking it, and then raising successively each of the two parts, and that it cannot be repaired there and relaid without splicing to the two broken ends new cable of a length equal to at least twice the depth of the sea at that point. Messrs. Morse propose to lay the cable on the whole line, in the first instance, in such a way that it can be raised at any time for repair, or for any other purpose, at any assigned station or stations on the line, and then relaid, without breaking it.

In laying a submarine cable entirely across the ocean, Messrs. Morse propose to employ two vessels. The first and larger vessel is to carry the telegraph cable in any required length, either enough for the whole line, or for one or more sections of the line, as may be desired, together with the ordinary apparatus for laying this cable on the bottom of the sea. The second and smaller vessel is to carry, first, a lifting cable, long enough at least to reach the bottom of the sea at the deepest point on the line, and strong enough to support a weight equal to the weight in water of ten miles of the telegraph cable, if the depth of the sea on any part of the line should be as much as two miles, and proportionally stronger if the water should be deeper, this lifting cable having firmly attached to its lower end a strong, heavy iron ring, seven or eight inches or more in diameter; and, secondly, as many properly-constructed iron hooks as there are stations on the line, at which provision is to be made for raising the telegraph cable; each hook to be strong enough to support the ten miles or more of telegraph cable; the shank of each hook to be provided at short intervals with five, six, or more barbs, all pointing downwards, but in various directions, each barb being as stout and strong as the hook itself, and the shank terminating in an eye, in which is firmly fastened the end of a galvanized-iron wire rope; it may be five or ten miles long, or more, and between one-eighth and one-fourth of an inch in diameter; the strands of this wire rope to be untwisted at suitable intervals to embrace wooden cases in the form of cylinders, about four inches in diameter and of indefinite length, but with tapering, conical ends; the cylindrical part of each wooden case to contain a sufficient number of three-and a-half-inch hollow glass spheres to give the wire rope any required buoyancy at any required intervals.

Thus freighted the two vessels leave a terminus, let us suppose, in France, to proceed along the arc of a great circle, nearly due west, to Newfoundland, a distance of about two thousand miles, to lay the telegraph cable so that it may be raised at any future time without breaking it, at any one of nineteen stations one hundred miles apart. The smaller vessel goes ahead on a nearly due west course, and is followed by the larger vessel, from which the telegraph cable is payed out and laid on the bottom of the sea in the usual way. After the smaller vessel has proceeded one hundred miles it stops, turns with its bow to the north, and, one of the hooks having been suspended from its stern, with the ring at the end of the lifting cable under one of the barbs on the shank of the hook, waits for the larger vessel, which, as it passes on its westerly course, deposits its cable in the hook and proceeds until the telegraph cable rests again on the bottom, leaving a certain length suspended from the stern of the smaller vessel in the form of two catenarian curves, extending each from the hook to the bottom of the sea, one in an easterly and the other in a westerly direction. If the depth of the sea at that point should be two miles, the speed of the larger vessel in laying the cable could be so regulated that the span between the two points at which the cable would touch the bottom would be eight miles, and in that case the length of cable included in the two catenarian curves would be about nine miles, and the hook and lifting-cable would support nine miles of telegraph cable at the stern of the smaller vesse The smaller vessel should then proceed due north for two miles, the lifting-cable meanwhile being allowed to sink and unwind itself from a reel till the whole of the nine miles of telegraph cable included in the catenarian curves is deposited on the bottom of the sea, as nearly as possible at right angles to the general course of the rest of the line. The lifting-cable should then be made, by the weight of the ring at its end, to detach itself from the hook, and should be drawn up and wound again around its reel in the smaller vessel, which should all the while be continuing on its course due north paying out the iron-wire rope and its inclosed glass-sphere buoys to any desired distance—five miles, or ten miles, or more if deemed expedient. The galvanized-iron wire rope should be made to terminate in an anchor, and when this anchor is dropped in the sea the rope may be made, by a previous proper disposition of the glass-sphere buoys, to assume any desired form, either that of one long arch or of a succession of arches, rising in the water from the bottom, and as near the bottom or as far from it as may be deemed best. The deposit of the anchor at the end of the galvanized-iron wire rope completes the laying of the first section of the line, and the other sections may be laid by repeating the whole process.

The process of raising again to the surface a telegraph cable thus laid is very simple. The latitude and longitude, both of the hook and of the anchor of the wire rope, it should have been remarked, must be accurately taken when they are deposited on the bottom of the sea. When the telegraph cable is to be raised, the smaller vessel, with the lifting-cable on board, and a small line, long enough to reach nearly to the bottom of the sea, and having a small hook or grapple of proper construction at its lower end, must be sent to any point of latitude between the latitude of the hook and the latitude of the anchor of the wire rope, and to any meridian within a few miles either east or west of that on which the wire rope is floating below, supported by the encased glass-sphere buoys. With the small line depending from its stern, and extending, with its sinker and hook, nearly to the bottom of the sea, the vessel must then be moved to the east or to the west, till this line shall cross the wire rope and bring it to the surface. When brought to the surface the wire rope must be parted, and the part connected with the anchor temporarily buoyed, while the end of the other part is taken on board the vessel, and, after passing the heavy iron ring of the lifting-cable over it, must be held on board until the ring carries the lifting-cable down to the bottom, the wire rope guiding it till the ring passes the barbs on the shank of the hook which holds the telegraph cable in its grasp. Then, by drawing up the lifting-cable the ring will catch under one of the barbs of the hook, and by continuing to draw up, while the smaller vessel is moved two miles on a southerly course, or on a course directly opposite to that pursued in laying it, the part of the telegraph cable included originally in the two catenarian curves will be raised again to the surface without being broken.

Among the advantages of this mode of laying submarine telegraph cables are the following:

1st. All risk of losing the cable while laying it is avoided. More than three hundred miles of the Atlantic telegraph cable of 1857 were finally lost, and more than half of the Atlantic telegraph cable of 1865 was temporarily lost, while the operators were in the act of laying them. These losses would not have occurred if those cables had been laid on the plan here proposed and described. After the parting of the telegraph cable in each case the vessels would have returned to the last raising-station with a lifting-cable, and after rais ing the telegraph cable from the bottom to the surface at that point, the operators would have underrun the raised part till they had come to the broken end, spliced this end to th broken end of the cable in the ship, and proceeded with the work of laying the cable on the bottom.

2d. The risk of losing the cable after it has been laid is divided by the number of raising-stations on the line. The Atlantic telegraph cable of 1858, although successfully laid through its whole line, after a few days of feeble life was totally and finally lost. No one knows where or what was its malady. It may have been confined to a few feet or to a single point on the line. If it had been laid on the plan herein proposed the place of the fault might soon have been found, the defective part might possibly have been easily removed, and the whole cable restored to permanent and efficient life.

3d. The danger of encountering storms and fogs while laying the cable is avoided. On the plan proposed by Messrs. Morse the cable is laid by sections, and after one section is laid the work may be left for weeks, or for any length of time, and then resumed. The sections may be of such length that a single section can be laid in a single day; and, if the day is judiciously selected, embarrassment from the weather will rarely occur, and, when it does occur, will be of comparatively little importance; but when the cable is laid in one continuous line for two thousand miles without stopping during the fourteen days neccessary to lay such a length of line, experience proves that it will be very difficult to avoid serious embarrassment from the weather, even in the most favorable season of the year.

4th. Less length of cable will be required to connect the termini of the line. The length of cable actually used to connect the termini in Ireland and Newfoundland of the Atlantic telegraph cable of 1858 was about fifteen per cent. greater than the distance of the two points from each other, measured on the arc of the great circle between them, and, in the cable of 1866, it was about twelve per cent. greater. As this distance in each case is nearly two thousand miles, it is clear that more than two hundred miles of telegraph cable were lost by *unnecessary slack* in attempting to lay the cable across the Atlantic Ocean in one continuous straight line under circumstances uncommonly favorable to economy in the length of cable used; for, in 1866, the weather was so favorable that the ships deviated very little from the true line in their course. The loss of these two hundred miles is not merely the loss of the cost of so much cable, but, as more words could be transmitted through the cable in any given time if it were two hundred miles shorter, the loss will continue to be felt through the whole life of the cable in the diminution of its capacity to earn income. If the cable had been laid in sections, on the plan proposed by Messrs. Morse, and had been carefully and deliberately laid upon that plan, after soundings at very short intervals along the line with the aid of the bathometer of Messrs. Morse, it could have been made to conform so accurately to the arc of the great circle, and to all the swells and hollows of the bottom of the sea, that the slack might have been almost confined to the stations at which it would have been purposely made, in order to furnish at those stations the necessary means for raising the cable from the bottom to the surface without breaking it. The loss of cable by slack at one of these stations, a loss by which an advantage so desirable is gained, need be only one mile, even when the water is two miles deep, as has been already stated in the account of the Morse process of laying the cable. The loss at twenty stations need, of course, be only twenty miles, or less than one-tenth part of the length superfluously expended in the method hitherto pursued in laying submarine telegraph cables.

Instead of a lifting-cable, Messrs. Morse propose, in some cases, to send down, to be attached to one of the barbs on the shank of the hook, a buoy, composed of very large hollow glass spheres, inclosed in a tube, the spheres being sufficient in number and buoyancy to support and raise through the water to the surface the whole of that part of the telegraph cable included originally in the catenarian curves. They would put the heavy iron ring over the end of the galvanized-iron wire rope held on board of the vessel, and then attach the buoy to the upper side of the ring, while to the lower side they would attach a weight sufficiently heavy to draw the buoy slowly to the bottom. After the ring, guided by the wire rope, has passed the barbs on the shank of the hook at its end, (the hook which holds the telegraph cable in its grasp,) Messrs. Morse would cause the weight, by a simple device, to detach itself from the ring, and the ring would then be drawn under one of the barbs by the buoy, which, at first very rapidly and afterwards slowly, would rise and draw the telegraph cable to the surface. The weight may be made at little cost by inclosing sand and stone in a bag, or in any suitable cheap material. By this mode of raising the telegraph cable the time and labor of men at a windlass would be dispensed with. The whole work would be performed automatically by the buoy and the weight, and at the expense only of the sand necessary to sink the buoy from the surface to the bottom, and the cable would be raised far more speedily and satisfactorily by this process than it could be by human labor.

Messrs. Morse also propose to apply their above-described method of laying and raising a long galvanized-iron wire rope, suspended by inclosed glass-sphere buoys in the form of an arch or arches near the bottom of the sea, to the end of a submarine telegraph cable laid in one continuous straight line from a station on shore to any assigned point of latitude and longitude in mid-ocean, which point would thus be constituted a telegraph station on the bottom of the sea, accessible for use by the master of any ship who should have a telegraph instrument on board, and a small line long enough to reach the bottom at that point, and who might be acquainted with the latitude and longitude of the mid-ocean terminus of this telegraph cable, and also with the latitude and longitude of the anchor at the outer end of the galvanized-iron wire rope. Knowing these points, and allowing the small line with a sinker and hook at its outer end to run out from the stern of his ship till the hook approached the bottom, this ship-master would cross the galvanized-iron wire rope with his small line, bring the rope on board, and, without breaking it, underrun it towards the telegraph cable till he came to the light insulated copper wire in which the telegraph cable, for a distance equal to the depth of the sea at that point, should be made to terminate, and then, by connecting this insulated copper wire with his telegraph instrument, he could send and receive communications to and from the shore. After doing this he might drop the iron wire rope and the light insulated copper wire into the sea, and they would automatically assume the position from which they were raised, and be ready to render their services to any other ship-master traversing that part of the ocean.

EXHIBITORS OF CABLES.

Specimens of cables were also exhibited by J. L. A. Machabée, 46 Rue de Veuves, Paris; by Rattier & Co., 4 Rue des Fosses, Montmartre; by A. Holtzman, of Amsterdam; by W. T. Henly, 27 Leadenhall street, London; by William Hooper, 7 Pall Mall, London; and by D. Nicoll, Oakland's Hall, Kilburn, London.

INSULATORS AND INSULATION.

THE BROOKS PARAFFINE INSULATOR.

This insulator was exhibited, but is not in the catalogue. The Brooks insulator has a wide popularity. The tests of its efficiency, in comparison with many other insulators, show it to be deserving of the popularity it has acquired. It is extensively sought after on European lines. The only plausible drawback is the apprehension that the paraffine may deteriorate in the course of time. Hitherto, however, it has stood the test of years. Whether the objection is a substantial one time alone can determine. In conversation with some of the jurors at the Exhibition, this insulator was spoken of as the best that had been submitted to them. There is an insulator in use in India called the "Brooke Insulator," which must not be confounded with the Brooks insulator. In alluding to the former, the director general of telegraphs in India, in his return to

Parliament, says: "I attribute the bad working of the better Indian lines to the department being inflicted with the Brooke bracket and insulator, both of which are most thoroughly unfit for the purpose for which they were designed." The American Brooks insulator is a totally different nvention.

Fig. 16.

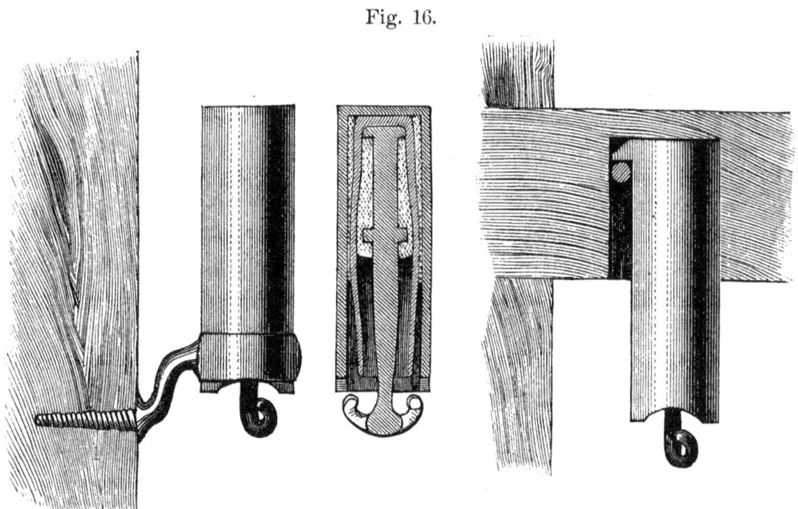

The Brooks Paraffine Insulator.

It is constructed as follows: An iron stem or wire holder is cemented into a glass bottle or vessel; the bottle is again cemented into a cylindrical iron shield. The cement is composed of sand and sulphur. The cement and cast iron are saturated with paraffine, and the whole surface of the insulator covered with paraffine.

Sulphur of itself is a great dialectric, or insulating material when dry, but upon crystallizing, it checks and becomes porous, admitting moisture when exposed to the air, which is prevented by the use of paraffine, as herein stated. Paraffine is repellant of moisture, and prevents it settling in continuous surface upon the insulator. In form the insulator has great length and small sectional area in order to obtain greatest current resistance.

Either point of the hook is nearer the iron shield than any other part of the hook, consequently surcharges of atmospheric electricity pass outside the glass and prevent fracture or injury to the insulator.

Insulation test of Brooks's and other insulators.

Description of insulator.						
	Date	March 1, 1868	March 9, 1868	March 20, 1868	March 26, 1868	March 31, 1868.
	Temperature	47° Fahr	49° Fahr	52° Fahr	48° Fahr	43° Fahr.
	State of weather	Very dull	During and after rain	Atmosphere damp	During and after much fine rain.	During a thick fog and frost.
	Constant of inst	334	336	335	333	327
	Number of cells	500	100	500	500	500
	Number of insulators tested.	Deflection (conductivity) in degrees on Thomson's astatic galvanometer per insulator.	Deflection (conductivity) in degrees on Thomson's astatic galvanometer per insulator.	Deflection (conductivity) in degrees on Thomson's astatic galvanometer per insulator.	Deflection (conductivity) in degrees on Thomson's astatic galvanometer per insulator.	Deflection (conductivity) in degrees on Thomson's astatic galvanometer per insulator.
United Kingdom Telegraph Company's large porcelain	4	3, 500	330	20, 000	10, 600	40, 000
Varley's double porcelain cup	4	4, 500	450	37, 500	25, 000	50, 000
British and Irish Magnetic Telegraph Company's porcelain	4	30, 000	1, 600	35, 000	18, 500	60, 000
United Kingdom Telegraph Company's small porcelain	4	800	150	11, 850	14, 500	50, 000
Brooks's patent insulator, with 6-inch screw shank and iron cap	5	2	0	2	1	4
Do........do........do	6	3	0	11	6	4
Do........do........do	6	7	0	4	6	1
Brooks's patent insulator, with 6-inch screw shank and iron cap lug for cross-arms	1	200	80	194	80	3

Constant of galvanometer. 1. Daniel Cell. Through 1,000,000 ohmads.

DAY'S KERITE INSULATOR.

The kerite compounds of Austin Goodyear Day, mentioned in the following memoir, were honored by two medals and an honorable mention by the jury of the Exposition Universelle, to whom the subject was referred. These awards covered other products than the electrical cables and insulators which are the special object of the descriptive memoir.

NOTE UPON INSULATION AND KERITE, BY PROFESSOR SILLIMAN.

The exhibition of the kerite, this product of the persevering labors and experiments of Mr. Day for so many years, furnishes an example of the not infrequent inappreciation, or rather overlooking, of an invaluable discovery, when modestly presented, as in this case, among the more showy articles by which it was surrounded.

True, it received honorable mention as "artificial India-rubber," and a bronze medal for its very limited application to "India-rubber cases;" but its superlative value as a substitute in insulation for India-rubber and gutta-percha was not, for it could scarcely be, appreciated, presented as it was simply in one of its more ordinary applications; so that heedless neglect is not charged upon the jury, but it is mentioned rather as an example of the existence of an unnoticed quality in an apparently trifling discovery, necessarily latent to superficial inquiry; a quality which is destined in this case to have a most important bearing upon submarine and subterranean telegraphy.

The kerite, in its condition simply as artificial rubber, is classed under Group V, Class 44; but in its application to telegraph wires as an insulator, is properly treated of in the present Group VI, Class 64.

The following memoir upon insulation and protection of electrical conductors for telegraphic purposes, describing the new insulating covering for telegraphic conductors known as kerite, of Austin G. Day, has been supplied for this report by B. Silliman, professor of general and applied chemistry in Yale College:

"Among the American products exhibited at the Exposition at Paris in 1867 was a series of specimens produced from a new artificial caoutchouc, prepared by Mr. Austin G. Day, of Seymour, Connecticut.

"Among these specimens was a new telegraphic covering and insulator, which constituted one of the applications of Mr. Day's invention. The product in this and many other forms is termed by the inventor 'kerite,' and at the Exposition it was presented as it existed in 1867. Since that date, however, some important improvements have been made in the preparation of this insulator, which render it yet more completely indestructible by natural and other agencies than any other material which has yet been discovered, leaving, in fact, nothing more to be desired in this direction. By means of these improvements the use of a considerable proportion of the sulphur previously employed in the vulcanization is dispensed with, a much less quantity of that agent sufficing to effect vulcanization on bodies thus oxidized, while at the same time new and highly useful properties are developed, in virtue of the less liability of the kerite produced to attack by oxidizing agents, like ozone. In this manner a body has been produced which resists in the most remarkable manner the solvent and destructive action of the most powerful chemical reagents, including ozone, while preserving all the required physical qualities of perfect insulation, resistance to extremes of heat and cold, and flexibility with firmness.

"ACTION OF OZONE UPON TELEGRAPHIC INSULATORS.—In the course of the investigation connected with this subject I have discovered that the most destructive of all agents upon these insulators is an ozonized atmosphere. Exposed for a short time to such an atmosphere, electrical conductors, covered with the most carefully prepared English gutta-percha or vulcanized caoutchouc, begin even in a few hours to show signs of disintegration, and shortly the covering breaks up and cleaves off, leaving the conducting wire exposed. The rapidity of this action is proportioned to the activity of the ozonized atmosphere. With the slow oxidation of phosphorus as the source of the ozone at temperatures below 12° C, the action is slow, requiring one or two days' time to manifest itself with gutta-percha, but with the same means at a temperature of 20° or 25° C, the action of the ozone becomes much more rapid, and will sometimes develop itself even in an hour or less.

"This is especially true if the covered conductor is coiled in a close spiral of short radius—*e. g.*, of two or three centimeters; the state of tension thus produced is peculiarly favorable to the rapid action of the destructive agency of the ozone.

"This important observation I have confirmed by many experiments variously modified, and upon every description of insulating material which I have been able to procure. The results explain why it is that no covering for aerial lines has yet been discovered which will withstand for any reasonable period the action of the atmosphere without soon cleaving off and hanging in shreds from the conductor. The atmosphere is never without this allotropic modification of oxygen, and its action upon the insulation is not the less certain because it is somewhat slow.

"The fact of greatest practical importance in this connection is that certain specimens of Day's kerite have withstood perfectly, in my experiments, this powerful agent of destruction, even where exposed to an atmosphere so highly charged with ozone as to destroy in thirty minutes other electrical insulators usually esteemed the best. I have continued such trials on the kerite in question for thirty consecutive days in such an atmosphere, without developing the slightest fault in the covering. By the use of this test I have been able to declare to the inventor, from time to time, which of his numerous products were worthless or imperfect, and thus to eliminate the valuable results of his synthetic experiments, until at last he has obtained a product which fully meets the requirements of the problem, leaving nothing more to be desired in this direction. For aerial and underground electrical cables this invention offers the solution of the great obstacle which has hitherto obstructed the progress of telegraphy; while for submarine cables the kerite offers a far more economical insulation than any which has yet been obtained, and one fully equal if not greatly superior to any other in its insulating power against electrical leakage. On this latter point I appeal to the electrical tests of Mr. Farmer, the well known electrician of Boston, which are appended:

"Of the value of this new insulator, as tested by the actual experience of telegraphic lines, we are fully assured by the experience of well known telegraphic constructors who have employed it. To this point is the testimony of Messrs. Chester, of New York, and of Mr. Callahan, whose opinions, founded upon their own experience, are given in their letters, which are also appended.

"ACTION OF OTHER CHEMICAL AGENTS UPON KERITE.—As respects the action of other chemical reagents upon the kerite covering, I have to add very briefly that I have submitted it to the test of numerous powerful bodies in contrast with other insulators or coverings, and always with the most marked advantage in favor of the kerite. The most important of these agents are carbonic disulphide, ($C S_2$), nitric acid, ($H_2 N O_4$), sulphuric acid, ($H_2 S O_4$), sulphuric dioxide, ($S O_2$), nitric per oxide, ($N_2 O_3$), chlorine gas and alkaline hydrates, *e. g.*, sodic hydrate (H Na O) and potassic hydrate, (H K O). Such reagents are useful in guiding the inventor in perfecting his synthetic experiments; but it is hardly necessary to say, that in the actual experience of telegraphy, cables are never exposed to these powerful reagents which the chemist resorts to in his laboratory. We may safely conclude, also, that a product which can withstand the continued attacks of atmospheric ozone must be regarded as safe from all other causes of destruction which may be encountered in nature.

"This last remark is open to only one important qualification. It remains to be seen whether the marine borers of tropical seas and the ravages of the white ants of tropical regions, which are known to destroy gutta-percha coverings, may not also attack with effect the kerite. I have caused cables to be prepared to test this question in the waters of the Bay of Aspinwall, and also to be buried in situations where they are fully exposed to the ravages of the white ant. These specimens of kerite have been prepared with carbolic acid, (phenol,) compounds of which, as applied to ship timber, I have found in certain investigations undertaken some years since for the naval department of the United States government, to offer the only effectual cure to the attacks of the marine animals.

"The trials now in progress in Aspinwall and upon the Isthmus of Panama will soon decide this question for the kerite cable.

"In conclusion, we are led as the result of this investigation to express the opinion, that in the present state of our knowledge the 'kerite' of Day is the best material yet found for telegraphic use, offering at once the greatest resistance to electrical leakage and to all the causes of destruction, whether chemical, atmospheric, or vital, to which electrical cables are liable, whether in air, earth, or water."[1]

LETTERS UPON THE VALUE OF KERITE AS AN INSULATOR.

The following is the letter referred to from Mr. Moses G. Farmer, dated at Boston, February 12, 1869, and addressed to Mr. Day:

"I have made numerous tests of the insulating power of your 'kerite' covering for telegraph wires.

"It is well known that in cables which have the same relation subsisting between the diameters of the core and of the contained strand, the relative insulating power is in proportion to the time which it takes for the cable to lose half of a given charge.

"The Atlantic cables fall to half charge in about one and one tenth hours, while a sample of your kerite-covered wire, which I operated upon, was thirteen hours in falling to half charge, showing it to be a most wonderful insulator.

"Wishing for you the utmost success in introducing this truly valuable invention, I remain."

The letter of Messrs. Charles T. & J. N. Chester, dated New York, November 13, 1868, is as follows:

"In reply to your inquiries as to our experience in the compound known as kerite wire, we would say that we have been familiar with your experiments and have examined your products during the last two or three years, and have been so well satisfied that this kerite-covered wire fulfilled many requirements not hitherto found in insulated wire, that we have induced many of our friends to purchase and test the wire, and the result of these tests has been to establish the excellence of the fabric as superseding any other for the purpose of insulation. These tests have been made in at least two hundred exposed places in the prominent cities of the Union and Canada, in connection with fire-alarm telegraphs. They have also been made with underground wires, as at Vassar College and Dartmouth College. Some of these wires have been laid two years; they have given excellent satisfaction. In the course of our experience we have had occasion to test many insulated wires under water, and find it rare to obtain a piece of much length without an escape, even with delicate instruments. A few days since we were about to ship one thousand feet of small size office kerite wire, not intended for subaqueous use. A test of this with a battery of fifty cells and a delicate acting apparatus, gave no deflection whatever. We believe its insulating properties very extraordinary."

Edward A. Callahan, esq., the superintendent of the Gold and Stock

[1] Dated at New Haven, Connecticut, January, 1869.

Telegraph Company, makes the following statement in his letter to Mr. Day, dated at No. 18 New street, New York, November 10, 1868:

"In reply to your inquiries with reference to your kerite insulated wire, I take great pleasure in making you the following statement:

"It has, under all circumstances, given us the fullest satisfaction. The peculiar nature of our business renders it necessary for us to use the most perfectly insulated wire. I have tried several and various kinds of insulated wire before using yours, but have been obliged to take it all down, and have now substituted your kerite insulated wire in its stead.

"Your wire, which I strung in December, 1867, is, so far as we are able to judge, as good as the first day we put it up. We have tested it after three days constant rain, and could not find one degree of escape. We use it in gas-pipes, where we twist six wires together. We hold this to be as severe a test of its insulating properties as it can be put to, and have never been obliged to look at one of these gas-pipes for crasses, grounds, or escapes. We now use it for office wire, where it is sometimes placed near furnaces, subjected to a very high temperature, and again where it is exposed to the most intense cold, and I have not been able to detect the slightest change from its original condition.

"I am very favorably impressed with it, and can see no reason why it will not last for an indefinite number of years.

"You ask my opinion for underground purposes. We have exposed it to the extreme cold and heat of the past year; strung over the roofs of buildings, which we consider the best test of its indestructible and insulating qualities that it can be submitted to, while placing it under ground would be favorable as a protection."

CHAPTER V.

AUTOMATIC RECORDING, TRANSMITTING, AND CONTROLLING.

Automatic recording—Improvement and modification not the same—The generic telegraph—The electro-chemical process—The electro-magnetic mode of recording—The pencil point—Inking processes—Triple pen—Steel point—Automatic transmission—Embossed paper process—Automatic apparatus of Siemens and Halske—Speed of transmission—Blavier on speed of transmission—Comparative speed by different instruments—Recent result in France in speed of transmission—Automatic transmission in Prussia and speed of transmission—Comparative speed of transmission—Critical review of the results—Automatic control—Morse's method—Sortais apparatus—Morse stopping apparatus.

AUTOMATIC RECORDING.

At the very earliest conception of the art of writing or imprinting at a distance, in one or more distant places at the same time, the best modes of practically demonstrating it were, as a matter of course, the subject of absorbing attention in the mind of the inventor. No sooner, therefore, did the idea of the possibility of making an automatic record of intelligence from a distance occur to its originator, than it became his main purpose to demonstrate by some means, and by the simplest means he could then devise, that it was not merely possible, but that it must be realized in some way, and made an accomplished fact. Indeed, the production in some way of this automatic record was the key-note of his whole theme.

It cannot, therefore, be thought strange, that a great variety of possible modes suggested themselves to him; nor is it more strange that, after he had demonstrated one mode as practicable, subsequent inventors, in following the original track which led to the demonstration of that mode, should find that many of the devices occurring to them in their speculations, which seemed to them new, had been anticipated by the original discoverer of the new road. It could scarcely be otherwise, nor does this consideration by any means involve a charge of plagiarism against claimants to these same devices; a more charitable position is that while pursuing the new route opened to them, the same objects would independently attract their notice. Such, however, would be ready to allow that the objects which to them are novelties may not be novelties to him who opened and first explored the new path.

The original proposition of writing or printing at a distance must not be considered as merely a brilliant but crude idea, sent forth by its originator to be developed and equipped by others; it was from the moment of its conception the hourly occupation of his thoughts for days and months, long before it was deemed by others to be more than the chimera of an ill-regulated imagination. These modes in their embryo state were conceived, indeed, in comparative seclusion, without even the opportunity or the means to put them except in part into tangible shape, other than in drawings, until months and even years had elapsed; for the first apparatus, although conceived in its essential characteristics as early as 1832, and mainly existing in drawings, (partly embodied, indeed, at that date,) was not in a shape to give a substantial practical demonstration of the successful result until 1835. This is not the date given by the inventor but by numerous witnesses, who are in agreement in testifying to seeing it in operation at that time.

That the earliest instrumentalities should be crude and capable of more or less improvement, every one experienced in invention will readily allow. But what is improvement? An improvement, or, as the French style it, *perfectionnement*, has a different meaning from improvement in the strict sense of that word. As often loosely used at the present day, the word modification would more accurately express the change or changes made in the instrumentalities of an invention. An improvement is a modification, but the reverse is not always true; a modification is not, of course, an improvement, but it would be technically styled so at the Patent Office. Even a change in an apparatus, for the purpose of gaining some presumed advantage, may accomplish its immediate purpose, while, at the same time, it may involve countervailing disadvantages in complication and expensiveness which may more than neutralize the advantage, and so the result of modification may be on the whole a loss and not a gain.

It is not uncommon to misapprehend the true nature and extent of a modification. While ignorant of the nature of that invention upon which a modification is based, it is not so easy to know if the modification is an unimportant change, or is, indeed, an improvement. A casual observer, without a thorough knowledge of an original invention is very apt to confound the new and the old, and in noticing a new arrangement is often led to consider the whole as new. Proper discrimination is necessary, that no injustice be done to any of the laborers in the same field of invention.

It will not be deemed egotistical on the part of an inventor, if in the attempts of others to improve his invention he should now and then recognize the familiar features of his own offspring, and claim their paternity. The attempts at improvement in the telegraph have been mainly directed to modes of recording, to wit: to modifications of the original inking apparatus; to modes of imprinting the ordinary alphabetic character; to automatic transmission of dispatches; to autographic transmission of dispatches and designs, and to automatic control of a distant apparatus. There have also been attempted improvements in batteries or generators of electricity.

In order, therefore, to demonstrate and elucidate any professed improvement upon an art in any of its processes, it becomes not a matter of choice but of necessity in the very outset, first, to set forth clearly the original processes or instrumentalities professed to be improved. This necessity must be an apology (if any apology is required) for so often recurring to the original invention of the Morse telegraph.

THE GENERIC TELEGRAPH.

The more thoroughly its early history becomes known the more clearly will it be erceived and acknowledged to be the generic telegraph. The means and processes of this first telegraph have been adopted, and have become not only the efficient instrumentalities of all the modern telegraphs, but the modern semaphores have also derived from the instrumentalities applied in the telegraph some of their most efficient means of accomplishing their more limited results; for example, the adoption of the electro-magnet, giving to the telegraph its semaphoric or acoustic quality.

Fig. 17.

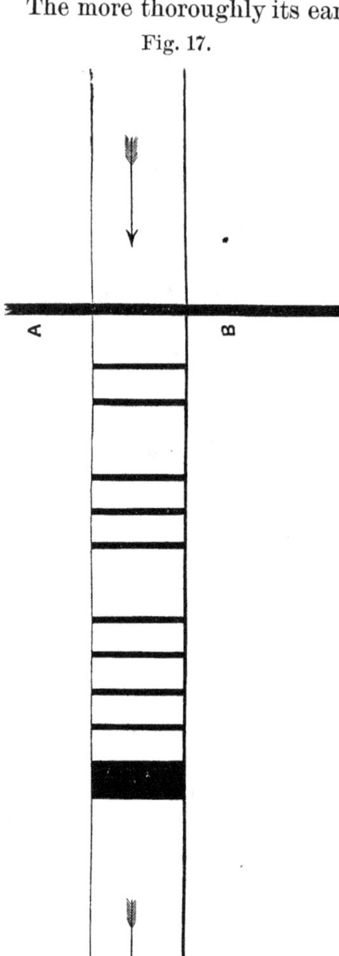

In illustration, therefore, of the earlier processes of the telegraph, diagrams of some of the modes of recording first tried by the inventor are given—modes used by him with more or less of success in the first constructed instruments.

THE ELECTRO-CHEMICAL PROCESS.

The earliest mode devised for producing a record was an electro-chemical process.

The inventor had the idea before landing from the ship in 1832 that his purpose of recording might be accomplished by the use of some salt, so easily decomposable, or so sensibly influenced by electricity in its passage through a conductor that a mark upon paper impregnated with such a salt might be the result, by simple contact with the conductor at the moment of an electrical charge. A magnetic effect was known to exist. Was there any other effect available to produce a mark? This was the problem to be solved.

With no means on board the ship for any experiment, this suggested mode was reserved to be tried at the close of the voyage. Coincident with the electro-chemical mode the electro-magnetic or mechanical mode of marking was elaborated, and the various devices for using the power of the electro-magnet reduced to drawings.

On testing the first electro-chemical mode by simple contact with a conductor in an electric state with the hope to produce the result in the diagram, the experiment failed with the salt that had been suggested, and with several other salts that were experimented upon in that manner. The paper impregnated with the salt in this case was made simply to pass beneath and in contact with the conducting wire. If no current was passing in the wire the paper would show no mark, but when a current was sent through the wire the paper should show marks across the strip like those in the diagram. The thinner lines represent the dots, the thicker lines the dashes of the conventional code, This was the theory. Submitted to experiment, as has been stated, it failed in practice. But by passing the electric current through the paper impregnated with various salts the marking was produced more or less perfectly, yet attended with so many inconveniences that the electro-chemical mode was temporarily reserved for future experimenting, in order to perfect the electro-magnetic mode, which promised a surer and better result. Perceiving that by the electro-magnet he had command of a power capable at will to make a line of any length upon a moving strip or ribbon of paper, the inventor found that the dots and spaces and eventually the dashes of the code he had already devised were readily made by any convenient marking instrument, such as a pencil or pen or printing wheel. The object, then, of the inventor was to adopt the best of the several devices which had suggested themselves to him.

THE ELECTRO-MAGNETIC MODE.

The first and most obvious was that of a pencil at one extremity of the lever, as in Fig. 18.

Fig. 18.

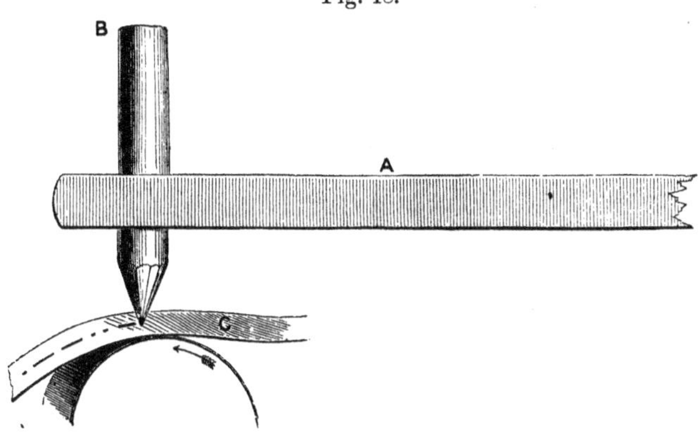

The Pencil Point.

The marking with the pencil B gave a successful result, but the blow in striking the paper often broke the point of the pencil and required constant attention, and produced many interruptions, so that the use in the manner seen in the diagram was early abandoned; but the pencil was immediately used in the manner shown in the first constructed instrument of 1835, as seen in Fig. 18, by which the damage to the point of the pencil was avoided, yet still the constant wearing away of the pencil presented a difficulty to be removed.

Fig. 19.

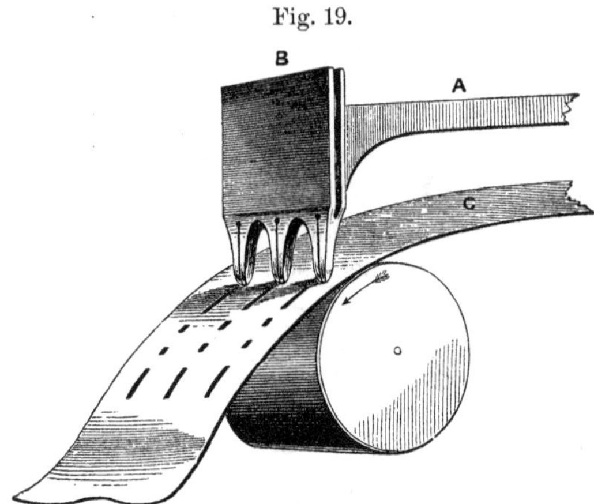

The Triple Pen.

This was attempted by the use of fountain pens of various construction; at first a single pen formed a capillary tube, which had the inconvenience of out not giving out its ink if of action for any length of time. To remedy this defect the form of the fountain pen was like that shown in Fig. 19.

THE TRIPLE PEN.

This gave the dispatch by a three-fold line, so that in case one pen should be clogged and fail to record, one or both of the other pen secured the record. This method for some time produced good results. It was the mode exhibited to the Congress at Washington in the session of 1837–'38, and to the Academy of Sciences in Paris in 1838, described by M. Arago from its appearance as " *un petit rateau*," or little rake.

THE PRINTING WHEEL.

There was also another mode successfully used in the early experiments, seen in Fig. 20, by a printing wheel, as in the modern ink-writers,

Fig. 20.

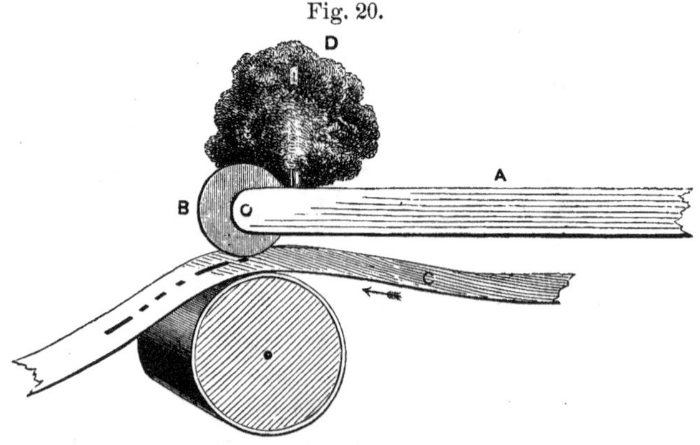

The Printing Wheel.

the only difference between this original mode and the present ink-writers being the supply of ink to the wheel originally by a sponge instead of the modern felt wheel. All these modes are distinctly specified in Morse's caveat of 1837, in the Patent Office at Washington. Why was not the last mode, so identical with the modern ink-writers, which are so popular, at once adopted in practice? The inventor was desirous of avoiding several inconveniences attendant on all the modes of using ink. The drying of the ink upon the ink-wheel, especially in dry climates and in warm weather, would often render the inking process unreliable. Again, unless care were specially taken there was constant danger of an over-charge of ink, soiling the paper and producing grave interruptions.

THE STEEL POINT.

To avoid these inconveniences a steel point *(point sèche)* was devised and used, which marked the paper strip, by the interposition of a blackened or colored paper between the point and the paper strip, as in the ordinary manifold copying process. This also was successful, but did not remove every inconvenience. It was then that the idea of embossing the paper directly with the same stylus, in the mode now known as the dry point or embosser, (the *point sèche*,) was conceived and adopted. Fig. 21 shows this mode.

Fig. 21.

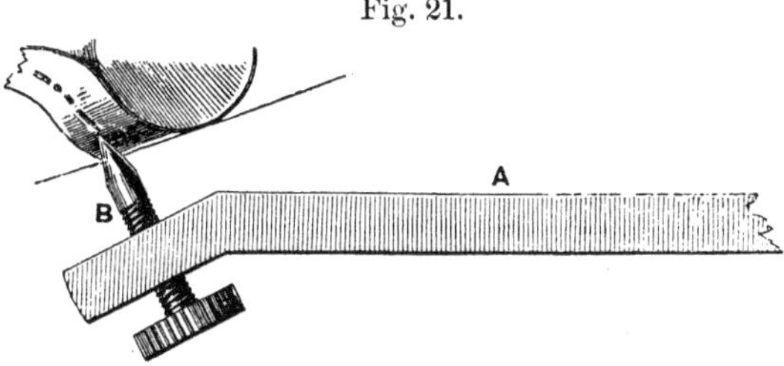

The Steel Point.

This was considered by him a substantial improvement, since the simple stylus at the extremity of the lever was always in order, requiring no attention. It dispensed with ink and all its inconveniences and complication, and reduced the apparatus to its minimum of simplicity.

MODES OF MARKING OR RECORDING.

It is customary, in treating of this part of the telegraphic apparatus, by many historians of the telegraph, to consider this steel point or embossing mode as the primary mode devised by the inventor, and the inking or printing wheel as a modern improvement upon it by others. This is a mistake. The inventor considered the dry point or embosser as an improvement on his original inking apparatus devised and used as early as 1845, and was patented in April, 1846, and in the employment of his inking wheel by modern mechanicians, he thinks that some of the advantages of the dry point have been overlooked, while some of its disadvantages have been unduly exaggerated. These latter are stated to be—first, the disadvantage of being obliged to read the letters by a particular light and shadow fatiguing to the eye. A simple remedy to this is the application of a light ink roller to the top of the embossed letter as it issues from the stylus, in such a way that the ink touches the top only of the raised letter. This has been successfully done, and is a mechanical arrangement easily made, and it obviates this disadvantage, and at the same time obviates the second disadvantage, which is, that an embossed message, when the paper is rolled up, loses its raised character, and leaves the paper blank, so that the record is obliterated. If inked in the way just suggested this difficulty disappears. The third disadvantage is, that it requires a relay in order to furnish the requisite power to emboss the characters. This is the most plausible of all, and so far as it is desirable to dispense with the relay, the mode of inking the characters devised by the Messrs. Digney frères, to wit: by bringing the paper up in contact with the ink wheel, instead of the ink wheel down upon the paper, as in the original mode, is a successful and valuable improvement. It must be said, however, on the other side that the dispensing with the relay, is, under some aspects, of doubtful economy, especially in view of the acoustic effect of the pen lever in the act of embossing; this effect is destroyed in the silent operation of the inking process, but with the relay and steel point is retained, and is of so important a character as to have modified to a considerable extent the whole process of telegraphic or rather semaphoric communication by the Morse apparatus.

To offset these disadvantages charged against the dry point there is one manifest advantage in its employment which seems so obvious that it is a matter of some surprise that no one of the ingenious mechanicians, who have been intent on improvements, should not have long since discovered and applied it. This advantage is the special applicability of the dry point process to automatic transmission.

AUTOMATIC TRANSMISSION.

The automatic process was the original mode devised for the first demonstration of a strictly telegraphic result. As special attention in the present day is being given to this mode, in the hope so to perfect it as to supersede other processes, it may not be amiss to dwell a moment upon its character.

The original automatic process of the first instrument in 1835 was accomplished by metallic type, set up in composing sticks or rules, and carried beneath the lever by an apparatus called the "port rule," which bore forward the prepared rules in proper succession. This mode required several distinct operations: First. The preparation of an indefinite quantity of the metallic type to be furnished to each office. Second. The setting up of these type in the rules or composing sticks. Third. The placing of these rules in their order in the transmitting apparatus. Fourth. The mechanical operating of the port rule. Fifth. The distribution of the type after the whole operation of transmission has been completed.

The automatic type process of Siemens, which we shall presently examine, requires the same several operations as the original automatic type process.

An automatic process by Wheatstone, not in the catalogue, requires, first, a peculiar apparatus, called the perforator, for punching holes in a strip of paper; second, another apparatus, called a transmitter, by which the paper thus prepared is carried forward to operate the levers of contact; third, another apparatus, called the receiver, which gives the recording result upon a strip of paper at a distance.

These last two—transmitter and receiver—are modifications of the original Morse manipulator or key, and the Morse register, in order to increase the speed of the mechanical movements of each instrumentality.

In Wheatstone's process the perforator is a different instrument from the Morse manipulating key, and much more complicated, and requires a different mode of operating it, a new manipulating process is to be learned by the operator in addition to his usual acquirements. The punched paper requires more time in its preparation than the usual embossing or writing process of the Morse system. When once prepared, however, it has the advantage over the type setting mode that no distribution of type is necessary after the transmission has been completed.

The transmission and reception of the message in all these modes differ very little from each other.

EMBOSSED PAPER PROCESS.

The general advantage proposed to be obtained by automatic transmission is that a greater quantity of intelligence can be transmitted in a given time by this mechanical mode than by the ordinary or hand manipulation with the Morse key, or manipulator, and that this may be accomplished by having the dispatch, if of great length, set up or prepared by dividing it into what are called by printers "takes" or convenient portions, and employing several operators who, at the same time, prepare their several takes, by setting up the type, or preparing the punched paper to be used in the transmission. The mode proposed by the writer of this report has the advantage of greater simplicity as a result of the embossing process with the *point sèche*. For this mode requires no type setting, no new instrument for preparing the paper; no new process of punching paper to be learned by the operators. The operator prepares his dispatch in the usual way, by embossing the paper, as if sending a dispatch. It is then at once ready for transmission; needing no perforations nor other preparation. The paper strip with the embossed characters is simply passed beneath a delicate lever like that of the relay magnet. As every embossed part passes under the lever, contact is made longer or shorter according to the length of the embossed line.

The result is the same as by the type process and the punched paper process.

The only variation which may possibly be required in the present Morse apparatus is a more perfect mechanical embossing point, a small wheel, for example, instead of a blunt point, by which the embossed characters shall receive a stronger and bolder relief, and paper more capable of this stronger embossing.

These are within the ordinary mechanical capabilities of good workmanship.

AUTOMATIC APPARATUS OF SIEMENS AND HALSKÉ.

No. 39 of the catalogue comprises the telegraphic and semaphoric instruments of those accomplished mechanicians and savans, the Messrs. Siemens and Halské, of Berlin, so profound in scientific research and prolific in every variety of ingenious and novel philosophical instruments. Among the most noteworthy in the Exposition is their automatic apparatus, which, it appears, has been operated with successful results upon the German lines. Those who are familiar with the early history of the generic telegraph will recognize the fact that the automatic mode of recording was embodied in the first telegraphic instrument devised by the writer in 1832, and it was the first mode by which the new art was demonstrated in 1835. At that early period the automatic was deemed to be the only practical, if not practicable, mode of insuring a perfect record. The details of this process are to be found in the earliest specifications and descriptions and models of the Morse invention in the Patent Office at Washington, and the instrumentalities are very fully described and illustrated by diagrams in Vail's earliest work on the telegraph, published in 1845.

The general features of this first Morse automatic process may be briefly stated to consist of—

First. The embodiment in a species of cogged type of the numerals to be recorded, consisting of lines, dots, and spaces—the elements of the Morse code. This was accomplished in November and December of 1832. Subsequently the inventor extended the principles of his code to the letters of the alphabet, which were added to the numerals, and, with some special signs for punctuation and office signals, completed his original code.

Second. Of rules or composing sticks, in which the desired type were set up.

Third. Of the port rule or instrument, by which the rules when prepared with their type were carried forward to operate.

Fourth. A lever to close and open the electric circuit at the regulated times.

In this part of the automatic process of the new art, the inventor early made many modifications, some of which are also fully described by Vail.

Experience soon suggested that however desirable on account of accuracy was this automatic mode, manipulation by the hand with a simple rocking lever possessed many advantages, among which was the dispensing with the complicated machinery of types, composing sticks, and port rules, and the consumption of time in preparation, and this simple manipulator was found to be sufficiently accurate for the ordinary requirements of the telegraph. This manipulator holds its place in the telegraph instruments at this day.

SPEED OF TRANSMISSION.

To ascertain the quantity of intelligence that could be recorded in a given time was not in the early period of the history of the telegraph so much a desideratum as to know that any could be recorded; and the comparatively little that was accomplished by the new art, in its first essays, was in such vastly greater quantity than could possibly be transmitted by any of the semaphoric modes previously in use, that for some time the public were content with the success already achieved.

In process of time, however, stimulated chiefly by the enterprising spirit of the conductors of the American Associated Press, the lightning was invoked to send what it sent more rapidly, or rather to send more in a specified time, and hence the minds of the ingenious were concentrated on modes of manipulating a greater quantity in a given time.

In estimating the speed of transmission, it is obvious that other circumstances than the time occupied in manipulation, whether by the hand key, (the circuit closer,) or by automatic machinery, must be considered in making a fair estimate.

Precedent to transmission there must be taken into the account, first, the cost and nature of the apparatus; second, the number of employés necessary to prepare the copy for transmission; third, the number of employés necessary to receive and prepare it for delivery at the distant station; fourth, the comparative time required to prepare the copy for transmission; and then follows, fifth, the time occupied in transmission; and, sixth, the distance to which it can be transmitted.

To illustrate the necessity for taking into the account these propositions, let a given quantity of intelligence, and the same intelligence, be presented at the same moment to be sent by the several apparatus respectively. That system which first delivers the intelligence complete at the distant station will (other things being equal) bear away the palm. I say other things being equal, for in an economic point of view, the first, second, and third propositions must be insisted on. For it is easy to conceive twenty wires with an apparatus and operators furnished to each, and the copy divided into twenty parts or "takes," (to use the nomenclature of the printing office,) and each operator sending his allotted portion or "take" at the same time, and thus the whole could be transmitted in a twentieth part of the time required to send the whole by a single wire, apparatus, and operator. It is at once perceived that, although this might be successfully accomplished, it could not be accomplished with economy. Hence the economic means enter materially into the estimate of the final result.

Again, in the test of the Morse apparatus, its semaphoric quality, by means of the simple acoustic arrangement, has shown, in mere rapidity of transmission, at least, its superiority over the proper telegraphic quality of the same apparatus. The telegraphic quality, however, is that which is considered in most of the European administrations as a necessity, because it furnishes, by its permanent recorded result, that control which the system of government surveillance makes absolutely necessary, and which does not belong to any mere semaphoric mode. This fact is to be taken into the account in estimating speed of transmission. All the automatic processes are telegraphic. There is a limit to the quantity that can be transmitted and recorded in a given time, for the most part quite inside of the result of the acoustic or semaphoric mode.

Experience alone can decide on the comparative advantages of these two modes.

The Morse process of recording by electro-chemical decomposition attracted early attention, and occupied the time and employed the skill of several ingenious men in Europe, but especially of Bain, who gave it greater efficiency by the application of a more sensitive salt than had been previously applied. This process is attended with great inconveniences, but these have not prevented its use to some limited extent. In theory, however capable of producing greater speed, (sometimes obtained in exceptional cases,) there are practical as well as theoretical difficulties which have hitherto disappointed the flattering expectations of its friends, and interposed serious obstacles to its general adoption.

The immense rapidity of the passage of the electric current suggests that there is scarcely a limit to the quantity of intelligence that might be transmitted in a given time. Theoretically, indeed, any speed yet attained could be increased almost indefinitely; but this speed is limited not by the speed of electricity, but by the action of the necessary intervening mechanical instrumentalities. Were the speed of electricity the sole element to be taken into consideration, the amount of intelligence that could be transmitted can scarcely be computed; but the mechanical agencies of a more sluggish nature which mingle in the process foreshadow a limit, and it is precisely here that the ingenious savant and mechanician find a profitable employment for their research and skill in modifying and improving the automatic process.

BLAVIER ON SPEED OF TRANSMISSION.

As pertinent to this subject, a quotation is made from the excellent work of M. Blavier, volume i, page 188, of his calculations of the possible speed of transmission:

"The speed of transmission which can be obtained with an instrument depends not only on the rapidity of manipulation that can be increased, by mechanical means, almost indefinitely, but also on the nature and length of the line. It depends, in fact, on the register itself, and it is well to ascertain for each instrument the maximum number of signs that it can give—that in which its power of transmission consists.

"For the Morse apparatus, the question reduces itself to know how many dots (or points) the register can receive in a minute.

"A movable armature over against an electro-magnet can, under the influence of interrupted currents, effect at least from five thousand to six thousand oscillations in a minute, but on condition that their extent shall be extremely small, and it would be insufficient to produce signs upon a band of paper, even admitting that the speed of unrolling the paper can be definitely increased. For, in order that the lever shall be lifted and mark a sign, there must be a determinate time which varies with the form of the apparatus, and above all with the mass of the lever.

"When in the Morse apparatus the *(point sèche)* dry point is used, the lever is always very massive; it allows also the addition of a relay, and even with a very rapid unrolling of the paper not more than 300 or 400 dots per minute can be obtained. An apparatus *(à molette)* with printing wheel, operating by the intervention of a relay, can give from 800 to 900 dots. In fact, a Morse apparatus *(à molette)* with printing wheel, without a relay, constituted in the best possible manner, that is to say, in which the armature, the lever, and the knife are as light as possible, a condition which may be obtained by reducing their dimensions, and even their densities, by the employment of aluminum, can give even 2,000 dots per minute.

"When the number of dots that can be transmitted is known, it is easy to estimate the corresponding number of words.

"In considering the duration or extent of a dot as unity, and in designating it by 1, the duration or extent of a line is 3; the separation (or space) between the signs in the same letter is 1; that of two letters, 3; that of words, 6 units. In taking at hazard a great number of words, (one or two pages of a book for example,) and in writing in the signs, every dot and line and space can be counted for the number of corresponding units, to calculate the total number of units necessary to express the aggregate of the words; and then, if the sum is divided by the number of words, we have the mean number of units which correspond to a word.

"Thus it is found that each word, including the blank space between the words, is represented by the average of 48 units.

"If, then, the apparatus can receive 2,000 dots in one minute, which with their blanks (or spaces) represent 4,000 units, the number of words which can be transmitted will be $\frac{4000}{48}$, or eighty-four words per minute. Besides, it is necessary that the signs be made distinct upon the paper band. In order to read them easily, the separation of the signs and the length of the dots ought to be at least three-quarters of a millimeter.[1]

"If the paper is unrolled at the speed of $1^{m}.20$ per minute, the

[1] A millimeter is .0394 of an inch, *i. e.*, about one twenty-fifth of an inch.

greatest number of units equal to three-quarters of the millimeter, .02955 of an inch, is 1,600, which corresponds to thirty-five words per minute. If this speed is to be surpassed, the speed of unrolling the paper must be increased either by employing a more powerful spring or by contracting the wings of the fly.

"The speed of unrolling the paper at the rate of $1^{m}.20$ is more than sufficient; for twenty-five words per minute can never be in practice surpassed, only in exceptional cases, and the space that each dot occupies must be above three-quarters of a millimeter to render the reading more easy."

"Manipulation by the hand, by means of the manipulator previously described, presents many inconveniences. It cannot be absolutely regular; it varies according to the skill and even to the character of the operator. Besides, it is forcibly limited, since the greater part of the operators attain with difficulty to fifteen or eighteen words per minute and the most skillful do not exceed twenty-five."

From this calculation of M. Blavier, therefore, it would seem to be demonstrated that twenty-five words in one minute, or fifteen hundred in one hour, is the greatest number that can be given by hand manipulation, yet this can only apply to the distinct recording of the signs upon the band of paper. The hand manipulation upon the sounder, which involves the use of the Morse manipulator in the same manner as if recording, gives a greater number of words in a minute than any automatic recording process yet practically employed, as will be presently shown.

COMPARATIVE SPEED BY DIFFERENT INSTRUMENTS.

The comparative speed of transmission, or the quantity of words in a given time, by different instruments is stated in the official documents of two national administrations as follows:

The single dispatch is calculated at *twenty words*, and the number of dispatches at so many in *one hour*.

Of such dispatches—

[1] In France the Morse is rated at twenty in one hour; the Hughes, at fifty in one hour; the dial system, at fifteen in one hour; the Caselli, (hesitatingly,) at forty in one hour.

In Prussia the Morse is rated at twenty to thirty in one hour; the Hughes, at forty to fifty in one hour; the Siemens, at sixty in one hour.

The distance or the length of the conductors, or their equivalent, in resistance, is an important element in the calculation. This element is not given in the French calculation.

In the Prussian experiments the distance measured by resistance coils is stated in one instance at 2,700 English miles, and in another at 540 English miles.

Not satisfied that justice had been done to the Morse system in this comparative statement by rating it at twenty telegrams in an hour, a

[1] See Chapter V, questions to, and answers of, Viscount de Vougy.

request was made to the president of the Western Union Telegraph Company to have the speed of transmission fairly tried upon the American lines. Accordingly, an executive circular was issued, and in conformity with its requirements the results were duly sworn to and attested by notaries public.

The following table embodies these results:

Table of results of the trial of speed by the Morse apparatus.

Name of operator sending.	Name of operator receiving.	Date of trial.	Number of telegrams of twenty words each in one hour.	Number of words in one hour.	Number of words in one minute.	Distance in English miles.
John H. French	John H. Dwight	Jan. 18, 1868	80	1, 600	26⅔	310
Charles F. Stumm	L. A. Somers	Jan. 28, 1868	96	1, 920	32	135
Thomas L. A. Valiquet and F. S. Kent.	A. B. Hilliker	Feb. —, 1868	99	1, 980	33	1, 650
Thomas L. A. Valiquet and F. S. Kent.	A. B. Hilliker	Feb. —, 1868	102	2, 040	34 2-7	1, 650
Thomas L. A. Valiquet and F. S. Kent.	A. B. Hilliker	Feb. —, 1868	111	2, 220	37 1-9	1, 650
G. M. Shape	E. Curry	Feb. 8, 1868	131½	2, 631	43 5-6	450
R. J. Hutchinson	L. A. Somers	Jan. 29, 1868	126½	2, 530	42 1-6	631
William S. Kettles	Reese and W. Sherman.	Jan. 19, 1868	94	1, 880	31⅓	1, 300
M. Mareau	William Wallace	Jan. 19, 1868	110	2, 202	36 1-7	700
M. Marks and J. Bagley, first trial.	N. J. Snyder	Jan. 21, 1868	125	*2, 500	41⅔	90
M. Marks and J. Bagley, second trial.	N. J. Snyder	Jan. 21, 1868	126	2, 520	42	450
James Fisher	James Leonard	Autumn, 1860	156	3, 120	52	
James Fisher	James Leonard	Autumn, 1860	165	3, 300	55	
R. J. Hutchinson	N. J. Snyder	Feb. 19, 1860	135	2, 704	45	100
Edward C. Stewart	N. J. Snyder	Feb. 20, 1860	127	2, 540	42⅓	100
M. Marian	William Wallace	Jan. 19, 1860	111¼	2, 224	37	663
P. H. Burns, Boston	Walter Phillips, Providence.	May 8, 1868	136½	†2, 731	45½	40

* By the repeating of a line, the number of words was actually 2, 510 in one hour.

FIRST TRIAL, (divided into six parts of ten minutes each.)	
First 10 minutes, M. Marks	410 words.
Next 10 minutes, Charles Bagley	404 words.
Next 10 minutes, Charles Bagley	369 words.
Next 10 minutes, Charles Bagley	454 words.
Next 10 minutes, Charles Bagley	434 words.
Next 10 minutes, Charles Bagley	429 words.
60 minutes	2, 500 words.

SECOND TRIAL—	
First 9 minutes, M. Marks	373 words.
Next 11 minutes, Charles Bagley	450 words.
Next 10 minutes, Charles Bagley	374 words.
Next 10 minutes, Charles Bagley	460 words.
Next 10 minutes, Charles Bagley	430 words.
Next 10 minutes, Charles Bagley	433 words.
60 minutes	2, 520 words.

† This recording of 2, 731 words in one hour, by Walter Phillips, of Providence, Rhode Island, and the recording of 2, 520 words in the same time, by N. J. Snyder, at Philadelphia, are the greatest feats in telegraphic transmission that have yet been accomplished by the Morse apparatus in any country. The instrumentalities were the Morse sounder, or acoustic instrument, (the cost of which is about eight dollars,) a battery, and two operators, one at each terminus of a line. In these seventeen trials the average is 119½ dispatches, of twenty words each, in one hour, or two dispatches in one minute.

Speed of the Hughes apparatus and of Siemen's automatic type-presses.

	Number of telegrams of twenty words each in one hour.	Number of words in one hour.	Number of words in one minute.
The Hughes apparatus—In France	50	1, 000	$16\frac{4}{6}$
In Prussia	40 to 50	800 to 1, 000	$13\frac{2}{6}$ to $16\frac{4}{6}$
The Siemen's process—In Prussia	60	1, 200	20

RECENT RESULT IN FRANCE IN SPEED OF TRANSMISSION.

At the late opening of the Legislative Assembly in Paris, (1869,) the speech of the Emperor on the occasion was transmitted from Paris to various capitals. It will be seen that extraordinary efforts were made to transmit it by telegraph with the utmost speed. We copy from the French journals the following account of the result:

"Nothing could be more curious and interesting than the aspect which was presented yesterday after the speech of the Emperor, in the central telegraph station.

"The day before, orders had been given that the lines and apparatus should be inspected with care and put in order. At half past 12 o'clock the entire body of officials were at their posts waiting the word of command.

"Scarcely had the first copies been distributed to them than *two hundred employés* were put to work, and the transmission was made with a dizzy rapidity, of which the following figures will give some idea:

"The imperial speech contains about 1,200 words.

"London received it in fourteen minutes; Berlin, in one hour and nine minutes; Florence, in one hour and forty minutes; Brussels, in forty-five minutes; Vienna, in one hour and fifty minutes.

"The difference in time to the advantage of London is explained by this fact: that four wires (or circuits) were used for the transmission of the speech to that capital, while only one was used for the others."

This feat of transmission by telegraph, scrutinized, gives the following comparative result. The speech containing 1,200 words was sent entire to London in fourteen minutes; but four wires (with, of course, as many instruments) were needed to accomplish the result, so that, divided between the four, each wire or instrument transmitted 300 words in fourteen minutes, equivalent to fifty-six minutes by one wire, to send the whole 1,200 words. By referring to the table of results in the trial of speed of the Morse apparatus, (in 1868,) it will be perceived that the minimum of the results, by the American operators, amounted to 1,600 words in one hour, which is in excess of the estimated number per hour of the greatest speed attained in this late European feat.

The time in which the speech was transmitted to Brussels upon one wire, to wit, forty-five minutes, is the greatest speed in this case; but this is equivalent to 1,500 words only per hour.

From these results it will be seen, in comparing them with the results of other modifications of the apparatus, that the original simple Morse apparatus maintains its superiority in the telegraphic field. Its simplicity of construction, its cheapness, its efficiency, its requirement of so few employés in its management, are the qualities which have given it its world-wide popularity, and have caused its universal adoption.

Notwithstanding this simple apparatus has proved its ability to accomplish so much, the desire for more has turned the minds of the ingenious upon devising many modifications of the apparatus.

The *automatic type telegraph* (No. 39) exhibited by Messrs. Siemens and Halské of Berlin is an apparatus of the same general character as the original Morse apparatus, but, it is scarcely necessary to add, of superior beauty of mechanical execution, like everything that comes from their extensive ateliers.

AUTOMATIC TRANSMISSION IN PRUSSIA.

Being in Berlin in February, 1868, the writer called on the courteous and obliging directors and superintendent of the Prussian telegraph, the Colonel Herr von Chauvin, and Herr von Frischen. By the latter officer he was shown into the apartment in which was arranged the automatic modification of Messrs. Siemens and Halské, a duplicate of their apparatus in the Exposition, (No. 39.) Besides the instruments for transmission, there were cases of type, (giving to the apartment the appearance of a printing office,) and a corps of some ten or twelve employés.

The following written questions were put to Herr von Frischen, to which he gave their annexed answers:

"1. Question. What instruments are necessary in this automatic process?

"Answer. Two instruments, a transmitter and receptor.

"2. Question. What is their respective cost?

"Answer. *Transmitter*, with 150 *long* rules and 35 *short* ones, and 15,000 types, cost 700 Prussian thalers, (or about $525 in gold.) *Receptor* costs 105 thalers, (or about $78 75 gold.)

"3. Question. What time does it take to prepare the message in type, for transmission?

"Answer. *Three minutes* to prepare a message of twenty words, together with eight words for the direction, or address, in all twenty-eight words; and half a minute to revise and see that all is right.

"4. Question. What is the practical speed of transmission and reception by the type process?

"Answer. *Forty-five* single messages in one hour by the present sized wire for 120 German miles, or 540 English miles. We can send at the same time in four different directions to Königsberg, Frankfort-on-the-Main, Cologne, and Brussels.

"5. Question. What is the practical speed of preparation, transmitting, and reception by the punched-paper process?

"Answer. Experiments in the room with 600 German miles (or 2,700 English miles) resistance, a single message of twenty words can be sent in half a minute with the magneto-electric current; and with double battery (galvanic) current, one minute. With better apparatus the same speed can be attained in both cases. The preparation of the paper by hand for a single message of twenty words takes three minutes; prepared by the key-board, like Hughes's key-board, a single message is prepared in one minute.

"6. Question. What distance is the magneto-electric current available practically in telegraphing?

"Answer. The same distance as the galvanic current.

"7. Question. What difficulties do you experience in the present mode of automatic transmission?

"Answer. The great number of employés necessary.

"8. Question. How many employés are necessary in preparing and transmitting a certain amount by one instrument?

"Answer. *Ten* (10) persons to prepare; *two* (2) to transmit; and *two* (2) to revise; in all fourteen (14)."

For the purpose of corroborating these statements, the following letter was addressed by the writer in February, 1868, to Messrs. Siemens and Halské, the mechanicians of the automatic type process, which was examined in the Prussian office, the counterpart of No. 39 in the Exposition:

"Will you oblige me with answers to the following questions, which I shall be happy to insert in my report?

"1. What kind of instruments, and how many, for one apparatus complete, are required in your automatic processes? How many in the *type process?* How many in the *punched-paper process?*

"2. What is the cost of each separate instrument in a single set, and what the cost of all together?

"3. How much time is required to prepare a message of twenty words for transmission by the type mode? How much by the punched paper mode?

"4. What is the regular practical speed of transmission and of reception by the type process, and what by the punched paper process?

"5. What are the difficulties you encounter in your automatic processes?

"6. How many employés are required to prepare, to transmit, and to receive messages?"

To the above questions the following replies were courteously accorded:

"We beg you to excuse the lateness of the answer to your favor of the 17th February. The delay was caused by the condition of the punched-paper apparatus, not so far finished as to be able to give you the desired information.

"1. The complete electro-magnetical type transmitter, sufficient for transmitting seventy messages in one hour, consists of—

	Thalers.
1 transmitting instrument	150 00
1 receiving instrument, inkwriter, with variable speed of its clock-work	110 00
150 letter rods (type rules) in which to set up the type, at 5 thalers	750 00
15,000 types, at 20 thalers per 1,000	300 00
6 letter cases, at 5⅔ thalers	34 00
15 cases for the rods, (type rules,) at 1½ thalers	22 15
The complete instrument, (about $1,024 in gold)	1,366 15

"The time for composing one dispatch of twenty words, five minutes; for distributing, four minutes; so that all preparations of every message require nine minutes.

"For the above-named speed of transmission there will be necessary, twelve men for setting up and distributing; two men for transmitting; and two men for receiving and writing down the messages.

"2. For transmission by the punched-paper arrrangement there will be required the following instruments:

	Thalers.
1 key-board puncher	250 00
1 handle puncher	80 00
1 magneto-electrical transmitter	125 00
One complete instrument	455 00

"The speed of transmission by this arrangement is one hundred and twenty messages in one hour. By the key-board puncher, one letter is completely finished as soon as the corresponding key is touched; therefore one man will be able to prepare the same number of messages as the transmitter gives away.

"However, we add the hand puncher for reserve or corrections. Instead of the magneto-electrical transmitter, we employ likewise a transmitter for reversed battery currents. The cost of such instruments is 120 thalers.

"This manner of transmission requires paper furnished with holes to drive it regularly.

"We manufacture also machines especially constructed for this perforation, at the price of 90 thalers each.

"For the service of this instrument are sufficient: one man for punching; one man for transmitting; two men for receiving and writing down the messages.

"This number of officers is necessary only if the automatic transmitter is continually in use, and it is only in this case the employing of the instrument seems lucrative.

"If there are always two lines at disposal, one for transmitting and the other for receiving, there is no difficulty in this automatic arrangement.

"Inclosed is a sample of a message prepared by the hand puncher, and transmitted by the magneto-electrical instrument. We have written on it the time occupied in preparation and transmission. The dispatch was worked through a resistance of 500 German miles, or 30,000 Siemens units of resistance," (equivalent to about 2,000 English miles.) * * *

Table of the comparative speed of transmission, by the different instrumentalities, on the basis of one dispatch of twenty words.

Kind of apparatus.	Time of preparation for transmission of one dispatch.	Time in transmitting one dispatch.	Number of employés.	Cost of the instruments, in gold.	Estimated average number of dispatches in one hour, taking into account time of preparation.	Stated average number in one hour.
	Minutes.	*Minutes.*				
Siemens & Halské's type process:						
According to Siemens & Halske, in their ateliers	9	½	16	$1,024 00	6⅔	70
According to Herr von Frischen, in the central office .	3½	½	14	603 75	20 to 60	40 to 45
Punched-paper process:						
According to Siemens & Halské..................	2½	½	4	431 25	*36	120
According to von Frischen...	1 to 3	½ to 1½	......	....	†20 to 60	....
Hughes	No time...	....	2	350 00	40 to 50	....
Morse..........................	No time...	....	2	14 00	119½	....

Remarks.—The discrepancy between the estimated average and the stated average arises doubtless from not taking into account, in the stated average, the time of "preparation for transmission."

* The sample referred to of the punched-paper process contains one hundred and fifty letters, occupying in the preparation and transmission two and a half minutes, equivalent to three hundred letters in five minutes, or sixty words, or three dispatches of twenty words each in five minutes, that is, at the rate of thirty-six dispatches in one hour.

† If it takes three minutes to prepare a single message of twenty words, it would take two hundred and ten minutes to prepare seventy dispatches for transmission, equivalent to three and a half hours. If one minute is required for preparing one dispatch, then one hour and ten minutes are required to prepare seventy dispatches previous to transmission.

CRITICAL REVIEW OF THESE RESULTS.

In presenting this table of results, it ought in fairness to be stated that, in all these automatic processes, the number of dispatches in an hour is estimated from a recorded dispatch made by the instrument itself, while the number by the Morse apparatus is the result of the acoustic method, recorded, indeed, but by an employé or clerk. The difference is in the efficiency of the two kinds of record for control. In the one case it is dependent on the automatic mechanism, which records upon the paper ribbon; in the other, it is dependent on the skill and faithfulness of the clerk transcribing as he hears it from the sounder. Sir Charles Wheatstone has recently devised an automatic punched-paper process, somewhat similar to the process of Messrs. Siemens and Halské, for a description of which we must refer to the jurors' reports of the London International Exhibition of 1862, Class XIII, pp. 69, 70. It is stated in that report that one hundred and sixty-six letters per minute were transmitted by it on a line of three hundred and twenty-four miles, equivalent to about one hundred dispatches in one hour. But in this case, as in the other automatic processes, the essential element of the time necessary to prepare the message previous to its transmission does not enter into the calculation. It is also stated in the same report that 1,476 words, equivalent to seventy-three dispatches per hour, are the greatest number that can be transmitted by the most expert clerk in the English telegraphic service. This rate, it will be seen, is greatly exceeded by the American operators in the late test of speed of transmission.

In making a comparison of the relative speed of transmission from the moment it is presented for that purpose until received at the distant station, it is necessary to take into the account—

1. The time required to prepare the dispatch for transmission.
2. The time of actual transmission.
3. The time for imbodying the received dispatch.
4. The number of employés necessary to accomplish the whole process.
5. The comparative cost of the apparatus.
6. The cost of maintenance of the employés, and the expense of repairs to the instruments.

For our purpose it is necessary at present only to consider the first and second of these points. On the supposition that a dispatch, say of 1,600 words, is presented at the office, at the same moment, for transmission, to be sent by the respective instruments, to wit, the Siemens and Halské automatic type telegraph, the Siemens and Halské punched-paper process, the Wheatstone punched-paper process, the Hughes apparatus, and the Morse apparatus, what would be the result of each?

The Siemens and Halské type-process takes three and a half minutes to prepare each dispatch of twenty-eight words for transmission; 1,600 words contain fifty-seven such dispatches, consuming, therefore, in the preparation, three hours and thirty minutes before transmission. Forty-five of these messages can then be transmitted in one hour, or the fifty-seven in one hour thirteen and a half minutes, which, added to the time of preparation, gives four hours forty-three and a half minutes as the time consumed in transmitting 1,600 words.

If the punched-paper process of Siemens and Halské be tested, the preparation of a dispatch of twenty words takes three minutes by hand; or one minute by a key-board instrument or perforator. Taking the lowest estimate, of one minute, then eighty messages, or 1,600 words, are prepared for transmission in one hour and twenty minutes, and in their transmission forty minutes more are consumed, making the time for completing the dispatch of 1,600 words two hours.

If from the data given of the capacity of the automatic punched-paper process of Sir Charles Wheatstone we make a comparative test, (the time of preparation not being stated,) we must assume that the time of preparation of a dispatch of 1,600 words previous to transmission can scarcely be less, by his perforator, than by the perforator of Messrs. Siemens and Halské. One hour and twenty minutes are therefore consumed in this preparation. If now the transmission of these eighty dispatches is accomplished at the rate given of one hundred dispatches in one hour, we must add forty-eight minutes, making the whole process two hours eight minutes.

The Hughes consumes no time in preparation, but commences transmitting at once, and the 1,600 words are, therefore, transmitted in one hour and thirty-six minutes.

The Morse consumes no time in preparation, but commences transmitting at once, and the 1,600 words are, therefore, transmitted in one hour.

This examination gives the following result:

	Hours.	Min.
The Siemens & Halské type-process, 80 dispatches..........	4	43½
The Siemens & Halské punched-paper process, 80 dispatches..	2	00
Wheatstone's punched-paper process, 80 dispatches...........	2	08
Hughes apparatus, 80 dispatches	1	36
Morse apparatus, 80 dispatches.............................	1	00

It is urged in favor of the automatic type-process, as well as the punched-paper process, that the preparation of the dispatches by type or punched paper can be expedited by multiplying the number of perforators and employés, and thus the difficulty of the time consumed in preparation (which is stated to be an objection) is obviated; for if 1,600 words, or eighty dispatches, be divided, for example, into eight "takes," or sections, and eight perforators be used by eight employés, each preparing his own "take" at the same time, then the whole eighty dispatches are prepared in one-eighth of the time, and the time by the—

Type process, 4*h.* 43½*m.*, is reduced to.......................... 35*m.*
Punched-paper process, 1*h.* 20*m.*, is reduced to.................. 10*m.*

To this time of preparation add time of transmission, respectively, and we have—

Type process, 40*m.*—altogether to........................... 1*h.* 15*m.*
Punched-paper process, 48*m.*—altogether to.................. 58*m.*

So that we have this result: The punched-paper process requires eight perforators and eight employés to accomplish what the Morse, with but one operator, accomplishes in the same time, (less only by two minutes.) Where wages are very low, and the employment, therefore, of an increased operative force is comparatively of little importance, there may be an advantage in employing the punched-paper process; but in an economic point of view, where the wages of employés are high, there would be no advantage in its adoption, except in exceptional cases.

AUTOMATIC CONTROL.

SORTAIS'S APPARATUS.

T. A. M. Sortais, of Lisieux, exhibited a mode of automatic control of a distant apparatus, (No. 7,) devised about the year 1861 or 1862.

It was early considered to be a great desideratum, so to have a distant apparatus under the control of a corresponding office, that even in case of the absence of the operator of that apparatus, a dispatch might still be recorded by the instrument, and so be independent of the presence of any attendant. One of Morse's earliest devices, for this purpose, patented in France in 1838, as well as in the United States, consisted of the union of two operations: 1st, of a means of setting in motion the distant recording apparatus; and, 2d, of a means of arresting the motion of the apparatus at any desired time. Both these operations being successfully accomplished, it is plain that a dispatch could be recorded, whether the attendant was present or not.

These means were based, first, on the sudden release of the fly that regulates the speed of the clock-work, by the first movement of the pen lever, in recording a dispatch. This part of the operation was simple enough. The detent that arrested the fly, being a small lever in contact with a friction wheel upon the axis of the fly, was easily removed by this first movement, and the clock-work set in motion, and the strip of paper was then ready to receive any amount of written characters. The second operation, that of arresting the apparatus, after the desired characters were completed, was based upon a replacement of the detent of the fly, or the small friction lever, upon the friction wheel, after the completion of the dispatch. This was accomplished in the very first instance successfully by an apparatus not now necessary to describe, in which there was the addition of a second electro-magnet, so adding complication to the instrumentalities. This was almost immediately modified by the improvement which Morse has described and specified in his French letters patent of August 18, 1838, as well as in his American patents. This improvement, in brief, consisted in slightly attaching, but not fixing, the detent or small lever by one extremity to the axis of one of the slower wheels of the clock-work in such a manner as to slip upon the axis when the friction lever was raised, but not so easily as not to hold its position when raised by the action of the pen lever. The other extremity of the small lever acted as a detent, by its friction, upon a friction wheel upon the fly axis, when brought in contact with it, and thus arrested the movement of the apparatus. The arm of the small friction lever was connected, by a thread or wire, with the pen lever above the friction lever, in such a manner, that when the pen lever rose it lifted the friction lever from the friction-wheel, and allowed the movement of the apparatus; but when the pen lever fell, it did not by that act abase the friction lever, which remained in its raised position, and was kept raised slipping on the axis of the slower wheel of the apparatus at every movement upward of the pen lever, and could only return to its position on the friction-wheel by the slower movement of the axis to which it was attached after the pen lever had for a given time ceased to act.

Another and an earlier mode, and the one fully described and illustrated by diagrams in Vail's work, of 1845, as well as in the specifications of Morse's patents, and which may also be found copied into the work of the Count du Moncel, is on the same principle. This earlier mode for automatic control is herein described with a diagram, following the description of M. Sortais's method.

The method of M. Sortais seems to have been devised without a consciousness that the same result had been already achieved by a mode similar in principle to his ingenious device.

The reasons so well given by M. Sortais for making this improvement upon the recording instrument, it will be seen by reference to Morse's patents, were those that suggested to him his original device for the purpose.

M. Sortais says: "The Morse apparatus, such as are in use at the present day, present a grave inconvenience. They can neither be put in motion, nor be arrested by themselves after being put in motion; in other words, they are not automatic. *Consequently, during the absence of the employé from the receiving office, no dispatch can be transmitted; it would be the same if this employé is absorbed in some urgent labor. As to the control of the service, no signal indicative of delay, is indicated either in the receptions or the expeditions.*

"An automatic system, on the contrary, will allow of the transmission and the recording of correspondence in the absence of the employés, and besides it offers to the administration the means of vigorously controlling the vigilance of the employés."

M. Sortais, in these remarks, was undoubtedly unaware that against the "grave inconveniences" he enumerates, Morse had already devised and applied a complete remedy more than twenty years before Mr. Sortais's modification of it.

M. Sortais has politely furnished a diagram, which illustrates his method of accomplishing this automatic control. It is an improvement on the Morse mode of automatic control, since it requires less power to put it in action, and it can be affixed to those Morse instruments of Messrs. Digney and Siemens's improvement, which dispense with the relays.

There has been a question of *utility* raised in regard to the advantage of this automatic control. Experience alone can determine the occasions when it may be of use.

The fact that the telegraphic service requires for the most part the constant presence of an operator would seem to indicate that this automatic control was considered more curious than useful; but upon lines established for infrequent or only occasional use, (for example such as may be established between the residence of a manufacturer and his distant workshops or offices,) there can be no doubt of its utility, since it enables him to dispense with the constant attendance of an operator. In such cases M. Sortais's ingenious and beautiful improvement is recommended as specially valuable.

The following is the description of M. Sortais's method of control:

The apparatus of M. Sortais consists of a ratchet-wheel G, bearing a lever *(d'embrayage) h*, and above which reacts one of the movable parts of the clock-work of the telegraph apparatus, and in a detent E, put in action by the aid of the printing lever of the electo-magnet, by the pin *d'*.

Fig. 22.

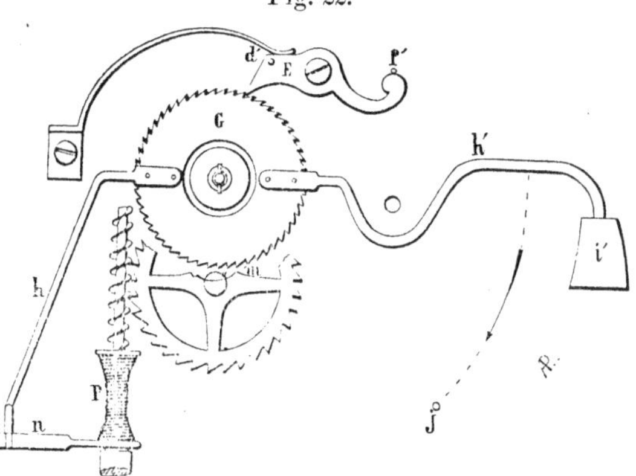

Sortais's Controlling Apparatus.

The lever *(embrayeur) h* is balanced by counter-weight *i'*, which has a tendency to disengage it from the fly-wheel upon which it should react to stop the mechanism. But in its normal state it cannot yield to this movement because of the catch of the detent which maintains the ratchet-wheel in a determinate position. At that time it strikes against the detent *n* fixed to the axis of the last but one wheel, which at each revolution of itself makes the rachet-wheel advance one notch.

When the apparatus is put in action by the electro-magnet the catch of the ratchet-wheel is disengaged, and as this is no longer sustained, the lever *h* which is upon it is disengaged by its counter-weight *i'*, and the *(déclunchment)* is in action. If this action is instantaneous, the catch of the ratchet-wheel moves with it, and at each turn of the last but one wheel in the clock train, the ratchet-wheel advances one tooth, the lever *(d'embrayage)* falls, to encounter, after a certain number of impulses of the ratchet-wheel, the finger *n* of the axis which commands the fly-wheel and stops the movement of the apparatus. If the play of the electro-magnet occurs in the slighter intervals corresponding to the signals, the ratchet-wheel will keep itself separated from the catch, consequently it will only be after interruptions of a sufficient length of time that the stopping will be produced.

MORSE'S STOPPING APPARATUS.

This was invented in 1837, and is here illustrated with the diagram from Vail's book of 1845.

Fig. 23.

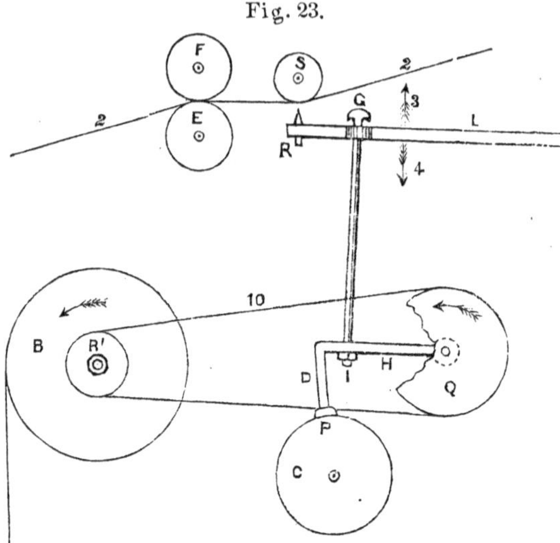

Morse's Stopping Apparatus.

B is the slowest wheel in the train. Upon its axle R′, prolonged outside the walls of the clock-work, is fixed a pulley wheel R′, of small diameter, and another pulley wheel Q, of much larger diameter, on the prolonged axle of another of the slow wheels of the train. An endless band 10 unites these two wheels. A bent arm H D fixed upon the axle of Q, under and parallel to the pen lever L, rests at P upon a friction wheel C, fixed upon the axle of the fly. The pen lever L having the stylus for marking, R, has a light rod or small wire A loosely hinged at I in the bent arm, and playing loosely through an aperture in the lever L, and held by its head G. The paper 2 2 passes under the groove cylinder S, drawn between the two rolling cylinders E and F.

When the pen lever L is brought into action in striking the stylus R against the paper at S, the rod A lifts the bent lever D H from the friction wheel C upon the fly shaft, and allows the movement of the clock-work. The endless band 10 is thus made to slip upon the smaller pulley wheel. But the pen lever in descending does not carry down the bent lever D H, because the rod A has free play, and rises in the lever at G; so that the lever L in descending does not replace P upon the friction wheel C. This can be accomplished only by the slower action of R′ gradually acting by the band 10 to replace P upon the friction-wheel. So long as the pen lever is in action, the rod A repeats its action upon the bent lever D H, and keeps the point P raised from the friction-wheel. But so soon as the pen lever ceases to act, the slow movement of the band 10 moving in the direction of the arrows, gradually replaces P upon the friction-wheel and stops the machinery.

This was one of the first modes devised and used by Morse to control the distant apparatus. By comparing this with the mode by which M. Sortais accomplishes the same result, it is perceived that although the original mode called the stopping apparatus, and early patented by

Morse, accomplished its result well, the more recent one of M. Sortais accomplishes it better.

The following appears in the New York Express of May 19, 1863, showing that the same result substantially was obtained by the ingenious Professor Wheatstone, apparently unconscious that it had been accomplished some twenty-five years previous in the United States:

"AUTOMATIC CONTROL OF THE TELEGRAPH.—Professor Wheatstone has just perfected a most extraordinary and valuable improvement in telegraphs—a private letter-printing apparatus working by itself, so that no clerk or attendant is required. A merchant can now lock up his counting-house, and on his return find every message faithfully recorded in legible type during his absence by this beautiful little machine. (So tells us the Boston Transcript.)"

The only novelty in this "improvement" is the adapting to machinery for printing the ordinary letters the automatic controlling apparatus invented by Professor Morse in 1837, and which he patented in France in 1838, and in Washington in April, 1846, and by which "no clerk or attendant is necessary at the distant terminus, and by means of which a merchant can now lock up his counting-house, and on his return find every message recorded during his absence." All this is substantially announced in the Report of the Committee of Commerce of the House of Representatives, December 30, 1842. In detailing the superior advantages of Professor Morse's invention, the chairman says: "Possessing an advantage over electric telegraphs heretofore in use, inasmuch as it records in permanently legible characters on paper any communication which may be made by it, *without the aid of any agent at the place of recording, except the apparatus*, which is *put in motion at the point of communication*. Thus the recording apparatus, called the register, *may be left in a closed chamber, where it will give notice of its commencing to write by a bell, and the communication may be found on opening the apartment.*"

CHAPTER VI.

INFORMATION CONCERNING TELEGRAPHS IN VARIOUS COUNTRIES.

THE UNITED KINGDOM OF GREAT BRITAIN AND IRELAND, STATISTICS OF ELECTRIC TELEGRAPHS IN—LETTER OF SIR CHARLES BRIGHT—INDIA—FRANCE, QUESTIONS TO AND ANSWERS FROM VISCOUNT DE VOUGY—HOLLAND—PRUSSIA—AUSTRIA—DENMARK—LETTER OF DIRECTOR GENERAL FABER—SWEDEN—LETTER OF DIRECTOR GENERAL BRÄNDSTRÖM—SPAIN—ITALY—EGYPT—TURKEY—AUSTRALIA—PERU.

GREAT BRITAIN.

The following questions were addressed by Professor Morse to the eminent secretary of the Submarine Telegraph Company, Sir James Carmichael, Baronet, London, directing the telegraphic correspondence between the United Kingdom and the Continent. Sir James has courteously sent the subjoined answers:

"1. What telegraphic systems are used in the British dominions?

"Answer. The system used by the Submarine Telegraph Company for correspondence between Great Britain and the continent of Europe is the Morse exclusively. The systems used by the United Kingdom Telegraph Company are the Morse and the Hughes type-printing instrument. The systems in use by the Magnetic Telegraph Company are[1] Bright's patent bells for the most important circuits, *i. e.*, for lines on which rapidity of working is essential, and on which there is a large amount of business. For other circuits (railway lines, &c.) Highton's single-needle instrument is used. The system used by the London District Telegraph Company is one brought out by Mr. Tyers, and is a single-needle instrument which is worked with the Morse code. The Electric and International Telegraph Company use the Morse system for international work, and also for large circuits; Dujardin's type-printing instrument, and the double-needle instrument, (Cooke and Wheatstone.)

"2. How many of each system?

"Answer. The number of instruments in use by each company is given in the accompanying table, extracted from the volume of miscellaneous statistics issued in March, 1867. A later volume, to the end of 1867, is now in course of publication. The number of instruments of submarine company is fifty-one, as per last return.

"3. What are the advantages and disadvantages of each system, in

[1] The "patent bells" instrument of Sir Charles Bright is an improvement, as well as a modification of the original Morse sounder. The improvement consists in utilizing the positive and negative currents, to vary the sound, creating an economy of time in transmission.—S. F. B. M.

cost of instruments and repairs, in rate of speed or quantity of intelligence in a given time?

"Answer. Highton's single-needle instrument is said to be the cheapest, costing only about 50*s.* or £3. The type-printing instruments are the most costly, but transmit with great rapidity. The instrument known as 'Bright's patent bells,' transmits an average of forty words a minute. The Submarine Telegraph Company working direct between London and Paris can transmit forty messages an hour, taking long and short together, by one Morse circuit.

"4. How many miles of conductors are constructed?

"Answer. This question is answered by the annexed extract. (See table.)

"5. What are the expenses and receipts per annum, and the net revenue to the state or to the companies?

Answer. Copies of the reports of the various companies, for the year 1867, are annexed and will show these particulars."

ELECTRIC TELEGRAPHS IN THE UNITED KINGDOM.

Statistics of electric telegraphs for the use of the public, in the United Kingdom, in each of the years 1863, 1864, *and* 1865.

Telegraph companies.	Length in miles of telegraph lines.			Length in miles of wires used.			Number of stations open for the public.		
	1863.	1864.	1865.	1863.	1864.	1865.	1863.	1864.	1865.
Electric and International	8, 282	8, 658	9, 306	39, 756	41, 691	45, 044	1, 022	1, 022	1, 022
British and Irish Magnetic	4, 196¾	4, 329½	4, 401	17, 257½	18, 554	18, 668	464	479	491
Southeastern Railway*	316	318	323½	2, 642½	2, 996½	3, 064½	94	102	104
London, Brighton, and South Coast Railway	212	217½	240¾	541½	583¼	688	46	48	57
London district†	107	115	123	430	454	470	81	80	83
The United Kingdom	‡831	1, 343	1, 672	‡5, 099	8, 096	9, 506	‡48	100	125
Total	13, 944¾	14, 981	16, 066¼	65, 726½	72, 374¾	77, 440½	1, 755	1, 831	1, 882
Submarine, (telegraph to Calais, 24 miles; to Boulogne, 25 miles; to Dieppe, 78 miles; to Jersey, 30 miles; to Ostend, 70 miles; to Hanover, 80 miles; and to Denmark, 380 miles.)	887	(§)	(§)	2, 683	(§)	(§)	(‖)	(§)	(§)

* The Southeastern Railway Company has no working arrangements with either of the electric telegraph companies.

† Exclusive of private telegraphs provided by this company for firms and persons having two places of business, and for the London fire brigade and general post office.

‡ This additional mileage and stations was only completed and opened in November, 1863.

§ No return.

‖ Upwards of 3,000 in foreign countries.

Statistics of electric telegraphs—Continued.

Telegraph companies.	Number of instruments.			Number of public messages.		
	1863.	1864.	1865.	1863.	1864.	1865.
Electric and International	4, 489	5, 136	5, 778	(*)	(*)	(*)
British and Irish Magnetic †	1, 042	(‡)	(‡)	827, 424	1, 030, 142	1, 251, 265
Southeastern Railway	142	158	159	62, 968	69, 623	88, 711
London, Brighton, and South Coast Railway	69	74	92	43, 208	52, 942	66, 523
London district	192	191	195	247, 606	308, 032	316, 272
The United Kingdom	172	285	358	226, 729	518, 651	743, 870
	....	....	6, 582	....	....	....
Submarine	§51	(‡)	(‡)	‖345, 784	(‡)	(‡)

* Not ascertained.

† The number of messages to and from the Continent transmitted jointly by this company and the Submarine Telegraph Company, and the number of messages for railway companies, newspapers, and news rooms, are not included with the messages for the public.

‡ No return.

§ Exclusively for continental traffic.

‖ To and from foreign countries.

LETTER OF SIR CHARLES BRIGHT.

From a letter received from Sir Charles Bright in August, 1868, at the moment of his leaving New York for Liverpool, the following extracts are made. Sir Charles says:

"Generally, as regards the instruments in the United Kingdom, the Electric Telegraph Company use the Morse instruments on the principal commercial circuits, and the needle instrument on small and unimportant circuits, and also for the railway stations and signaling.

"The magnetic company use my sound instrument since 1854, for nearly all the circuits, (some railway stations excepted, where a single needle system is used.) The railway companies seem to prefer the needle instrument; so we supply them.

"The Submarine Company use the Morse instrument only, their wires being all in circuit with the continental system.

"The United Kingdom Company, (a small company, started since you were in England in 1857,) use the Morse instruments, and also several Hughes type-printing instruments.

"The only modification in the Morse instrument is the use of ink instead of the point in registering the marks. The needle instrument is much the same as of old, except that a single wire and single needle is used.

"The sound instrument, which I adopted for the Magnetic Company, consists of two bells, dull in sound, and differing in note, placed on each side of the operator about on a line with his ear. These are worked by a relay sending currents through one or the other, according to the signals required. Two keys are used for sending; one for the right or positive (+) current; the other for the left or negative (—) current. One wire is, of course, used. There is no difference in the duration of either signal, and this is the saving of time, compared with one of the sounders used here, (in the United States,) where, in employing dots and dashes, the latter, (I take it,) require three times the duration of a dot. In the other the signals are all dots; but a Morse operator can use it by considering one key as a *dot*, the other as a *dash*, but sending dots on both. It is the quickest instrument of a non-mechanical kind."

INDIA.

The total number of miles of telegraph lines in India, in 1866, was 13,390⅛ miles, and of offices 174. At the rate of three instruments to two offices, there would be 261 instruments.

FRANCE.

QUESTIONS TO, AND ANSWERS FROM, VISCOUNT DE VOUGY.

In January, 1867, the following questions were addressed to the administrator of the French telegraphs, the Count de Vougy, at the request of the Western Union Telegraph Company:

"Can you oblige me by furnishing me with—

"1. A copy of the tariff of charges on telegrams in France, and, so far as practicable, in other European countries?

"2. The number and names of the telegraph systems in use in France; how many of each system are employed, and their adaptedness or fitness for particular service?

"3. The average number of messages or telegrams, of a certain length, sent daily?

"4. The comparative number capable of being sent by each system?

"5. The proportion between those for the government service and for private or commercial service?

"6. Where can be obtained telegraphic maps of lines in France and in other countries?

"7. Is the English needle system anywhere in use in France?"

The following is the answer of Count de Vougy, dated Paris, February 20, 1867:

"I have collected the different documents that you had the goodness to request from me, and I have the pleasure of sending them to you:

"I. [1]The first is the general tariff of telegraphic dispatches of the French empire. It comprises two distinct parts—the one relating to the interior correspondence, the other to the international correspondence. There is, besides, as complementary, the Moniteur Télégraphique

[1] The documents here mentioned were sent to the company in New York three months before my appointment as United States Commissioner.—S. F. B. M.

of December, 1865, remaining in use, to determine the taxes of the offices (not numerous) elsewhere, which have not yet adhered to the rules of the international convention, concluded at Paris the 17th of May, 1865.

"I have also added to the tariff the text of their convention, and the regulations made in consequence.

"A note, in which is collected the information that the administration in France possesses on the interior tariffs of different states of Europe, in short, completes this first series of documents.

"II. Four systems of apparatus are employed by the French administration: 1. The Morse apparatus. 2. The dial apparatus. 3. The Hughes apparatus. 4. The Caselli apparatus. There are counted in the service of the Morse system, 1,600; dial system, 1,180; Hughes system, 135; Caselli system, 6.

"The inherent merits of the Morse system, and of which the principal ones are its marvelous simplicity, and great reliability in its action, maintain its use on the greatest number of the net-work of lines.

"The Hughes apparatus replaces it, however, with advantage upon the conductors of great length, when the quantity of dispatches to be transmitted is in abundance.

"The apparatus *à cadran*, or dial apparatus, is employed in a certain number of city and semaphoric offices, the agents of communes and of the marine, who manage these posts, not being always in a condition to acquire the knowledge necessary to work an apparatus less elementary.

"As to the pantelegraph of Caselli, the public has not been permitted to make use of it but upon two or three principal lines, and besides has not shown much eagerness to profit by the advantages it presents. A printing dial apparatus, invented by M. d'Arlincourt, has been tried with success upon some lines of small extent, but it has not yet been admitted into definite practice.

"III. Statistics, drawn up in 1860, have permitted us to ascertain that the number of telegrams of twenty words, transmitted during this same year, amount to sixty-three per cent. of the telegrams of all lengths sent in the same period. There has not been kept an account since then, in a precise manner, of the comparative number and extent of these dispatches. I am inclined to think, nevertheless, that the proportion of these telegrams which do not exceed twenty words, the minimum limit of the tax, is augmented during the last years in the same proportion as telegraphic correspondence has been popularized.

"The pamphlet bearing the title '*Tableau des produits des bureaux de l'état en* 1865,' will furnish you with many interesting indications upon the extent of the French net-work of wires, and upon the results of its working. It is in place to remark, at all times, that these results do not include the state correspondence, free from tax, and of which the receipts, estimated by order, have amounted for the year 1865 to the sum of 1,800,631 francs 18 centimes. The French administration publishes this document every year. I will hasten to send to you that which relates to the year 1866 as soon as it shall appear.

"IV. The productive power of the different apparatus used in the service is represented in practice by the following means, determined (upon the interval in the space of an hour) for telegrams composed uniformly of twenty words:

The Hughes apparatus	50
The Morse apparatus	20
The dial apparatus	15
The Caselli apparatus	40

The mean attributed to this last cannot, however, be considered as precise, the surface of the paper, which serves as the basis of the tax, bearing a number of words, more or less large, according to the form of the writing of the sender.

"V. In 1864 the total number of private dispatches has been 1,967,748; that of the official dispatches, 526,613; 1865 has furnished for the one 2,473,747, and for the other 568,647. The approximative proportion between the transmissions of the state and those of private persons is then about one-fourth.

"VI. The map or chart of the telegraphic net-work in France is not in the market. It is published by the administration, but the works executed in the last year have rendered it incomplete and inexact upon so many points that it cannot at the present time give a just idea of the state of our telegraphic communications. A new edition is going to be put to press, and you may be sure, my dear sir, that you shall receive one of the first proofs.

"I send you, to supply in some degree, in the absence of this document, and also to inform you upon the telegraphic net-work of the different European states, a copy of a chart published about a year ago by the Prussian government. But I expect, likewise, to transmit to you soon a more detailed document on the international net-work of our continent.

"VII. The English needle system is not in use in a single office in France.

"I add to the different pamphlets, which answer the questions contained in your letter, a late document which includes the complete collection of the laws, decrees, rules, and instructions which regulate the French telegraphy. It bears the title of "*Recueil Administratif*," and comprises five volumes bound, and a bundle destined to form the sixth volume, to the end of 1867.

"If these different publications, and the indications contained in this letter, do not entirely meet the wishes of the Western Union Company, I remain, my dear Mr. Morse, with pleasure, at your disposal to complete them as far as possible.

"I avail myself of your obliging offer to furnish, on the part of the company, all the information that may appear interesting to my administration to obtain upon American telegraphy. For this purpose I am preparing a series of questions, and I will have the honor of soon sending them to you.

"In conclusion, I take advantage of this communication to give you, as a mark of my personal respect, a volume, in which is collected the diplomatic documents of the international conference of Paris." * *

HOLLAND.

The following is a letter of M. Faring, the referendary charged with the direction of the state telegraphs in Holland, to Hon. Hugh Ewing, United States minister to Holland, dated the Hague, April 27, 1868:

"In answer to the letter of Professor Morse, of the 22d instant, which I have received through you, I have the honor to communicate to you that the telegraphic system known by the name of the English needle system is not employed anywhere by us, neither on the lines of the state, nor on those of private companies.

"I propose to send you soon an answer to the other questions of Professor Morse, which were addressed to me in your letter of the 22d instant." * * *

As proposed in the preceding, the following letter of the referendary Faring to the minister resident of the United States at the Hague, the Hon. Mr. Ewing, dated the Hague, May 7, 1867, was written as a further answer to the questions proposed by Professor Morse:

"In accordance with the promise of my letter of the 27th April last, No. 3,188, I have the honor to address you the inclosed information respecting the Netherland telegraphs, requested by Professor Morse, in your letter of 22d April last.

"In that which follows, the order of the questions proposed has been observed:

"I. There are two telegraphic systems now established upon the telegraphic state lines, the Morse system, (*à molette*,) with the inking wheel, after the construction of Messrs. Digney, and the Hughes system. This last has been but lately introduced, and is not used but upon the most frequented lines.

"On the 1st of January, 1868, there were in use, of the Morse apparatus, 216; of the Hughes, 3.

"The railroads which are operated by private companies, (and of which I cannot give more precise information,) employ about 150 instruments, of which the greater part are constructed after the Morse system, with or without a constant current. Upon some of these railroads the dial instruments are still used, but these instruments are rapidly disappearing.

"II. On the 1st of January last the net-work of telegraph lines of the state had an extension of 2,328.3 kilometers, with a total length of wire of 6,863.2 kilometers.

"III. From the preceding, it results that the telegraph service of the state, as well as of the railroad, is almost exclusively performed by instruments constructed after the Morse system, the Hughes instrument doing service only on the most frequented lines, and the dial instruments disappearing more and more. It is not, therefore, necessary to discuss the question of the relative value of the different systems for greater or lesser distances, nor for the railroad service.

"The use of the telegraph for domestic life or for cities scarcely exists with us.

"IV. The receipts of the state telegraphs amounted in 1867 to about 500,000 florins of Holland; the expenses to 750,000 florins. The expense of the maintenance of the lines during the same year was about 175,000 florins; the expense of new constructions, 240,000 florins.

The price of a Morse apparatus (*à molette*) constructed by Digney frères, Paris, is	180 florins.
Of a relay magnet	80 florins.
Of a key or manipulator	14 florins.
Of a commutator	10 florins.
Of a galvanometer	15 florins.
Total Morse apparatus	299 florins.
Total cost of a Hughes instrument constructed by P. Dumoulin Froment	800 florins.

"V. The number of persons attached to the state telegraphs are found in a circular to the different European telegraph administrations, a copy of which I have the honor to inclose herewith. I also inclose a copy of the report to the King upon the condition of the Netherland telegraphs in 1866, and a copy of the new map of our telegraph lines."

* * * * * *

The circular alluded to in the foregoing letter is here given. It is signed by Faring, charged with the direction of the telegraphs, and dated the Hague, February 11, 1868:

"Conformably to the article 57 of the convention of Paris, I have the honor to send to you below some statistical information upon the personnel and the offices on the 1st January, 1868, the extent of lines and telegraphic wires, as well as the number of dispatches over the net-work of the Netherlands during the year 1867:

"DIRECTION.—The referendary, charged with the direction of the telegraphs of the state; the controller, charged with the working and responsibilities of the lines; three principal clerks; the engineer, charged with the technical service; two assistant engineers.

"EMPLOYÉS OF THE OFFICES.—Nine inspectors of the lines, directors of the offices; 44 directors of offices; 23 sub-directors; 225 telegraphists, (operators;) 49 clerks; 142 manufacturers of instruments.

"PERSONNEL OF TECHNICAL SERVICE.—Ten conductors; 10 inspectors.

"NET-WORK OF THE STATE.—Length of lines, 2,328.3 kilometers, (about 447 English miles;) length of wires, 6,863.2 kilometres, (about 1,340 English miles.)

"NUMBER OF OFFICES.—Of the state, including four auxiliary, 87; of private companies, 107. (Among those last offices, there are 38 which, being established, [*dans des localités de service,*] by the bureaus of the state, are not inserted in this list.)

"NUMBER OF APPARATUS.—Morse system, 216. Some steps have been taken to introduce the Hughes apparatus upon some of the lines of the Netherlands net-work.

"WORK OF 1867.—	
Number of internal dispatches	492,733
Number of international dispatches...	370,340
Number of *in transitu* dispatches	249,964
Number of dispatches (*de service*) in service of the line....................	7,188
Total	1,120,225

"Receipts, 495,800.40 florins Holland.

"The uniform tax for the telegraphic correspondence between two Netherland offices, whether they pertain to the state or to some private company, has been reduced since the 1st of January, 1868, from 0.50 to 0.30 florins of Holland for one simple dispatch." * * *

PRUSSIA.

In a letter from Professor Morse, dated February 15, 1868, to Herr von Chauvin, director general of the Prussian telegraphs, he requested answers to the following questions:

"1. Can you oblige me by furnishing me with a copy of the tariff of charges on telegrams in Prussia, and, as far as practicable, in other countries?

"2. The number and names of the telegraph systems in use in Prussia; how many of each system are employed, and their adaptedness or fitness for particular service?

"3. The average number of messages or telegrams of a certain length sent daily?

"4. The comparative number capable of being sent by each system?

"5. The proportion between those of government service, and for private or commercial service?

"6. Where can telegraphic maps be obtained?

"7. Is the English needle system anywhere in use on the Prussian lines?"

To these questions the obliging director general made the following answers, in a letter dated March 6, 1868:

"1. The tariff applicable to the telegraphic correspondence of North Germany is determined as follows:

"*a.* For dispatches exchanged between the bureaus of the North German Confederation: First zone, (distance of 14 German miles,) 5 silver groschen; second zone, (distance of 50 German miles,) 10 silver groschen; third zone, (distance over 50 German miles,) 15 silver groschen.

"*b.* For dispatches exchanged between North Germany and the other states belonging to the South German Telegraphic Union, (Austria, Bavaria, Wurtemberg, and Baden:) First zone, (distance of 10 miles,) 8 silver groschen; second zone, (distance of 45 miles,) 16 silver groschen; third zone, (over 45 miles,) 24 silver groschen.

"*c.* Dispatches destined for other European states are taxed in conformity with the tariff prescribed by the convention of Paris. * * * (This tariff fixes the terminal or final tax, which reverts to each state for the correspondence, (*en provénance,*) or at the destination of its offices, and that of transit, which reverts to each state for the correspondence which passes through its territory.) The taxes mentioned above apply to the simple dispatch of twenty words.

"2. The telegraphic systems adopted by my administration are the Morse apparatus, the Hughes apparatus, and the Siemens type apparatus.

"The Hughes apparatus is principally fitted to operate upon the direct lines which are freed from the labor of the intermediate offices, and upon which the correspondence is very active and continuous. It operates between Berlin on the one side, and Paris, Vienna, Warsaw, Frankfort-on-the-Main, Breslau, Koenigsberg, Hamburg, Cologne, on the other side.

"The type apparatus of Siemens is employed in the exchange of correspondence between the large cities of Prussia.

"In the North German offices, (not including those of the railways,) there are in actual use of the apparatus Morse, 2,692; apparatus Hughes, 24; apparatus Siemens, 6.

"3. The mean number of dispatches daily transmitted by the North German offices (not including the dispatches in transit) is 7,075.

"4. The comparative number of dispatches which can be transmitted by the different systems in the space of one hour is, [1] 20 to 30 for the Morse apparatus; 40 to 50 for the Hughes apparatus; 60 for the Siemens apparatus.

"5. The dispatches indicated above are in the following ratio: 2.6 per cent. dispatches of the state; 2.2 per cent. dispatches of the service; 95.2 per cent. private dispatches.

"6. The English needle apparatus has never been in use in Prussia."

Two Morse instruments cost 111 florins each, or 222 florins. The

[1] See Chapter V for a correction of this estimate.

two together cost less than one-third of the cost of one of the Hughes apparatus. If, then, 'two Morse instruments are employed, with one operator to each instrument, which is equivalent to the manning of one Hughes, we have the means of doubling the number of dispatches, in the comparison of the two apparatus, (the Morse and the Hughes.) But the recent tests of the capacity of the Morse show that a single Morse instrument can transmit even as high as 130 dispatches, of twenty words each, in one hour, while a single Hughes instrument can transmit at the utmost from fifty to sixty per hour.

We have, therefore, this result: Two Morse: two operators; cost, 222 florins; 260 dispatches. One Hughes: two operators; cost, 700 florins; 60 dispatches.

REMARK.—If two Morse apparatus are employed at the same time, each requires a circuit, that is, two circuits, while the Hughes requires but one. This makes an important difference in the calculation; but still the result is one hundred and forty in favor of the work of the two Morse apparatus against the work of one Hughes apparatus.

DENMARK.

LETTER OF DIRECTOR GENERAL FABER.

In answer to questions similar to those addressed to the telegraphic administrations of other countries, the following information has been furnished by the director general of Danish telegraphs in a letter to the Hon. George H. Yeaman, United States minister to Denmark, dated May 2, 1868:

"1. Throughout this kingdom the Morse telegraphic system is the only one used on the government lines as well as on private and railway lines, the instruments being partially of an older construction with relays, partially newer ones without relays, and writing with ink. The fire telegraph in this city has magnetic-induction dial instruments o the manufacture of Messrs. Siemens and Halske, in Berlin. The English needle system is nowhere in public use in Denmark. On the lines of the government we have 124 Morse instruments; on private lines, 21 Morse instruments; on railway lines, 58 Morse instruments; on the fire telegraph line in Copenhagen, 22 induction dial instruments.

"2. The government lines have an extension of 950 miles English, containing 2,298 miles of single wire; the private lines have an extension of 324 miles, with 338 miles of single wire; the railway lines have an extension of 265 miles, with 275 miles of single wire; the fire telegraph in this city contains 11 miles of line by 20 miles of single wire.

"3. According to the experience made in this country, I should prefer:

"For long distances and for short ones, the Morse system with a line current; for railway service, the same with constant current; for city or domestic use, the magnetic-induction dial apparatus of Messrs. Siemens and Halske.

"4. The account of the last year, as we take it here from April 1 to March 31, having not yet been quite finished, an exact indication of the aggregate receipts and expenses cannot be given. Approximately the receipts of the government telegraph have amounted to 151,500 rigsdaler, and the expenses to 142,330 rigsdaler, of which latter 24,650 rigsdaler are costs of maintenance. One hundred and fifty functionaries are engaged in the telegraph service of the government. The number of those in private and railway telegraph service I cannot state exactly, but calculate it to be about eighty.

"5. According to the desires expressed by Professor Morse, I append to this a map of the telegraph lines and stations in Denmark, a statistical survey of the traffic on the Danish lines in the year 1867, and a representation of the extension of the government, from their first establishment to the expiration of the year 1866."

SWEDEN.

LETTER OF DIRECTOR GENERAL BRÄNDSTRÖM.

The following is a letter from the director general of Swedish telegraphs to his excellency General Bartlett, United States minister resident at the court of Sweden, dated Stockholm, April 19, 1868:

"I have the honor to acknowledge the receipt of your letter of the 14th instant accompanied with that of Professor Morse, addressed to you of the date of March 18 last, and I hasten to answer the questions of the professor respecting Sweden.

"As to Norway, whose offices and telegraph lines are under the jurisdiction of a special administration, I am persuaded that you will obtain all necessary explanations by addressing the chief of this administration, M. le Directeur Nielson, whose address is Christiania.

"It is the system Morse, which is exclusively adopted for all the offices of the administration of telegraphs in Sweden. This system is also employed for all the telegraph offices of the railways, except in some small offices where the dial apparatus is used.

"The English needle system has not been used in any part of Sweden.

"It is probable that sooner or later the administration of the telegraphs will adopt, for some of the principal lines, the Hughes system, but at the present time we have none of this apparatus.

"In regard to the organization of the Swedish telegraphs, the extension of the lines belonging to the administration of the telegraphs, the expenses for repairs of these lines, the internal taxes of the country, &c., I hope that Mr. Morse will find sufficient explanations in consulting the accompanying printed papers, to wit: First, notices of the organization of the Swedish telegraphs, and statistical table of the action *(du mouvement)* of the dispatches during the year 1866; and, second, international notification of the Swedish administration of the telegraphs, to the date of April 27, 1868, containing statistical information for the year 1867.

"The accompanying map indicates all the telegraph offices of the country. The lines marked as being in construction are already completed." * * * *

The following is the information alluded to in the foregoing letter, issued as a circular by Director General Brändström, and dated April 27, 1868:

"Conformably to article 57 of the convention of Paris, we have already had the honor to send to you, on February 27 last, the map of our telegraphic net-work prepared to the end of the year 1867.

"Here is some statistical information upon the personnel, the offices in service, and the extent of the lines and the telegraph wires at the same epoch, as well as a table of the action of the dispatches upon the Swedish net-work during the said year.

PERSONNEL.

a. Central administration.—One director general, 2 inspectors general, 2 assistant inspectors general, 1 professor of physics, (*physicien,*) 1 intendant general of economy and accounts, 1 secretary-in-chief, 1 keeper of the records, 1 keeper of the books, 1 cashier, 1 intendant of the materials, 2 examiners, 5 other employés—total, 19 persons.

"*b. Employés in the electric offices.*—Thirteen directors, chiefs of the principal offices; 86 commissaries, chiefs of offices of the second and third classes, or placed in an office of the first class, either as assistants of the chief or as cashiers; 169 assistants, chiefs of the smaller offices, (of whom 21 are women,) or employed in the others—in all, 268 persons.

"*c. Employés in the optical offices.*—Eighteen chiefs of offices; 22 employés, subalterns—in all, 40 persons.

"TELEGRAPHIC OFFICES.—Offices belonging to the telegraphic administration—

(*a.*) Electric	96
(*b.*) Optical	18
	114
Offices of state railways, (of which 21 are open for international correspondence)	91
Offices of private companies, (of which 23 are open for international correspondence)	70
Total	275

"The number of apparatus, (Morse system,) employed in the offices of the telegraph administration is 277.

"*Lines of the telegraph administration.*

	Length of lines.	Length of wire conductors.
	Kilometers.	*Kilometers.*
Lines established on the railways	1, 033	3, 420
Lines established on the great roads	4, 525	8, 273
Submarine cable between Sweden and the Isle of Gotland	103	103
Submarine cable between Sweden and the Isle of Oland	3	3
	5, 664	11, 799

	Kilometers.
Lines with one wire	2, 089
Lines with two wires	1, 903
Lines with three wires	1, 172
Lines with four wires	312
Lines with five wires	82
Lines with six wires	45
Lines with seven wires	30
Lines with eight wires	31
Total length of the wires	5, 664

"The submarine cable between Sweden and Prussia, which is seventy-three kilometers in length, and contains three wire conductors, belongs in common to the two countries.

"At the same time Sweden possesses, in conjunction with Denmark, the cable laid in the Sound. This cable is fifteen kilometers long, and contains four wire conductors, of which, however, only two are in use.

"*International correspondence in* 1867.

Names of the states.	Number of dispatches from the state, and private dispatches sent from Sweden for Norway and foreign countries.	Number of dispatches from the state, and private dispatches received in Sweden from Norway and from foreign countries.	Total.
Norway	14, 802	11, 532	26, 334
Algiers and Tunis	85	61	146
North America	4	8	12
Austria	112	141	253
Baden	37	46	83
Bavaria	58	42	100
Belgium	704	711	1, 415
Bremen	345	254	599
Denmark	14, 705	16, 698	31, 403

"*International correspondence in* 1867—Continued.

Names of the states.	Number of dispatches from the state, and private dispatches sent from Sweden for Norway and foreign countries.	Number of dispatches from the state, and private dispatches received in Sweden from Norway and from foreign countries.	Total.
Egypt	2	3	5
Spain	354	351	705
Finland	1,989	2,057	4,046
France	3,295	3,256	6,551
Great Britain and Ireland	9,702	10,598	20,300
Hamburg	4,587	4,911	9,498
Italy	234	252	486
Lubec	1,201	988	2,189
Malta	1	8	9
Mecklenburg	344	407	751
Moldavia, Wallachia	5	2	7
Holland	1,053	1,010	2,063
Portugal	124	140	264
Prussia	4,004	3,743	7,747
Russia, European, (except Finland)	2,144	1,967	4,111
Saxony	144	98	242
Switzerland	131	126	257
Turkey, European	5	19	24
Tnrkey, Asiatic	1	1	2
Wurtemberg	21	16	37
Other German states	84	94	178
	60,277	59,540	119,817

"*Comparative table of the transmission of dispatches, and their receipt in* 1866, 1867.

	1866.			1867.			Increase in 1867.			
	Number of dispatches.	Proportional number.	Receipts.	Number of dispatches.	Proportional number.	Receipts.	Dispatches.		Receipts.	
		P'r ct.	*Francs.*		*P'r ct.*	*Francs.*	*Number.*	*P'r ct.*	*Francs.*	*P'r ct.*
Service, interior	272,834	64.2	402,645	314,025	63.3	528,894	41,191	15.1	66,249	14.3
Service, international	94,974	22.3	440,909	120,943	24.4	441,991	25,969	27.3	1,082	0.25
Transit	57,098	13.5		61,137	12.3		4,039	7.1		
Total	424,906	100	903,554	496,105	100	970,885	71,199	16.8	57,774	7.45

"*Revenues and receipts for the year* 1867.

"For the electric lines:

1. Revenues:

	Francs.
a. Receipt proceeding from the correspondence........	961,328
b. Contribution from certain communes for the rents of the offices, &c........	9,556
c. Subsidy accorded by the government for the construction of new lines, and the multiplication of wire conductors........	263,320
Total........	1,234,204

2. Expenses:

a. Salaries of the officers, repair of the old lines, &c....	905,150
b. Construction of new lines, and multiplication of wires.	248,504

"For the optical lines, (semaphores:)

1. Revenues:

a. Receipts proceeding from correspondence........	3,332
b. Subsidy accorded by government........	40,781
Total........	44,113

2. Expenses:

Salaries of officers, and repairs of the telegraph, &c....	42,066

SPAIN.

LETTER FROM DIRECTOR GENERAL SANZ.

The following is a letter from the director general of Spanish telegraphs to the minister of the United States, John P. Hale, dated Madrid, April 27, 1868:

"In reply to your valued favor of the 21st instant, I, to-day, have the pleasure of giving you the following information, which you have requested of me:

"The system of telegraphs used in the government lines in Spain is solely and exclusively that of Morse. As an auxiliary to this apparatus, there is also used an English needle for the purpose of observing the calls at one end of the line when the Morse apparatus is being used at the other.

"The extent of the lines is 10,735 kilometers, and of the wires 24,134 kilometers.

"As the Morse system is the only one used, there is, of course, no means of comparing it with others.

"The railway companies use for their purposes Breguet's dial apparatus.

"The receipts for charges on dispatches amount to 8,424,510 reals, (equal to $42,122 55 gold.)

"The personal expenses (pay of officers, operators, &c.) amount to 9,044,500 reals, ($45,222 50 gold,) and the expenses for working materials (wires, chemicals, &c.) to 3,704,020 reals, ($18,520 10 gold.)

"I inclose a telegraphic map and other documents, which may serve to give a detailed knowledge of the organization of the telegraphic system in Spain, and also the letter which was put into my hands at the central office."

ITALY.

From Italy, in addition to answers to questions, there have been received, through the prompt attention of the United States minister to Italy, his excellency George P. Marsh, a large number of valuable public documents, relating to the telegraph, which have been sent to the department at Washington.

The following are the statistical data of Italian telegraphs furnished by the director general, in answer to the same questions which had been addressed to other telegraph administrations:

"I. On January 1, 1868, there were in operation—

Morse apparatus	1,017
Hughes apparatus	14
Total	1,031

"II. Miles of line, 9,496 English miles; miles of wire, 22,211 English miles.

"III. Apparatus best adapted for long distances and for short ones: The Hughes, if the lines are in the best condition, and with much difficulty, otherwise the Morse. For railway service: The Morse. For city or domestic use: This service has not yet in Italy had any great development. What there is now in the city is done by the Morse apparatus. If this service becomes more active the Hughes may be better, or better the tubular system adopted in Paris and Berlin.

"Effective revenues for private dispatches of 1867, 4,278,925 francs; ordinary expenses, 4,100,000 francs; extraordinary expenses, 180,000 francs; cost of apparatus and other material, (see allegato *o*;) personal expenses for maintenance of the apparatus of 1867, 24,168.50 francs, adding a small sum for the purchase of small materials for repairs. Total number of employés, 2,374. (For distinction of grades and classes see table marked *a*, and the manuscript of the allegato *a*.)

"IV. No English system is in use in any part whatever of Italy.

"V. For fuller information on the condition of the telegraph in Italy see the accompanying documents."[1]

---

[1] The documents alluded to have been forwarded to the department, and are as follows:

(*a*.) Organico dell' Amministrazione dei Telegrafi Italiani, del 18 Settembre, 1865, e successive variazioni, 17 Ottobre, 1866, e 8 Dicembre, 1867.

(*b*.) Regolamento pel servizio dei telegrafi, del 4 Marzo, 1866.

EGYPT.

The telegraph administration in Egypt was addressed through the United States consul general, Hon. Charles Hale, in Alexandria, and, through his prompt attention, the following information, supplied by Hartley J. Gibson, esq., director of Egyptian telegraphs, was received in reply to questions proposed:

"Question 1. Please give the names of the telegraph systems employed in the Egyptian dominions, and the number of each system.

"Answer. The Egyptian government telegraphs under my direction are confined to those in the Soudan country, the whole of which are worked on the 'Morse' system.

"Question 2. How many miles (English) of telegraph connection, and how many miles of telegraph wires?

"Answer. They commence at Assouan, and are all in construction. The whole lines are constructed with two wires, (No. 8, not galvanized,) thus affording two lines.

Telegraph lines in Egypt.

	Miles line.	Miles wire.
Assouan to Wady Halfa	215	430
Wady Halfa to Ourdeh	260	520
Ourdeh to Ambaked	120	240
Ambaked to Berber	170	340
Berber to Metammeh	110	220
Metammeh to Khartum	112	224
Berber to Kassala	240	480
Kassala to Souakim	270	540
Massouah to Kassala	250	500
	1,747	3,494

(*c*.) Regolamento per la correspondenza telegrafica nell' interno dello stato, del 10 Dicembre, 1865.

(*d*.) Servizio dei vaglia telegrafici.

(*e*.) Servizio dei vaglia semaforico.

(*f*.) Servizio dei nell' interno delli cittá.

(*g*.) Tariffa generale dei despacci.

(*h*.) Guida indice dei circuiti e uffici del regno.

(*i*.) Casta delle linea telegrafiche di correspondenza generale ed internazionale, 1 Giugnio, 1867.

(*k*.) Casta delle linea telegrafiche di tutti i fili, 1 Giugnio, 1867.

(*l*.) Casta delle linea telegrafiche delle distanze del 1865.

(*m*.) Tavola delle communicazione pel systema "Morse."

(*n*.) Modelli degli isolatori in uso.

(*o*.) Nomenclatura e prezzi del materiale.

(*p*.) Relazione statistica pel biennio 1865'-66.

(*q*.) Bullettino telegrafico. Publicazione mensile còntinente disposizioni ufficiali, e una parte non ufficiale di studi, invenzioni e notizie diversa si unisce quello, di Marzo, 1868.

"The line between Assouan and Berber is completed, with the exception of the section between Wady Halfa and Ourdeh. This part of the country is so infested with white ants that iron posts are a necessity. These have accordingly been procured and sent to their destination, and before the end of November, (1868,) this section will be completed.

"The section between Massouah and Kassala has not yet been commenced. That between Berber and Kassala is under construction, and on its completion in November next, that between Berber, Metammeh, and Khartum will be undertaken.

"Independently of the towns mentioned, there are others on the route where stations exist, and many intermediate ones will be hereafter organized.

"Of the delta telegraph lines I refrain now from speaking; but I believe there are about 820 miles of line, a considerable portion of which comprise two or more wires.

"Between Alexandria and Cairo (135 miles) they have one wire, worked on the 'Morse' system. The line also from Cairo to Gaza (300 miles) is worked by that system; on all the rest, including about 600 miles from Cairo to Assouan, the double needle is used.

"Question 3. Which system has experience shown to be best adapted to the following purposes, to wit: A, for long distances; B, for short distances; C, for railway service; D, for city or domestic use?

"Answer. With regard to your question 3, my experience goes to prove the following: A, the 'Morse;' B, the 'needle;' C, the 'needle;' D, the 'Morse.'

"Question 4. What are the aggregate expenses and receipts, cost of instruments, of maintenance, and number of employés?

"Answer. Quite unanswerable.

"As a postscript to my note, I add, that the telegraph lines owned by foreign nations in Egypt are three, to wit: 1st. The Mediterranean and Malta Company's line, Alexandria to Suez, 220 miles of line, 440 miles of wire. 'Morse system.' 2d. The Suez Canal Company, from Zagazig to the Isthmus, (distance unknown.) 'Morse system.' 3d. The Alexandria and Ramleh Railway Company's line, (five miles,) ten miles wire. 'Needle.'

"A line is proposed by the Egyptian government from Zagazig to Wady."

TURKEY.

LETTER FROM HON. J. P. BROWN.

The following letter, of the date of June 1, 1868, has been received from Hon. John P. Brown, secretary of legation to the Ottoman Porte, in answer to one addressed to him in relation to Turkish telegraphs:

"Many thanks for your interesting pamphlets on the subject of your invention of the telegraph. Dr. Staniatades, of this city, was a pupil at the college, (New York City university,) when your discovery was originally made known, and can vouch for what you have stated therein. He remembers clearly that you were the sole inventor. I feel much interest in all that concerns yourself and the telegraph, from the fact that I first spoke of it personally to his late Majesty Sultan Abdul Mejid, and with Dr. J. L. Smith, of Louisville, Kentucky, and Dr. C. Hamlin, exhibited the wonderful invention to his Majesty and all of his ministers and others at the palace of Beyler Bey on the Bosphorus.

"His Majesty wished them to have it put up between his capital and Smyrna, and I told him that I feared the people would cut the wires. Since then 'Morse's telegraph' is spread over the whole of the empire.

"The minister resident has sent me your two letters of inquiry, and I will in a day or two report to him on the same. In the mean time I have been able to report to him that the 'English needle system' is *not* used in any part of this empire. The present minister of public works, telegraphs, &c., is H. G. Daûd Pacha, a Catholic Christian, (late governor general of the Lebanon,) and a very learned and intelligent man.

"A Mr. Hughes (an American) was here some time since, at the request of the Porte, to instruct pupils in his system, (I believe one which prints the letters;) and I suppose the report which I am promised from the director will show this. At all times ready to be of any service to you."

The following is a letter to his excellency E. Joy Morris, United States minister to the Ottoman Porte, from James Millingen, esq., director of telegraphs, dated Pera, June 4, 1868:

"I have the honor to communicate, according to your request, the information respecting the Ottoman telegraph administration, accompanied with a map of the telegraphic net-work.

"In 1863 our net-work comprised 6,490 kilometers of lines, and 13,821 kilometers of wires, and 52 stations.

"To-day we possess 27,500 kilometers of lines, 56,230 kilometers of wires, and 310 stations, divided into stations of international service, and stations of interior service. Consequently, in the space of five years, our net-work has more than quadrupled.

"We are connected directly with Austria by three routes, Mostar-Melkovich, Scodra-Castellastua, and Gradiska; Italy, by Valona, Otrente; the principalities Moldo-Valques, by three routes, Tultcha-Ismail, Tultcha-Galatz, and Rustchuk-Giurgevo; Serbia, by two routes, Nissa-Alexinatz and Widdin-Negotin; Persia, by Hannokin (haggi Cara) Kirmanohah; Egypt, by Gaza-Elarich; Greece, by Polo-Lamia; and, finally, with the Indian telegraphic net-work, by the cable ending at Fao.

"The cables which put the Ottoman empire in communication with the Archipelago, and which belong to an English company, are nearly all interrupted; but, according to advices we have recently received, we hope they will shortly be re-established.

"We have but a few small cables in the Bosphorus, to the Dardanelles, and in the Danube: four in the Bosphorus, of 1,500 meters each, of which two are for the Indian transit; two to the Dardanelles, of 3,000 meters each; five in the Danube, of which two above Ismail, of 1,000 meters each; one above Galatz, of 1,500 meters; one above Soulina, of 1,500 meters; and one above Rustchuk, of 1,500 meters.

"All our great lines are constructed with two wires of galvanized iron of four millimeters in diameter. Some small branch lines, or for interior service, are constructed with wire of three millimeters diameter.

"The great Asiatic line from Constantinople to Fao has been constructed with two wires of six millimeters, because of the great distances of the stations. In fact, the mean distance of these stations is 102 kilometers; but from Kerhuk to Bagdad it is calculated at little less than 350 kilometers; and, in short, Moussoul works with Bagdad, a distance of 520 kilometers, without intermediate relays.

"Upon the line from Asia, Pera works sometimes direct with Sivas, a distance of 910 kilometers, without intermediate relays. All these wires of the first quality are annealed with charcoal.

"The insulators employed are, of the Siemens model, in castings of metal; the French model, in porcelain, furnished by the house of Brequet. For some time we commenced to employ the Belgian collar-model.

"In consequence of the difficulties of the ground, the want of railroads, and of carriage ways, the lines followed tracts for the most part arbitrary. But the present direction is turning its attention to rectifying these, as far as possible, by taking advantage of new routes, which are being constructed in different parts of the empire.

"Our posts are of oak, and some of them of pine, (spruce.) They are neither injected nor carbonized at their base.

"The administration thinks seriously of the improvement of construction, which owes its delay only to some local difficulties.

"The apparatus employed are all of the Morse system, furnished by the manufacturers, Bréguet, Siemens & Mouilleron, to the number of 1,020. We employ, also, the apparatus Hughes, upon the great line of transit from Pera to Valona, and also between Pera and Semlin; soon it will be put between Pera and Bagdad to facilitate the Indian correspondence. This apparatus is better for a long line, while for shorter distances the apparatus Morse is more convenient.

"The dial apparatus are no longer employed upon our lines. They require to operate all these apparatus about 16,000 Daniel elements, French model.

"Towards Bagdad we have some posts *(en fonte)* of cast iron, which have not given the results that we expected, as the administration has given them up to be employed on other lines. During the winter we have had to contend against violent winds, tempests, and inundations, which have raised and prostrated the posts, for our lines traverse forests, precipices, ravines, and some abrupt mountains, where the superintendence and the repairs were difficult to be executed, but with the actual repairs of the tracks these inconveniences have nearly completely disappeared. In certain countries some turbulent hordes often interrupt the communication from malevolence or from simple curiosity, believing that they can by this means discover the mysteries of the telegraph. Accustomed to-day to this new mode of correspondence and influenced by such measures that they are interested in the good repair of the line, we have no longer any fear on that score.

"Upon certain parts of our lines the wires are covered every winter with a layer of frost which attains sometimes a prodigious thickness, so as to render the wires ten times heavier than in their normal state, producing numerous breaks.

"This fact, which occurs always in the same places, and the results of which are so difficult to avoid, is not known to be explained but by a special meteorological tendency of the places.

"The direction seeks to avoid these places in removing the lines every time that repairs are necessary. In spite of these inconveniences without number, thanks to an inspection well organized, the interruptions are of less duration, and for nearly five months the Indian transit has not been interrupted a single instant. In fact, Constantinople is in direct communication every night with Vienna on the one side, and Fao upon the Persian Gulf on the other. Vienna has worked many times with Diarbekir, Alexinatz, and Semlin with Fao. Pera, at the same time, communicates with Bushire, in the south of Persia, and with Kurachée, the first Indian station, a distance of about five thousand kilometers.

"Notwithstanding the above-mentioned obstacles, results like these make comment unnecessary, for they suffice to give an exact idea of the actual Ottoman telegraph.

"These ameliorations are due to measures taken nearly two years ago at the creation of responsible inspectors, and, in short, to the complete reorganization of the direction.

"Before closing it will not be amiss to notice the existence of two services, distinct and very different—the international service in the European languages, and the interior service in the Turkish language, services which cannot be confounded, seeing the impossibility of assimilating the letters of the two alphabets, that which requires a double personnel and involves a multitude of other difficulties that cannot be overcome, but by practice the experience of many years, and some recent improvements.

"The Indian dispatches reach us ordinarily on the same day, and are transmitted immediately to Valona, Belgrade, or Vienna; but the English public has raised many complaints on the subject of the delay experienced in these dispatches. We ought to remark on this subject, that the said dispatches do not come all the way in our territory, and that we often even receive them from the foreign post offices with an ancient date, and that, in short, the person to whom they are addressed seldom knows by what way his dispatch is to come to him.

"Dispatches for India can go three different ways: 1. The way through Turkey to Fao, and the cable in the Persian Gulf. 2. The way through Turkey as far as Hannékin, and from there the Persian route by Bushire. 3. Finally, the Russo-Persian way, without passing through Turkey.

"After a special convention the dispatches we receive from Europe for the Indies ought to be transmitted by us in equal parts by the way of Fao and by the way of Hannékin. We receive them ordinarily from Europe by the way of Valona or Belgrade.

"There are also some errors which render the dispatches sometimes undecipherable. The Turks, to remedy these inconveniences, have placed upon all the lines of the great Asiatic line special employés, for the most part English, and who are charged with the control of these dispatches. Further, it is a recognized fact that nearly all our employés are more or less linguists, a fact which necessarily facilitates the exchange of international correspondence." * * *

AUSTRALIA.

Samuel W. McGowan, esq., general superintendent of electric telegraph in Victoria, (Australia,) has politely furnished two reports of the advancement and condition of his department for 1867 and 1868, which have been forwarded to the State Department at Washington. They contain maps of telegraph lines in a portion of Australia, and tables of the financial condition of the department under his charge.

In his report of 1867 he alludes to orders for two of "Messrs. Siemens & Halske's patent rapid writing type instruments," and also for "one of Professor Wheatstone's patent rapid writing instruments," which it was thought would afford greater facilities for speedy transmission. Respecting these, Mr. McGowan remarks: "In working either apparatus it is essentially necessary that the line should be in the best possible state of electric conductivity and insulation. Atmospheric disturbances or other existing cause would militate much more against successful transmission than under ordinary circumstances. It must also be borne in mind that in using the rapid writing instruments, the *staff of operators* at each terminal of the line will require to be largely augmented—the one for preparing the type or other transmitting material, the other for effecting the task of transcribing the matter as received from the recording instrument."

This necessity for the augmentation of the number of employés is a disadvantage complained of at Berlin as one of the great difficulties in the automatic type-printing apparatus of Messrs. Siemens & Halske.

By reference to Mr. McGowan's report for 1868, this remark will be found: "The order for a supply of the rapid writing automatic instruments mentioned in my last report has been canceled, owing to the enhanced cost of manufacture, and the probable gain in the working of the lines being overborne by the large expenditure involved."

The following questions were addressed to Samuel Walker McGowan, esq., superintendent general of telegraphs in Victoria, Australia, and the answers annexed returned under date of November 9, 1868:

"1. What systems of electro-telegraphic communication are in use in Australia?

"2. How many instruments of each system?

"3. Which system has your experience shown to be the best adapted to the various services required?

"4. Is the English needle system in use in Australia; and if so, to what extent?"

"Answer 1. The system known as Morse's electro-magnetic recording telegraph, and (to a small extent for local purposes,) Wheatstone's visual alphabetical magneto-induction telegraph.

"Answer 2. Of the Morse system there are—

In Victoria	87
In New South Wales	62
In Queensland	33
In South Australia	66
In New Zealand	25
In Tasmania	7
Total	280

"I do not take into account any other system, as none other is employed on the lines throughout the country. Professor Wheatstone's instruments are employed for local lines between the government offices, &c., and are not, so far as I am aware, used on any of the ordinary lines.

"Answer 3. I have no hesitation in giving my opinion in favor of the Morse system for all purposes requiring the transmission of large correspondence, where simplicity, accuracy, and the retention of a record of all messages, as actually transmitted, are matters of importance. During an experience of nearly twenty-two years solely devoted to my present profession, I have seen many other systems in practical operation, but none with which I am acquainted appears to me to fulfill so thoroughly all the requirements of a really efficient telegraph as the particular system now under mention.

"Answer 4. The English single and double needle system (Henley's magneto-induction instruments) was in use on some short railway lines in South Australia for a few years, but it has since been replaced by Morse instruments."

The expansion of the telegraph in Australia, in the three years 1863, 1864, 1865, is indicated in the following table:

Telegraph lines in Australia.

Year.	No. of stations.	No. of miles wire.	No. of telegrams.	Receipts.
1863	66	2, 585¼	234, 520	£24, 733
1864	70	2, 626¼	256, 380	29, 122
1865	79	3, 110½	279, 741	*34, 770

* In 1867 there were in the colony of Victoria 86 stations, 2,526¼ miles of line, and 3,119½ miles of wire.

In the Australian Return to Parliament for 1867, in the Appendix B, at p. 26, there is a column headed "Average number of words per hour." The minimum is 800 words = 40 dispatches; the maximum is 1,500 words = 75 dispatches per hour. It is worthy of notice that these dispatches are sent by the Morse apparatus, and that, therefore, the skill of the Australian operators is far greater than that of their European brethren, their minimum being double the number of dispatches sent by the same apparatus in Europe, and nearly equal to the number ordinarily transmitted by the operators in the United States, while their maximum number is triple the number of the European operators in the same time.

PERU.

Through the courtesy of his excellency Signor Bareda, the Peruvian minister to the United States, the following information has been obtained in answer to questions proposed to the Telegraph Administration of Peru:

"Question 1. What systems of telegraphy are in use in Peru, and the number of instruments under each system?"

"Answer. In the first line established in Peru (from Lima to Callao) the French system of Bréguet (the dial system) was used. This was changed on the formation of the 'National Telegraph Company,' which substituted that of Morse with closed circuit, *(circuito cerrado.)* There is a double line between those places, and four apparatus are employed. Since the years 1865, 1866, two lines were built by the government, one between Tacua and Arica, (44 miles,) and another between Arequipa and Islay, (90 miles,) and both of these lines employ the Morse system. Each line is simple, and consequently only four apparatus are in use, (one for each station.")

"Question 2. How many English miles of telegraph *connection*,[1] and how many miles of wire?

"Answer. By supreme decree of July 26, 1867, permission was given

[1] From some cause this question was misapprehended, and is answered as if it had been "telegraphic concession," instead of "telegraph connection."

to Don Carloz Paz Soldan, without guarantee or subsidy, to organize a 'National Telegraph Company,' which should build a line between Callao and Lima, and as far as Lambayeque, (500 miles,) with stations in Chaneay, Huacho, Casma, Santa Trujillo, San Pedro, Chiclayo, and Lambayeque, and permission to extend lines to intermediate points.

"The government, by way of protection, and as compensation for a discount of fifty per cent. from the tariff in its favor, on messages, gave (as a loan at six per cent., payable in twenty years,) $50,000 worth of materials and telegraphic articles, which it had in the custom-house, at the cost of the whole at Callao.

"The company has already in operation the line between Callao and Lima, and to Huacho, (90 miles,) and is constructing between Huacho and Casma, (60 miles of this finished, and the work goes on.) Also it has a line to Chorillos, which is being extended to Pisco and Ica, and the completion of this line, already built as far as Mala, (60 miles from Lima,) is expected by the end of September, (160 miles to Ica.)

"The company has also commenced work on the line from Lima to Cerro de Pasco, (180 miles,) and this will be extended to Iarma, Jauja, Huancayo, Ayaeucho.

"At the time of giving the concession named to Paz Soldan, the government conceded permission to build the line between Lima and Ica, to one Morse, an American, with concession also of $25,000 in materials. This individual did not do anything, and has since died, and the concession now remains void, as the National Telegraph Company is finishing this line.

"The government of the dictator, Colonel Prado, offered $46,000 subsidy to an American company, which proposed to place a cable from Panama to Chiloe.

"As the acts of the dictatorship have been annulled, that concession also remains void.

"Recapitulating, there is no other pending concession than the one granted to the 'National Telegraph Company' for the line to Lambayeque, (500 miles.)

Lines already built:	
Arequipa to Islay, on account of government	90 miles.
Tacua to Arica, on account of government	44 miles.
Lines of National Company:	
Lima to Callao	6 miles.
Lima to Huacho	90 miles.
Lima to Mala	60 miles.
Line completed in Casana and Huamey	60 miles.
Total already built	350 miles.
In construction:	
Mala to Yca	100 miles.

Huamey to Huacho	66 miles.
Lima to Cerro de Pasco	180 miles.
Total	346 miles.

"It can be stated that at the end of this year (1868) we will have in operation 700 miles of telegraph.

"Question 3. Which system has experience shown to be best adapted to the following purposes, to wit: A, for long distances; B, for short distances; C, for railway service; D, for city or domestic use?

"Answer. To this question we cannot give particulars, on account of our short experience.

"Question 4. What are the aggregate expenses and receipts, cost of instruments, and maintenance, and number of employés?

"Answer. The expenses have not as yet been very large. You can state them now at $200 per mile. The receipts are calculated to give nine per cent. now, but when all the lines are in operation, will be twenty-five per cent. on capital. The cost of instruments is the same in all the markets from which we ask them, adding exchange. The number of employés which the government has on the two lines, between Arequipa and Islay, and Arica and Tacua, is twelve, and four directors, which is more than necessary. The National Company has now in five stations already opened, and three about to be opened, (also one at the palace for the use of the government,) say nine stations altogether, nineteen employés and ten conductors, and four horses, for the use of these; altogether twenty-nine employés.

"All its service is American. It has a building in Lima, with its various departments separate; another in Callao, and is about to buy in Huacho and Chancay—twelve instruments altogether.

"Question 5. Have you maps, documents, or other works illustrative of the extent and condition of the telegraph in any part of South America?

"Answer. We have no maps. By next steamer I will send more particulars, regulations, &c., and a letter I have written for the instruction of telegraphers.

"Question 6. Is the English needle system employed on any of the lines in South America?

"Answer. No."

APPENDICES.

A.—NUMBER OF THE MORSE APPARATUS USED IN EUROPE.

The following is the number of the Morse apparatus employed in the various European and Australian telegraph administrations in the year 1867:

France	1,600
Holland	216
Italy	1,017
Denmark	203
Austria	1,300
Switzerland	478
Belgium	590
Prussia	2,692
Ottoman Empire	1,020
Sweden	277
Australia	280
	9,673

In England, in one company, (the Electric and International Telegraph Company,) it is stated that there are 7,245 instruments. From this statement, taken in connection with another by the chairman of the company, that "the needle system first used had been superseded by the Morse," and "the ink-writer," which is also a Morse instrument, it may be inferred that the greater part of the 7,245 instruments are the Morse. Mr. Sabine, however, states that—

This company has in use of the Morse instruments	662
The United Kingdom Company	300
British and Irish London District Company	100
Total	1,062

From Russia, Spain, and Norway no official statement of the number of Morse instruments has been obtained; but an estimate made from a comparison of the proportion between the number of stations and instruments in other countries, renders it safe to estimate at a minimum—

Russia	624
Spain	262
Norway	110
	996

Exclusive, therefore, of the number of Morse instruments employed in the entire western continent, and Greece and Egypt, on the eastern continent, the numbers amount to 11,731 Morse instruments in use on the eastern continent. No direct statement of the number of Morse instruments in India has been obtained, but from the "return" to the House of Commons on the East India telegraphs, made June 22, 1868, sufficient information is gathered to give an estimate of the probable number. In casual conversation with one of the firm of a house which furnishes a good proportion of the telegraph apparatus for the United States, and mentioning the estimate of the number of Morse apparatus in use exclusive of America, (placing it at nearly 12,000,) he was asked for an estimate of the number in America. He replied that that number might be safely doubled for America alone, stating at the same time that every office had at least two instruments, and that in the last two months alone he had filled orders for 500 of the Morse sounder.

In the appendix of the "Return," D, p. 52, under "Tests upon which a signaller" (operator) "is to be promoted," one of the tests is "proficiency in transmitting and reading Morse signals." If, therefore, the Morse is employed in the same proportion to the number of offices as in other countries, the number of offices in 1866 is found to be 172, which makes the number of instruments 258. This number, added to the aggregate of 11,731, gives a total of 11,989 Morse instruments. Most offices or stations have two Morse instruments, sometimes more; hence in estimating the number of instruments, it has been assumed that the proportion between offices and instruments may safely be estimated at one and a half instruments to an office, or three instruments to two offices. On this basis the number of instruments in countries where the number is not definitely given has been estimated.

B—INVENTION OF THE TELEGRAPH.

TWO LETTERS ON THE QUESTION: "IS THE WORLD INDEBTED TO THE UNITED STATES FOR THE INVENTION OF THE TELEGRAPH?"

PARIS, *July* 18, 1868.

DEAR SIR: Being in company with some English friends a few evenings ago, there was a sharp controversy (conducted, however, with general good feeling) on the subject of the telegraph, and the question was raised: "To whom is the world indebted for the invention of the modern telegraph?" I contended that it was to the United States, while my English friends insisted that it was to England. On asking their authority for such a dictum, one of the gentlemen referred me to an article in the London Times, published in March or April, in which it was distinctly claimed that the world was indebted to England for the telegraph. He also seemed well posted in other documents, which he took from his library. I asked the favor of a loan of them for a few days. Let me quote from them:

1. In presenting the Albert Gold Medal of the Society of Arts in London, in November of last year, (1867,) to William Fothergill Cooke, esq., the chairman of the society claimed that it was conferred for the "practical introduction of the electric telegraph, not only to this country, (England,) but to every country in the world."

2. In a note also (p. 6) of editor's preface of a pamphlet by Rev. T. F. Cooke, (brother of the distinguished introducer of the electric semaphore into England,) he thus writes in commenting on the award of the society: "The award says, speaking of Mr. Cooke, 'To whom this country (England) is indebted.' Mr. Varley extends this claim, 'To whom *Europe* is indebted;' and another writer makes the claim absolute, 'To whom the *world* is indebted,' including *America*."

3. Then follows a note, which requires some explanation. He says: "This country (Great Britain) was the only country in which practical telegraphy was introduced at the date of the award, (April 27, 1841.) And on Dr. Hamel's authority we learn that Mr. Samuel Morse, of America, dates back his idea of an electric telegraph to 1832, and seems not to have known that the idea had existed for a century before. His signal apparatus, original, simple, and highly meritorious, was worked out gradually and very much later. It was not till 1844 that the first telegraph line from Washington to Baltimore was completed; when, on the 24th March, the first short telegram of four words (dictated by a Miss Ellsworth, and still preserved in the Historical Museum at Hartford, Connecticut, as the *first*,) announced the existence of a practical telegraph on the American continent. This was just five years after the Great Western Railway Telegraph was at work daily between London and Drayton, and after the varied experience of England was known and studied, both in Europe and America; and three years after the Brunel award was made publicly known."

4. In the very able pamphlet, "Government and the Telegraphs," presented to Parliament in opposition to the bill for the government purchase of the telegraphs, (attributed to the distinguished chairman of the Electric and International Telegraph Company, (Mr. Grimston,) the same claim is made to having given the telegraph to the world. It is in these words, at page 19: "The system they (the company) introduced has become, within a period of about twenty years, the basis from which has sprung not only all the systems of the United Kingdom, but the entire net-work of telegraphs throughout the globe."

5. As pertinent in this connection, I quote from page 11 of the same pamphlet the following passage relating to the instruments used by the company. After stating that "everything that has ever been proved to be practically useful had been adopted," he says: "This has been specially the case with regard to instruments. The earlier needle

instruments used in the principal circuits were soon superseded by Bain's printer. That again was superseded by the Morse instruments, which are now gradually giving way to the *ink writer*, an improved instrument on the same system."

These are a few of the extracts made from the journals and pamphlets which my English friend thought substantiated the English claim to the position, "that to England the world was indebted for the electric telegraph." I called at your hotel yesterday to show them to you, but to my grief you had left the country. I feel an interest, in common with some others of our countrymen, to know the truth in this matter, and I am sure I cannot apply to a more competent person than yourself for the facts. Will you not spare a little time to give them to me? I know some English women of high intellectual position who are quite as enthusiastic in espousing my side of the question as any American can be. Please direct care of C. B. Norton & Co., 16 Rue Auber.

I remain, with friendly regard, yours,

C.

Prof. S. F. B. MORSE, *New York, U. S. A.*

POUGHKEEPSIE, *September* 25, 1868.

MY DEAR SIR: Although absorbed just now in the labors of arranging my materials for my commissioners' report on the telegraph apparatus of the Paris Exposition, I snatch a few moments to answer your letter of the 18th July, and to remark on the extracts which you have quoted from publications, some of which I had already seen. Although the position taken by the English writers, from whose works you have made your extracts, is certainly untenable in the sense of having given the modern instrumental system of telegraphs to the world, yet the boast, regarded in the sense of extending the telegraph wires, cables, and land lines throughout the world, has some plausibility, since this extension, particularly in submarine lines, is greatly due to English capital, energy, and skill. But even in these qualities, the palm must be divided with the United States, France, Prussia, and Russia, to say nothing of the local assistance of other states through which the wires are carried.

If we look more closely into the composition of the telegraph as a whole, it will be seen that it is divided into two very distinct, yet correlative parts, to wit: The wire conductors or electrical thoroughfare, and the terminal instruments using this thoroughfare. A good illustration of these correlative parts is found in the railway system; there is the iron roadway and the locomotive. So, in the telegraph system, there is the iron roadway (the electrical conductors) and the instrumental system, for transmission over the way. The two parts, both in the railway and the telegraph, separated, would be inoperative for any useful purpose. The locomotive without the rail, and equally the rail without the locomotive, are inoperative. So the recording or signal instruments, without the conductors and the conductors without terminal instruments, are equally inoperative for any useful purpose.

There may be a difference of opinion regarding the relative importance of these two correlated parts, as there once was between the organist and the bellows-blower, (excuse the badinage,) the latter contending that in the production of the music the organist must use the copulative pronoun "*we*," when boasting of his performance, since without the labors of the blower the organ would be dumb.

Yet, to revert to the railroad illustration, the inventor of the locomotive, or its improver, works in a distinct department, and the builder of the road would not be entitled to claim for himself the merit of an improved locomotive, or the whole railroad, because he had extended the latter to a greater distance.

Since you have numbered your extracts, I will allude to them by their numbers.

Nos. 1, 2, and 4. On these extracts I observe that they furnish good examples of history made erroneous, by confounding things wholly unlike, by not regarding proper distinctions. Many errors proceeding from this source made it necessary for me to draw attention to the important distinction between the *semaphore* and the *telegraph*. I say important, because the proper definition of these terms removes from conflict the *meum* and *tuum* of two modes of communicating at a distance, differing in essential particulars in process and means from each other, yet treated of as conjoined under the name "telegraph" by most writers. The general use of the word, as applied to all modes of communicating at a distance, ought not to be cited as an objection to strict definition, when the progress and accuracy of history render such a definition a necessity. The improvement of the semaphore—indeed, the invention of the *electric needle semaphore*, so far, at least, as the making it a *practical instrumentality*—belongs to William Fothergill Cooke; but the telegraph, in its strict definition as a means of recording at a distance, belongs to Morse. The philological or etymological distinction, therefore, is not a fanciful, or captious, or capricious quibble.

3. In the note here quoted the telegraph and semaphore, as you perceive, are assumed to be the same invention, whereas the invention of Morse is a telegraph, and the invention of Cooke is a semaphore. Hence the events and dates set forth in this note are inapposite to prove priority. The question, which of the two systems was first practically introduced to public use, is discussed by the writer as if the date of the introduction settled the date of the invention.

The invention is one thing; its practical introduction quite another. They are referable each to different times. The time of the invention is one time, the time of its practical introduction is another; they may or may not be coincident. The invention, strictly speaking, must be precedent to its practical introduction. The agencies for the latter may be indefinitely delayed, without affecting the fact of the previous existence of that which is to be practically introduced.

There was no necessity for the writer's citation of Hamel as an authority that Morse dates back his idea of an electric telegraph to 1832. (Hamel, I may say in passing, is no authority for any statement affecting me.) This citation is accompanied by a reflection upon my supposed ignorance of the fact that the "idea" had existed "a century before." What idea? The idea of the possibility of using electricity as a means of communicating at a distance may have been a century old, but that was not my idea of 1832. The idea of 1832 was the possibility of *producing an automatic record at a distance by means of electricity*—the idea of a true telegraph—and this original idea was immediately followed by devising the process and means for carrying the idea into effect. This was the new idea of 1832, now realized in the adoption of the Morse telegraphic system throughout the world.

If it was necessary for the writer to cite an authority to prove that I dated back my idea of an electric telegraph to 1832, there was better authority at hand than that of the prejudiced Dr. Hamel to show what that idea was. The Chief Justice of the United States, in delivering the decision of the Supreme Court, says: "The evidence is full and clear that when he (Morse) was returning from Europe in 1832, he was deeply engaged upon this subject during the voyage, and that *the process and means were so far developed and arranged* in his own mind that he was confident of ultimate success."

Now, "process and means, developed and arranged," pertain to something more than a barren idea.

The note further says: "It was not till 1844 that the first telegraph line from Washington to Baltimore was completed, when the first short telegram announced the existence of a practical telegraph on the American continent." In other words, 1844 was the date of the practical introduction of the invention of 1832; and the "first telegram of four words" was, indeed, the first on this first public line, but not the first produced by the invention.

The electric semaphore of Mr. Cooke was demonstrated and practically introduced on a short line on the 25th of July, 1837. This is the date of its practical introduction, but not the date of his invention.

His invention goes back to an earlier date, at least to 1836.

The electric telegraph of Morse was demonstrated in 1835, before many witnesses; it was practically introduced for public use in 1844; but neither of these dates is the date of the invention, to wit: the date when "the process and means were developed and arranged." This was in 1832.

5. From the statement in this extract, it appears that on the lines of the company in Great Britain, which has the greatest extent in the United Kingdom, (the Electric and International Telegraph Company,) the electric needle semaphore was originally practically introduced through

the genius, skill, and energy of Mr. Cooke. But the writer, the chairman of the company, says, "this system was superseded by what is called the Bain printer;" and that was in turn "superseded by the Morse instruments," (that is, by the American telegraph.) But this again, it seems, was superseded by an instrument, which has received the name of "Ink-writer," a new name only for the original Morse instrument—one of his earliest modes of recording.

On the general subject of your letter I would say, if England's claims are sound, and the world is indebted to England for the telegraph, there should be the evidence of it in every country. The English needle system ought to be seen in use everywhere, not merely in Europe, but in America also, since America is included, by the writer you quote, in the class of debtors to England for the telegraph. It may be well, therefore, to inquire in what countries of the world the English needle system is in use. In reply to this question, I have the means of correct information from the highest sources, elicited in the answers from the various national administrations to the direct question I proposed to them, when engaged in my labors at the Exposition in 1867, "Is the English needle system in use in your country?"

The several administrations have given the following answers:

FRANCE.—"Not in a single office."—*Count de Vougy, Administrator of French Telegraphs.*

HOLLAND.—"It is not employed anywhere with us, neither on the lines of the state, nor of private companies."—*Referendary's letter.*

ITALY.—"The English needle system is no longer in public use in any part of Italy."—*United States Legation, Florence.*

DENMARK.—"The English needle system is not in use anywhere in Denmark."—*United States Minister, Copenhagen.* "Throughout the kingdom the Morse system is the only one in use, whether on government, private, or railroad lines. The English needle system is nowhere in public use in Denmark."—*Director General Faber.*

AUSTRIA.—"The English needle system is nowhere in use in this empire."—*United States Chargé d'Affaires in Vienna.*

SWITZERLAND.—"There is no use made in Switzerland of the English needle system; in fact, none other than the Morse system."—*Superintendent Telegraph Bureau, Berne.* "The only telegraph system employed in Switzerland is that of Morse. We do not hesitate to express our conviction that no known system at this day better fulfills the required conditions than that which we have in use, and of which M. Professor Morse is the inventor."—*Director General of Telegraphs.*

BELGIUM.—"It is long since the Belgian telegraphs have used the English needle apparatus."—*Farsia.*

EGYPT.—"The Egyptian government lines are confined to those in the Soudan country, the whole of which are worked on the Morse system."—*Director of Telegraphs.*

SPAIN.—"In Spain the telegraph system employed on the government lines is solely and exclusively that of Morse."—*Director General of Spanish Telegraphs.*

PRUSSIA.—"The systems of Prussia are Morse, Siemens, and Hughes. The English needle system has never been in use in Prussia."—*Director General De Chauvin.*

SWEDEN.—"It is the Morse system which is exclusively adopted for all the offices of the telegraph administration of Sweden. The English needle system has not been employed in any part of Sweden."—*Director General Brandstrom.*

OTTOMAN EMPIRE.—"The English needle system is not used in any part of this empire."—*United States Secretary of Legation, J. P. Brown.* "The English needle system is not in use in any part of the Ottoman Empire."—*United States Minister E. J. Morris.*

Indirectly I learn it is not used in Russia. It is nowhere used in North or South America, not even in the British possessions.

To these facts, from so many of the telegraph administrations of the world, add the significant additional facts, stated by Mr. Grimston in your extract No. 5, which shows that the English needle system, at first so widely extended and used in the United Kingdom, is now for the most part abandoned in Great Britain, as it has been universally on the continent, and its place supplied by other systems, the Hughes and the Morse, but chiefly the latter, (both American systems.) If, therefore, in every nation where the telegraph has been established, it is the original Morse system, or in part the Hughes, which is adopted, and that even in the United Kingdom itself the English system has been abandoned for the American, it appears to me you have the facts you have desired to sustain your position that the world is indebted to the United States rather than to Great Britain for the modern telegraph. If these facts are not in accord with the preconceived opinions of your English friends, I wish I had the time, and indeed the ability, to do anything like justice to the multitude of Britain's master-minds in science and inventions, for whom I have the highest admiration. My list of these honored names would swell this already prolix letter to too great a bulk. At the risk, nevertheless, of making an invidious selection, I cannot forbear mentioning the names of Professor Faraday, of William Fothergill Cooke, esq., of Sir William Thompson, of Dr. Whitehouse, of Sir Charles Bright, and of Cromwell F. Varley. The labors of the last four savans in giving effect and practicality to the Atlantic telegraph ought to be held in lasting remembrance.

But I must close with the assurance of my sincere respect.

Your friend and servant,

SAMUEL F. B. MORSE.

C. ———,

Care of C. B. Norton & Co., 16 Rue Auber, Paris.

C.—TELEGRAPH STATISTICS.

[Compiled by George Sauer, Esq.]

Through the courtesy of George Sauer, esq., who has bestowed much labor and statistical talent in collating and arranging telegraph statistics, and who has prepared for publication a valuable work on the telegraph, interesting tables have been furnished in proof-sheets, which he has kindly transmitted in advance of the publication of his work. And in this connection, the opportunity is improved to acknowledge obligations not only to him, but also to very many distinguished men in various countries. General acknowledgments are made to the United States diplomatic agents at the various courts of the Eastern Continent, and also to the chiefs of the telegraph administrations of the various countries, for their prompt, courteous, and satisfactory replies to the inquiries addressed to them. An indebtedness is also felt to many individual friends in the United Kingdom for valuable information; among these are Sir James Carmichael, Bart., Sir Charles Bright, M. P., and Robert Sabine, esq., the latter the author of a valuable treatise on the telegraph. From Australia also statistics have been received from the energetic and experienced general superintendent of telegraphs in Victoria, S. W. McGowan, esq., the first introducer of the telegraph into Australia.

Statement showing the average number of messages per mile and per station in Europe.

Years.	MESSAGES PER MILE OF TELEGRAPHIC LINE.							MESSAGES PER MILE OF TELEGRAPHIC WIRE.							MESSAGES PER STATION.						
	France.	Belgium.	Switzerland.	Prussia.	Russia.	Norway.	Great Britain.	France.	Belgium.	Switzerland.	Prussia.	Russia.	Norway.	Great Britain.	France.	Belgium.	Switzerland.	Prussia.	Russia.	Norway.	Great Britain.
1851	6	54	......	......	......	......	......	......	22	......	......	......	......	......	530	......	......	......	......	......	......
1852	22	65	......	23	......	......	......	......	27	......	11	......	......	......	1, 002	927	......	1, 016	......	......	......
1853	32	119	......	24	......	......	......	......	40	......	14	......	......	......	1, 561	1, 239	1, 169	1, 109	......	......	......
1854	51	111	105	45	......	......	......	......	39	......	24	......	......	......	1, 844	1, 342	1, 439	2, 280	......	......	......
1855	39	125	120	54	......	49	127	......	32	......	24	......	44	22	1, 709	1, 284	1, 679	2, 282	......	1, 041	1, 501
1856	51	158	152	67	......	122	123	......	59	......	28	......	94	25	2, 157	1, 985	2, 162	2, 323	......	2, 557	1, [illegible]53
1857	58	219	170	67	27	89	131	......	63	......	26	20	56	27	2, 419	1, 920	2, 098	2, 464	1, 690	1, 888	1, 580
1858	57	220	150	57	26	62	130	......	70	114	22	20	49	27	2, 399	1, 043	1, 946	2, 268	1, 964	1, 552	1, 386
1859	60	221	261	77	26	74	156	......	81	120	28	21	60	33	2, 496	2, 308	2, 113	3, 181	2, 057	2, 255	1, 762
1860	53	246	167	80	37	85	171	......	88	119	28	24	67	22	1, 880	1, 568	2, 096	3, 202	2, 509	2, 412	1, 806
1861	56	250	168	87	43	76	184	......	96	126	30	26	61	38	2, 023	1, 630	2, 114	3, 381	3, 194	2, 134	1, 527
1862	89	250	194	109	43	81	211	......	97	132	37	27	66	46	2, 988	1, 489	2, 161	3, 353	3, 318	2, 571	1, 656
1863	100	263	230	122	42	92	228	3[illegible]	107	138	40	24	75	48	3, 268	1, 726	2, 296	2, 985	2, 626	2, 937	1, 818
1864	107	293	250	125	40	103	262	33	123	153	50	2[illegible]	84	54	3, 209	1, 960	2, 309	3, 247	2, 723	2, 112	1, 034
1865	125	335	277	182	......	114	290	40	124	159	57	......	94	60	2, 596	2, 195	2, 346	3, 287	......	3, 690	2, 287
1866	134	513	277	209	......	122	......	42	187	163	63	......	99	......	2, 351	3, 168	2, 355	3, 650	......	......	......
1867	139	533	297	193	......	......	......	42	174	154	51	......	......	......	2, 163	3, 460	......	3, 013	......	......	......

Telegraph statistics of France.

Years.	NUMBER OF STATIONS, LENGTHS OF LINES, ETC.					NUMBER OF MESSAGES.			PRODUCE OF MESSAGES.			PROFIT AND LOSS.			
	Lengths of lines.	Lengths of wires.	Number of stations.	Number of instruments.	Number of persons employed.	Inland.	International.	Total.	Inland.	International.	Total.	Gross receipts.	Expenditure.	Profit.	Loss.
	Miles.	*Miles.*							*Francs.*	*Francs.*	*Francs.*	*Francs.*	*Francs.*	*Francs.*	*Francs.*
1851	1, 325	...	17	...	...	...	...	9, 014	...	...	76, 722	99, 582	1, 194, 467	...	1, 094, 884
1852	2, 149	...	43	...	...	...	...	48, 105	...	...	542, 891	565, 751	1, 299, 739	...	733, 988
1853	4, 440	...	91	...	...	...	...	142, 061	...	...	1, 511, 909	1, 617, 166	1, 794, 090	...	176, 923
1854	5, 745	...	128	...	...	...	...	236, 018	...	...	2, 064, 983	2, 284, 274	2, 393, 769	...	109, 495
1855	6, 540	...	149	...	...	...	...	254, 532	...	...	2, 487, 159	2, 860, 919	3, 066, 149	...	205, 229
1856	7, 000	...	167	...	...	...	...	360, 299	...	...	3, 191, 102	3, 494, 719	3, 364, 479	130, 239	...
1857	7, 100	...	171	...	...	...	...	413, 616	...	...	3, 333, 695	3, 690, 939	3, 759, 526	...	68, 587
1858	8, 098	...	193	...	...	349, 887	114, 086	463, 973	1, 794, 918	1, 721, 715	3, 516, 633	3, 902, 078	4, 398, 627	...	496, 549
1859	10, 000	...	240	...	...	453, 998	144, 703	598, 701	2, 072, 314	1, 950, 485	4, 022, 799	4, 450, 270	4, 659, 106	...	208, 835
1860	13, 620	...	383	...	...	568, 365	151, 885	720, 250	2, 358, 525	1, 829, 540	4, 188, 065	4, 770, 240	5, 570, 064	...	799, 824
1861	16, 468	...	455	...	...	734, 252	186, 357	920, 357	2, 840, 445	2, 079, 292	4, 919, 737	5, 676, 864	6, 594, 407	...	917, 542
1862	17, 113	...	508	...	...	1, 291, 774	226, 270	1, 518, 044	2, 984, 490	2, 317, 950	5, 302, 440	6, 265, 683	7, 301, 046	...	1, 035, 363
1863	17, 518	57, 455	537	...	...	1, 490, 023	264, 844	1, 754, 867	*3, 305, 993	2, 631, 911	5, 937, 904	6, 987, 521	8, 163, 423	...	1, 175, 900
1864	18, 222	60, 458	610	...	...	1, 654, 406	313, 342	1, 967, 748	3, 565, 933	2, 557, 338	6, 123, 272	7, 315, 922	8, 373, 098	...	1, 057, 175
1865	19, 763	63, 591	953	...	...	2, 098, 640	375, 102	2, 473, 747	4, 159, 445	2, 892, 694	7, 052, 139	8, 161, 218	8, 983, 460	...	822, 241
1866	21, 264	70, 351	1, 209	...	...	2, 379, 681	462, 873	2, 842, 554	4, 513, 095	3, 194, 495	7, 707, 590	8, 810, 283	8, 983, 460	...	73, 157
1867	23, 090	70, 330	1, 486	...	...	2, 682, 810	531, 185	3, 213, 995	4, 969, 618	3, 690, 226	8, 659, 845	...	...	...	...

* The receipts are exclusive of government business, amounting in the aggregate to about 1,000,000 francs annually, which, if added, would show an increase in lieu of a deficiency.

Telegraph statistics of Belgium.

Years.	NUMBER OF STATIONS, LENGTHS OF LINES, ETC.					NUMBER OF MESSAGES.			PRODUCE OF MESSAGES.			PROFIT AND LOSS.			
	Lengths of lines.	Lengths of wires.	Number of stations.	Number of instruments.	Number of persons employed.	Inland.	International.	Total.	Inland.	International.	Total.	Gross receipts.	Expenditure.	Loss.	Profit.
	Miles.	*Miles.*							*Francs.*	*Francs.*	*Francs.*	*Francs.*	*Francs.*	*Francs.*	*Francs.*
1851	257	626	10	20	32	6, 652	7, 373	14, 025	....	....	88, 674	88, 674	309, 116	220, 441	....
1852	420	993	28	60	40	9, 807	17, 410	27, 217	....	....	165, 973	165, 973	102, 947	....	63, 025
1853	437	1, 312½	42	74	57	14, 159	38, 195	52, 050	....	....	265, 536	265, 939	170, 735	....	94, 800
1854	454	1, 550	45	87	71	16, 719	43, 696	60, 415	....	....	280, 845	280, 845	139, 795	....	141, 050
1855	490	1, 596	50	97	75	17, 279	44, 154	61, 433	....	....	265, 939	265, 379	161, 500	....	104, 439
1856	501	1, 676	50	113	90	32, 862	66, 411	99, 273	....	....	359, 979	395, 579	202, 599	....	156, 980
1857	543	1, 835	62	138	113	41, 434	77, 616	119, 050	....	....	407, 011	407, 011	283, 171	....	123, 840
1858	661	2, 077½	75	155	126	47, 673	98, 053	145, 726	....	....	413, 926	413, 926	293, 891	....	120, 035
1859	887	2, 402	85	178	144	65, 465	130, 775	196, 240	....	....	506, 006	506, 006	375, 343	....	130, 662
1860	916	2, 569	144	234	158	80, 216	145, 603	225, 819	142, 344	382, 846	527, 743	527, 743	403, 500	....	124, 243
1861	1, 079	2, 808	165	265	155	97, 945	171, 023	268, 968	171, 225	396, 306	588, 532	588, 532	408, 261	....	180, 271
1862	1, 174	3, 002	196	271	167	105, 274	186, 513	291, 787	176, 643	428, 401	605, 044	605, 044	515, 800	....	89, 244
1863	1, 655	3, 875	241	365	185	188, 825	227, 288	416, 113	211, 063	401, 299	612, 363	612, 363	653, 780	41, 417	....
1864	1, 867	4, 421	279	421	217	252, 301	294, 196	546, 497	282, 591	506, 806	789, 399	789, 399	670, 424	....	118, 974
1865	2, 012	5, 433	307	481	267	332, 721	341, 316	674, 037	345, 289	520, 350	865, 640	865, 640	948, 516	82, 876	....
1866	2, 200	6, 243	356	556	309	692, 536	435, 469	1, 128, 005	407, 532	553, 580	962, 213	962, 213	1, 217, 496	255, 282	....
1867	2, 424	7, 444	374	603	336	819, 668	474, 202	1, 293, 870	471, 279	602, 935	1, 074, 214	....	....	....	....

Telegraph statistics of Switzerland.

Years.	NUMBER OF STATIONS, LENGTHS OF LINES, ETC.					NUMBER OF MESSAGES.			PRODUCE OF MESSAGES.			PROFIT AND LOSS.			
	Lengths of lines.	Lengths of wires.	Number of stations.	Number of instruments.	Number of persons employed.	Inland.	International.	Total.	Inland.	International.	Total.	Gross receipts.	Expenditure.	Loss.	Profit.
	Miles.	*Miles.*							*Francs.*	*Francs.*	*Francs.*	*Francs.*	*Francs.*	*Francs.*	*Francs.*
1852	....	....	34	....	....	2, 876	....	2, 876	3, 541	....	3, 541	6, 507	424, 081	417, 573	....
1853	....	....	70	....	....	74, 095	8, 491	82, 586	77, 388	50, 481	127, 870	144, 645	289, 120	144, 475	....
1854	1, 228	....	90	....	....	109, 599	18, 568	129, 167	109, 927	98, 959	208, 887	235, 688	218, 718	....	16, 970
1855	1, 354	....	97	....	....	133, 936	28, 915	162, 851	133, 563	117, 828	251, 391	305, 821	324, 520	18, 698	....
1856	1, 494	....	105	....	....	169, 376	57, 696	227, 072	178, 896	141, 050	319, 947	393, 441	367, 312	....	26, 129
1857	1, 535	....	124	....	....	192, 664	67, 500	260, 164	206, 130	163, 095	369, 226	450, 529	406, 045	....	44, 484
1858	1, 649	2, 161	127	200	....	180, 489	66, 613	247, 102	191, 109	152, 487	343, 597	462, 279	428, 892	....	33, 386
1859	1, 774	2, 380	131	215	....	196, 425	90, 451	286, 876	213, 072	212, 515	425, 587	631, 327	504, 963	....	126, 364
1860	1, 857	2, 549	145	246	249	208, 311	95, 619	303, 930	224, 484	183, 944	408, 429	488, 286	439, 856	....	48, 329
1861	1, 970	2, 623	157	249	265	217, 700	114, 233	331, 933	233, 631	214, 424	448, 056	502, 429	421, 039	....	81, 389
1862	1, 970	2, 901	177	280	294	241, 814	140, 638	382, 452	259, 308	271, 109	530, 418	583, 915	502, 002	....	81, 913
1863	1, 982	3, 080	199	308	322	298, 778	158, 093	456, 871	318, 495	312, 253	630, 749	676, 885	570, 846	....	101, 03
1864	2, 062	3, 360	223	....	346	325, 165	189, 787	514, 952	344, 829	270, 488	615, 318	657, 583	572, 083	....	85, 499
1865	2, 132	3, 720	252	410	373	364, 118	227, 096	591, 214	381, 376	345, 186	726, 564	768, 582	657, 533	....	111, 048
1866	2, 410	4, 098	284	441	417	383, 158	285, 758	668, 916	400, 152	284, 319	684, 471	727, 615	687, 390	....	40, 225
1867	2, 395	4, 612	333	463	....	397, 289	311, 685	708, 974	412, 019	363, 004	775, 024	....	....	....	....

Telegraph statistics of Norway.

Years.	NUMBER OF STATIONS, LENGTHS OF LINES, ETC.					NUMBER OF MESSAGES.			PRODUCE OF MESSAGES.			PROFIT AND LOSS.			
	Lengths of lines.	Lengths of wires.	Number of stations.	Number of instruments.	Number of persons employed.	Inland.	International.	Total.	Inland.	International.	Total.	Gross receipts.	Expenditure.	Loss.	Profit.
	Miles.	*Miles.*									*Rixdolls.*	*Rixdolls.*	*Rixdolls.*	*Rixdolls.*	
1855	471	532	22	....	44	19, 253	3, 663	22, 916	....	....	29, 422				
1856	481	625	23	....	55	47, 943	10, 839	58, 812	....	....	78, 925				
1857	824	1, 310	39	....	98	57, 273	16, 402	73, 675	....	....	110, 544				
1858	1, 468	1, 847	52	....	125	73, 848	16, 860	90, 708	....	....	136, 021				
1859	1, 571	1, 955	52	....	129	95, 505	21, 745	117, 250	....	....	171, 894				
1860	1, 571	1, 955	52	....	129	106, 665	26, 629	133, 294	....	....	217, 490	2,061,173 (1855–1865)	2, 610, 854	459, 681	....
1861	1, 690	2, 087	53	....	130	98, 165	29, 662	127, 827	....	....	229, 976				
1862	1, 700	2, 115	65	....	130	106, 060	32, 650	138, 710	....	....	247, 041				
1863	1, 808	2, 234	65	....	131	130, 218	36, 918	167, 136	....	....	251, 228				
1864	1, 931	2, 358	68	....	138	159, 968	39, 766	199, 734	....	....	280, 810				
1865	1, 931	2, 358	71	....	138	169, 386	51, 608	220, 994	....	....	307, 822				
1866	2, 205	2, 710	73	....	152	191, 563	77, 812	269, 375	....	....	343, 645	343, 645	345, 776	2, 131	....
1867	....	....	....	....	....	....	....	....	....	....	....	....	....	....	....

Telegraph statistics of Prussia.

Years.	Number of stations, lengths of lines, etc.					Number of messages.			Produce of messages.			Profit and loss.			
	Lengths of lines.	Lengths of wires.	Number of stations.	Number of instruments.	Number of persons employed.	Inland.	International and transit.	Total.	Inland.	International and transit.	Total.	Gross receipts.	Expenditure.	Loss.	Profit.
	Miles.	*Miles.*							*Thalers.*	*Thalers.*	*Thalers.*	*Thalers.*	*Thalers.*	*Thalers.*	*Thalers.*
1852	2, 070	4, 232	48	....	306	....	....	48, 751	....	....	114, 539	114, 539	173, 993	59, 454	....
1853	2, 328	3, 927	50	....	266	....	....	55, 161	....	....	209, 944	209, 944	266, 689	56, 745	....
1854	2, 595	4, 803	51	....	298	....	....	116, 313	....	....	328, 506	328, 506	374, 062	45, 556	....
1855	2, 821	6, 492	67	....	409	83, 737	68, 983	152, 820	168, 725	265, 397	434, 122	434, 122	265, 038	....	169, 084
1856	3, 314	7, 837	91	....	540	159, 975	61, 436	221, 411	283, 785	307, 253	591, 038	591, 038	388, 571	....	202, 467
1857	3, 580	9, 128	98	....	568	179, 340	62, 205	241, 545	313, 383	413, 134	726, 517	726, 517	431, 175	....	295, 342
1858	4, 384	10, 981	109	....	596	159, 685	87, 517	247, 202	210, 900	519, 644	730, 584	730, 584	551, 317	....	158, 693
1859	4, 513	12, 493	110	....	659	284, 812	65, 185	349, 997	257, 601	550, 920	808, 521	808, 521	571, 791	....	257, 204
1860	4, 785	13, 774	120	....	722	239, 781	144, 554	384, 335	214, 476	576, 625	791, 101	791, 101	587, 769	....	203, 332
1861	5, 269	15, 609	136	....	780	289, 381	169, 621	459, 002	244, 236	631, 547	875, 783	875, 783	588, 998	....	286, 785
1862	6, 034	17, 946	197	....	936	462, 996	197, 505	660, 501	258, 386	696, 164	954, 550	954, 550	690, 066	....	264, 484
1863	7, 150	21, 851	294	....	1, 169	639, 486	238, 102	877, 583	313, 362	726, 499	1, 039, 961	1, 039, 961	787, 710	....	252, 251
1864	8, 086	25, 230	388	....	1, 508	1, 012, 040	247, 550	1, 259, 590	340, 165	809, 848	1, 150, 008	1, 150, 008	951, 312	....	198, 696
1865	8, 787	28, 254	486	....	1, 758	1, 133, 624	383, 831	1, 527, 455	402, 832	839, 657	1, 242, 489	1, 242, 489	1, 068, 337	....	174, 152
1866	9, 386	30, 970	538	....	1, 976	1, 483, 415	480, 615	1, 964, 030	487, 758	788, 027	1, 275, 785	1, 275, 785	1, 149, 527	....	126, 258
1867	13, 364	43, 072	857	....	2, 816	1, 885, 452	697, 948	2, 582, 400	624, 912	793, 178	1, 418, 090	1, 418, 090	1, 216, 285	....	201, 805

Telegraph statistics of Russia.

Years.	NUMBER OF STATIONS, LENGTHS OF LINES, ETC.					NUMBER OF MESSAGES.			PRODUCE OF MESSAGES.			PROFIT AND LOSS.			
	Lengths of lines.	Lengths of wires.	Number of stations.	Number of instruments.	Number of persons employed.	Inland.	International.	Total.	Inland.	International.	Total.	Gross receipts.	Expenditure.	Loss.	Profit.
	Miles.	*Miles.*							*Roubles.*	*Roubles.*	*Roubles.*	*Roubles.*	*Roubles.*		*Roubles.*
1857	4, 840	6, 715	79	....	....	78, 047	55, 509	133, 556	248, 500	208, 492	456, 992	412, 250	322, 955	....	89, 295
1858	6, 175	8, 042	90	....	....	98, 256	58, 538	156, 794	276, 711	245, 141	521, 852	457, 569	359, 980	....	97, 589
1859	9, 417	11, 343	118	....	....	164, 293	78, 456	242, 749	411, 497	329, 129	740, 626	656, 045	556, 688	....	99, 357
1860	10, 904	16, 745	160	....	....	303, 008	98, 471	401, 479	735, 427	296, 794	1, 032, 221	940, 009	828, 861	....	111, 148
1861	12, 926	21, 402	175	....	....	433, 110	125, 919	559, 029	965, 473	333, 831	1, 299, 304	1, 176, 762	1, 020, 616	....	156, 146
1862	15, 070	24, 086	195	....	....	512, 685	134, 557	647, 242	1, 155, 989	346, 035	1, 502, 024	1, 368, 953	1, 268, 071	....	100, 882
1863	17, 445	30, 364	281	....	....	589, 554	148, 299	737, 853	1, 341, 271	362, 183	1, 703, 454	1, 534, 830	1, 497, 125	....	37, 705
1864	21, 119	37, 330	308	....	....	677, 911	160, 742	838, 653	1, 464, 750	407, 909	1, 872, 659	1, 724, 118	1, 674, 236	....	49, 882
1865	....	....	....	....	....	....	....	....	....	....	....	....	....	....	....
1866	....	....	....	....	....	....	....	....	....	....	....	....	....	....	....
1867	....	....	....	....	....	....	....	....	....	....	....	....	....	....	....

Statement showing the progress of telegraphy in France, Belgium, Switzerland, and Austria.

Years.	FRANCE.			BELGIUM.			SWITZERLAND.			AUSTRIA.		
	Number of messages.	Gross receipts.	Average cost per mess'ge.	Number of messages.	Gross receipts.	Average cost per mess'ge.	Number of messages.	Gross receipts.	Average cost per mess'ge.	Number of messages.	Gross receipts.	Average cost per mess'ge.
		Francs.	*Francs.*		*Francs.*	*Francs.*		*Francs.*	*Francs.*		*lorins.*	*Florins.*
1851	9, 014	76, 722	7. 84	14, 025	88, 674	6. 32	....	....	....	44, 911	128, 736	2. 86
1852	48, 105	542, 891	11. 28	27, 217	165, 973	6. 10	2, 876	3, 541	....	62, 716	209, 547	3. 34
1853	142, 061	1, 511, 909	10. 64	52, 050	265, 536	5. 07	82, 586	127, 870	1. 55	109, 347	308, 158	2. 82
1854	236, 018	2, 064, 982	8. 14	60, 415	280, 845	4. 65	129, 167	208, 887	1. 62	190, 552	549, 697	2. 88
1855	254, 532	2, 487, 159	9. 77	61, 433	265, 939	4. 33	162, 851	251, 391	1. 53	204, 221	607, 745	2. 97
1856	360, 299	3, 191, 102	8. 68	99, 273	359, 579	3. 62	227, 072	319, 947	1. 41	251, 948	778, 294	3. 08
1857	413, 616	3, 333, 695	8. 06	119, 050	407, 011	3. 42	260, 164	369, 226	1. 42	381, 720	888, 905	2. 33
1858	463, 973	3, 516, 633	7. 60	145, 726	413, 926	2. 84	247, 102	343, 597	1. 37	419, 449	760, 811	1. 81
1859	598, 701	4, 022, 799	6. 72	196, 240	506, 066	2. 57	286, 876	425, 587	1. 48	692, 379	951, 240	1. 37
1860	720, 250	4, 188, 065	5. 81	225, 819	527, 743	2. 34	303, 930	408, 429	1. 34	700, 795	991, 275	1. 41
1861	920, 357	4, 919, 737	5. 34	268, 968	588, 532	2. 19	331, 933	448, 056	1. 35	846, 953	1, 226, 404	1. 44
1862	1, 518, 044	5, 302, 440	3. 49	291, 787	605, 044	2. 07	382, 452	530, 418	1. 42	946, 675	1, 267, 966	1. 34
1863	1, 754, 867	5, 937, 904	3. 38	416, 113	612, 363	1. 47	456, 871	630, 749	1. 38	1, 130, 625	1, 290, 447	1. 14
1864	1, 967, 748	6, 123, 272	3. 11	546, 497	789, 399	1. 44	514, 952	615, 318	1. 20	1, 610, 663	1, 322, 948	0. 82
1865	2, 473, 747	7, 052, 139	2. 85	674. 037	865, 640	1. 28	591, 214	726, 564	1. 23	1, 786, 955	1, 435, 478	0. 80
1866	2, 842, 554	7, 707, 590	2. 71	1, 128, 005	962, 213	0. 85	668, 916	684, 471	1. 03	2, 507, 472	1, 644, 742	0. 66
1867	3, 213, 965	8, 659, 845	2. 69	1, 293, 870	1, 074, 214	0. 83	708, 974	775, 024	1. 00	....	....	....

Statement showing the progress of telegraphy in Prussia, Spain, Russia, and Norway.

Years.	PRUSSIA.			SPAIN.			RUSSIA.			NORWAY.		
	Number of messages.	Gross receipts.	Average cost per mess'ge.	Number of messages.	Gross receipts.	Average cost per mess'ge.	Number of messages.	Gross receipts.	Average cost per mess'ge.	Number of messages.	Gross receipts.	Average cost per mess'ge.
		Thalers.	*Thalers.*		*Dollars.*	*Dollars.*		*Roubles.*	*Roubles.*		*Rixdollars.*	*Rixdolls.*
1851												
1852	48, 751	114, 539	2. 35									
1853	85, 161	209, 944	2. 46									
1854	116, 343	328, 506	2. 82									
1855	152, 820	434, 122	2. 84	2, 085	38, 042	18. 290				22, 916	8, 414	0. 36
1856	221, 411	591, 038	2. 67	4, 346	76, 084	17. 530				58, 812	22, 572	0. 38
1857	241, 545	726, 517	3. 01	26, 772	146, 911	5. 480	133, 556	456, 992	3. 42	73, 675	31, 615	0. 42
1858	247, 202	730, 584	2. 95	113, 171	303, 665	2. 686	156, 794	521, 852	3. 33	90, 708	38, 902	0. 43
1859	349, 997	808, 521	2. 31	210, 426	523, 807	2. 450	242, 749	740, 626	3. 05	117, 250	49, 161	0. 42
1860	384, 335	791, 101	2. 06	230, 108	558, 227	2. 420	401, 479	1, 032, 221	2. 57	133, 294	62, 256	0. 46
1861	459, 002	875, 783	1. 90	236, 089	620, 678	2. 650	559, 029	1, 299, 304	2. 32	127, 827	65, 773	0. 51
1862	660, 501	954, 550	1. 45	282, 098	526, 079	1. 850	647, 242	1, 502, 024	2. 32	138, 710	70, 653	0. 52
1863	877, 583	1, 039, 961	1. 18	433, 110	587, 218	1. 350	737, 853	1, 703, 454	2. 31	167, 136	71, 851	0. 42
1864	1, 259, 590	1, 150, 008	0. 91	613, 265	611, 644	0. 980	838, 653	1, 885, 355	2. 25	199, 734	80, 331	0. 40
1865	1, 527, 455	1, 242, 489	0. 81	767, 909	631, 682	0. 810				230, 994	88, 037	0. 40
1866	1, 964, 030	1, 275, 785	0. 65	666, 462	533, 558	0. 800				269, 375	98, 282	0. 36
1867	2, 582, 400	1, 656, 419	0. 64	533, 376	554, 476	1. 030						

D.—FRANKLIN AND ELECTRICAL SEMAPHORES.

It has frequently been asserted (on what authority I know not) that the first idea of an electric semaphore originated with Franklin. I have sought in vain in the publications of Franklin's experiments and works for anything confirmatory of this assertion. On mentioning the subject to my friend, Professor Blake, he kindly proposed examining the writings of Franklin in order to elicit the truth. From him I have received the following:

"I have consulted several works for the purpose of ascertaining, if possible, the foundation for the statement that Franklin suggested the idea of semaphores by static electricity. I have not yet found any such suggestion, but I have noted that following the experiments by Dr. Watson, and others, in England, to determine the *velocity* of the electric discharge, and the time supposed to be required for the electrical discharges across the Thames, by which spirits were kindled, &c., (in 1747,) Dr. Franklin, in 1748, made some similar experiments upon the banks of the Schuylkill, and amused his friends by sending a spark 'from side to side through the river without any other conductor than the water.'[1] (This was in 1748, at the end of the year.) In 1756, 'J. A. esq.,' of New York, (James Alexander,) presented to the Royal Society a proposition 'to measure the time taken by the electric spark in moving through any given space' by sending the discharge or spark down the Susquehanna or Potomac, and around by way of the Mississippi and Ohio rivers, so that the 'electric fire' would have a circuit of some thousands of miles to go. All this was upon the supposition or assumption that the electric fire would choose a continuous water conductor rather than to return or pass through the earth. Franklin presented a paper in reply, in which he says, 'the proposed experiment (though well-imagined and very ingenious) of sending the spark round through a vast length of space, &c., &c., would not afford the satisfaction desired, though we could be sure that the motion of the electric fluid would be in that tract, and not underground in the wet earth by the shortest way.'[2]

"Can it be possible that Franklin's experiment of firing spirits and showing the spark and other effects of the electric discharge across the river originated, or forms the foundation for, the statement that he suggested the semaphoric use of electricity?"

---

[1] Vide Priestley's History of Electricity.

[2] Franklin's Experiments on Electricity, and Letters and Papers on Philosophical Subjects. 4to. London, MDCCLXIX, pages 282, 283.

E.—CATALOGUE OF WORKS ON TELEGRAPHY.

The following are the titles of a few of the constantly increasing number of treatises on the telegraph:

Title of works.	Names of authors.	Place of publication and date.
Telegraphie	Prof. Steinheil	Munich, 1838.
The American Electro-magnetic Telegraph	Alfred Vail	New York, 1845.
Traité de télégraphie électrique	L'Abbé Moigno	Paris, 1849.
Elektrische Telegraphie	F. Kohl	——, 1850
Electric Telegraph Manipulator	C. V. Walker	London, 1850.
Manuel de telegrafia electrica	Matteuci	Pisa, 1850.
Kurze Darstellung, &c	W. Siemens	Berlin, 1851.
Mémoire, &c	W. Siemens	Berlin, 1851.
Die elektromagnetische Telegraphie	T. Bauerbaum	Berlin, 1851.
Recherches sur la télégraphie électrique	Gloesner	Liége, 1851.
Traité général des applications	Gloesner	....
Ueber elektrische Telegraphie	Pelchrzun	Potsdam, 1853.
Katechismus der elektrischen Telegraphie	J. A. Forsach	Leipzig, 1853.
The Electric Telegraph	Dr. Lardner	London, 1855.
Exposé, &c	Du Moncel	Paris, 1855.
Revue des applications, &c	Du Moncel	Paris, 1857.
Télégraphie électrique	Du Moncel	Paris, 1864.
Traité d'électricité	De la Rive	Paris, 1858.
L'électricité et les chemins de fer	De Castro	Paris, 1858.
Cours théorique, 2 vols	E. E. Blavier	Paris, 1859.
Telegraph Manual	T. P. Schaffner	New York, 1859.
Electric Telegraph	Highton	London, 1860.
Handbuch der Telegraphie	Kuhn	Leipzig, 1866.
Die electromagnetische Telegraphie	Schellen	Brunswick, 1866.
Manuel de la télégraphie	Breguet	Paris.
Anwendung des Electromagnetismus, &c	Dub	....
Electromagnetismus	Dub	....
Telegraph History	A. Jones	New York.
Telegraph History	—— Turnbull	Philadelphia.
Telegraph History	George Prescott	Boston, 1860.
The Electric Telegraph	Robert Sabine	London, 1867.
The Electric Telegraph	Lardner & Bright	London, 1867.
Télégraphie électrique	J. Gavarret	Paris, 1861.
Telegraph Manual	R. S. Culley	London.
Manual of Telegraphy*	Prof. J. L. Smith	New York
Modern Practice of the Electric Telegraph, a handbook for electricians and operators	Frank L. Pope	New York.

* An excellent compendium, brief but lucid.

F.—MATERIALS AND APPARATUS EXHIBITED.

The following catalogue of the apparatus and articles exhibited in Class 64, Group VI, is from the French catalogue of the Exposition, arranged under the various countries exhibiting them, but renumbered for the greater convenience of reference.

For reasons given in the introduction, many of these are unnoticed in the report.

FRANCE.

1. MINISTRY OF THE INTERIOR.—Exhibit by the administration of the telegraph lines, the various instruments employed on their lines.
2. A. JOLY, 29 rue Saint Sulpice, Paris.—A printing telegraph apparatus.
3. J. L. A. MACHABÉE, 46 rue de Veuves, Paris.—Telegraphic cables.
4. E. HARDY, 21 rue de Sèvres, Paris.—The telegraphic apparatus of M. M. Vavin, of Fribourg, the autographic apparatus of M. David, and the printing apparatus of M. Hughes.
5. A. CAUMONT, 79 boulevard Malesherbes, Paris.—Telegraphic apparatus, &c.
6. CH. CROS, 14 rue Royale, Paris.—Telegraphic apparatus.
7. T. A. M. SORTAIS, of Lisieux, (Calvados.)—The Morse apparatus.
8. LECLANCHÉ ,22 rue Fontaine St. Georges, Paris.—Galvanic battery.
9. E. GRENET, 14 rue Castiglione, Paris.—Galvanic battery.
10. P. DUMOULIN FROMENT, 85 rue Notre Dame des Champs, Paris.—Telegraph apparatus, Hughes & Caselli.
11. P. A. J. DUJARDIN, of Lille.—Telegraph apparatus and battery.
12. ZALINSKI MIKORSKI, 103 rue d'Enfer, Paris.—Galvanic battery.
13. E. LENOIR, 109 boulevard du Prince Eugène, Paris.—Autographic telegraph.
14. H. LÉGER, 24 rue des Bourdonnais, Paris.—Acoustic apparatus.
15. P. GUILLOT, 29 route de Choisy, Paris, and J. GATGET, 90 boulevard Mazas, Paris.—Magneto-electric telegraph apparatus.
16. L. BRÉGUET, 39 quai de l'Horloge, Paris.—Telegraphic apparatus, paratonneres, &c.
17. G. A. TABOURIN, of Lyons.—Telegraph, called hydro-dynamic.
18. DIGNEY FRÈRES & Co., 8 rue de Poitevins. Paris.—Telegraph apparatus.
19. THE ABBÉ J. CASELLI, 20 rue de l'Ouest, Paris.—The pantelegraph.
20. RATTIER & Co., 4 rue des Fossés Montmartre, Paris.—Telegraph cables.
21. L. GUYOT D'ARLINCOURT, 3 bis rue de la Bruyère, Paris.—Printing telegraph.
22. A. F. CACHELEUX, 103 rue de Grenelle St. Germain, Paris.—Telegraph apparatus.
23. E. E. BLAVIER, of Nancy, (Meurthe.)—Treatise on the telegraph, 2 vols.
24. P. D. PRUD'HOMME, 4 bis rue St. Martin, Paris.—Telegraph apparatus.

HOLLAND.

25. A. HOLTZMAN, of Amsterdam.—Telegraphic cable.

BELGIUM.

26. LÉON DELPERDANGE, 15 rue Zérézo, Brussels.—Work respecting subterranean telegraph lines.

27. CH. DEVOS, 8 rue des Croisades, St. Josse-ten-Noode, Brussels.—A commutator for 40 lines for the bureau central of the telegraphs.
28. ANT. J. GÉRARD, 5 Place St. Lambert, Liège.—Autographic telegraph.
29. MICHAEL GLOESENER, 55 rue des Augustins, Liège.—Telegraphs, electric, ordinary, and submarine; printing telegraph; autographic telegraph; needle telegraph; dial telegraph; model of electric bells; paratonneres, or lightning arresters.
30. LESAGE & CO., 8 rue du Gazomètre, Brussels.—Telegraph apparatus.
31. JEAN MICHAEL J. NAPLE, of Farciennes, (Namur.)—Telegraph apparatus, comprising two systems, that of the dial and letters, and that called artistic. They can be alternately used. Another apparatus with keys. The clock-work serves alternately for sending or receiving.

ENGLAND.

32. JOSEPH BOURNE & SON, Denby Potteries, Derbyshire.—Vitrified stone-ware insulators.
33. W. E. HENLEY, 27 Leadenhall street, London.—Submarine telegraph cables.
34. WILLIAM HOOPER, 7 Pall Mall east, London.—Telegraph cables.
35. D. NICOLL, Oakland's hall, Kilburn, London.—Wire and telegraph cables.
36. SIEMENS BROTHERS, 3 Great George street, Westminster, London.—Telegraphic apparatus.

CANADA.

37. ERNEST CHANTELOUP, of Montreal.—Telegraph apparatus.

PRUSSIA, AND STATES OF NORTHERN GERMANY.

38. ROYAL DIRECTION OF THE PRUSSIAN TELEGRAPH, Berlin.—Insulators complete.
39. WERNER SIEMENS AND J. G. HALSKE, Berlin, and CHARLES H. SIEMENS of St. Petersburg, &c.—Apparatus for distributing type dispatches; machine for composing; machine for distributing; apparatus for rapid writing; three apparatus for writing in color; apparatus for writing in relief; apparatus of wheels, *(appareils à roues;)* magnet indicators; two small magnet indicators for a private telegraph; an electric indicator of the height of water; small bridge in portable boxes for measuring resistance, &c.
40. GUILLAUME HORN, 45 Brandenburgstrasse, Berlin.—Polarized telegraph for writing in blue, with its accessories.
41. W. GURLT, 61 Krausenstrasse, Berlin.—Telegraph complete of Morse.
42. LEVIN & CO., Berlin.—Two telegraph apparatus.

43. BERNARD BEHREND, Coeslin.—Specimens of paper for the telegraph.
44. CHARLES JULES VOGEL AND A. HABERSTOLTZ, 39 Ritterstrasse, Berlin.—Specimens of copper wire, and (*de maillechort recouverts de soie et de coton*) for telegraph and offices.
45. RICH. BELLÉ, Aix-la-Chapelle.—Electric bells.

GRAND DUCHY OF BADEN.

46. H. MEIDINGER, of Carlsruhe.—Electric battery.

BAVARIA.

47. THE SOCIETY OF PASIGRAPHY, of Munich.—Pasigraphic books, in eighteen sheets, for the use of international telegraphy.

AUSTRIA.

48. THE CHEVALIER CH. ADOLPHE DE BERGMÜLLER, 8 Augustiner-strasse, Vienna.—Telegraph for the service of the police and fire-department.
49. LÉON DE HAMAR, Pesth, Hungary.—Telegraph apparatus of Morse, with key.
50. JEAN LEOPOLDER, 3 Theresianumgasse, Vienna.—Station telegraphs typographic telegraph, with the Morse characters; portable telegraph.
51. JEAN MÖERÄTH, 25 Alsengrund, Vienna.—Plan and process for laying submarine cables.
52. IMPERIAL ROYAL DIRECTION OF TELEGRAPHS, Vienna.—Telegraphic materials adopted for war service; carbon battery.

SWITZERLAND.

53. THE FEDERAL MANUFACTORY OF TELEGRAPHS, HASTER & ESCHER, Berne.—Telegraph apparatus.
54. M. HIPP, Neufchatel. Apparatus for the telegraph, clocks, and chronographs.

SPAIN.

55. THE DIRECTION GENERAL OF TELEGRAPHS, MOREUIL & BONET, Madrid.—Printing telegraphs, and material for telegraph stations.

PORTUGAL.

56. MAXIMILIAN HERMANN, Lisbon.—Electric telegraph apparatus.

DENMARK.

57. S. HJORTH, of Copenhagen.—Magneto-electric battery.
58. JULES THOMPSEN, of Copenhagen.—Battery of polarization.

RUSSIA.

59. RUSSIAN COMPANY FOR THE MANUFACTURE OF CAOUTCHOUC, at St. Petersburg.—Telegraph wire and insulators.
60. GALVANIC ESTABLISHMENT OF ENGINEERS, at St. Petersburg.—Electric telegraph apparatus.
61. JOSEPH PIK, Warsaw.—Telegraph, Morse system.

ITALY.

62. THOMAS PICCO, Alexandria.—A lightning arrester.
63. GASPARD SACCO, Turin.—Telegraph apparatus.
64. THE LONGONI & DELL'ACQUA, Milan.—Morse Telegraph, modified by Moroni, with accessories.
65. GAETAN BONELLI, Florence.—A type telegraph called "Telegraph with a shuttle," by Bonelli & Hipp; the simple autographic apparatus; the accessories for the use of this last.
66. JOSEPH POGGIALI, Florence.—The Morse apparatus complete.
67. JOSEPH AND IGNACE TREVISANI, and FRANÇOIS ERNEST HALLIE, of Ascoli Piceno.—A submarine cable.
68. BÉLISAIRE DETTI & SON, Naples.—A submarine cable; pen proper to substitute for the pencil for writing telegraphic dispatches.
69. ALBERT BALESTRINE, Paris.—Electric plummet with its line, called the sounding line; model of submarine stations, for the telegraph; model of a machine for laying the cable; plan of a transatlantic line; profile of five stations.

TURKEY.

70. HARISCHE OGLOU, of Eyalet and city of Sivas.—Electric batteries for the telegraph.

EGYPT.

71. Porous cups of the earth of Keneh, for the electric batteries.

UNITED STATES OF AMERICA.

72. S. E. AND G. L. MORSE, of Harrison, New Jersey.—Model of a new mode of laying and raising submarine cables, and a bathometer for deep-sea soundings.
73. Mrs. M. J. COSTON, Washington, D. C.—Telegraphic night-signals.
74. M. G. FARMER, Boston, Massachusetts.—Thermo-electric battery.
75. J. D. CATON, Ottawa, Illinois.—Pocket field-telegraph apparatus; the Morse sounder.

www.ingramcontent.com/pod-product-compliance
Lightning Source LLC
LaVergne TN
LVHW021357110826
845150LV00007B/1691

* 9 7 8 1 4 2 5 5 1 2 9 9 6 *